1 MONTH OF
FREE
READING

at

www.ForgottenBooks.com

By purchasing this book you are eligible for one month membership to ForgottenBooks.com, giving you unlimited access to our entire collection of over 1,000,000 titles via our web site and mobile apps.

To claim your free month visit:

www.forgottenbooks.com/free922487

ISBN 978-0-260-01740-6
PIBN 10922487

Forgotten Books is a registered trademark of FB &c Ltd.
Copyright © 2018 FB &c Ltd.
FB &c Ltd, Dalton House, 60 Windsor Avenue, London, SW19 2RR.
Company number 08720141. Registered in England and Wales.

For support please visit www.forgottenbooks.com

GOVERNMENT VERSUS PRIVATE RAILROADS

JOURNAL

OF

THE NATIONAL INSTITUTE OF SOCIAL SCIENCES

FOUNDED IN 1912 UNDER THE CHARTER OF THE

AMERICAN SOCIAL SCIENCE ASSOCIATION

INCORPORATED BY ACT OF CONGRESS, JANUARY 28, 1899

VOLUME V.   JUNE 1, 1919.

THIS VOLUME ALSO REPRESENTS No. 51 OF THE
JOURNAL OF THE AMERICAN SOCIAL SCIENCE ASSOCIATION

———

SELLING AGENTS

F. W. FAXON COMPANY, BOSTON, MASS.

Press of
J. J. Little & Ives Co.
New York

OFFICERS OF THE INSTITUTE

President
EMORY R. JOHNSON

Honorary President
WILLIAM H. TAFT

Vice-Presidents

JANE ADDAMS, LL.D.
MRS. GEORGE C. AVERY
HON. ROBERT BACON
HON. SIMEON E. BALDWIN
HON. JAMES M. BECK
MABEL T. BOARDMAN, LL.D.
MARSTON T. BOGERT, LL.D.
NICHOLAS MURRAY BUTLER, LL.D.
HON. WILLIAM H. CROCKER
H. HOLBROOK CURTIS, M.D.
CHAS. B. DAVENPORT, PH.D.
MRS. HENRY P. DAVISON
MRS. HENRY F. DIMOCK
TYSON S. DINES, ESQ.
CHARLES W. ELIOT, LL.D.
JOHN H. FINLEY, LL.D.
PROF. IRVING FISHER
REAR-ADMIRAL B. A. FISKE
HARRY A. GARFIELD, LL.D.
VIRGINIA C. GILDERSLEEVE, LL.D.
S. S. GOLDWATER, M.D.
FRANK J. GOODNOW, LL.D.
HON. MADISON GRANT

MRS. E. H. HARRIMAN
MRS. J. BORDEN HARRIMAN
HON. MYRON T. HERRICK
HON. DAVID JAYNE HILL
MRS. RIPLEY HITCHCOCK
ARCHER M. HUNTINGTON, LITT.D.
MRS. H. HARTLEY JENKINS
HON. JAMES G. JENKINS
MRS. ST. CLAIR MCKELWAY
A. L. METZ, M.D.
HARRIS P. MOSHER, M.D.
MRS. FREDERICK NATHAN
HENRY FAIRFIELD OSBORN, LL.D.
CORNELIA B. S. QUINTON, LITT.D.
HON. ELIHU ROOT
LEO S. ROWE, LL.D.
HERBERT L. SATTERLEE, PH.D.
MRS. C. LORILLARD SPENCER
HON. OSCAR S. STRAUS
ROLAND G. USHER, PH.D.
MISS LILLIAN D. WALD
TALCOT T. WILLIAMS

Treasurer
HENRY P. DAVISON, LL.D.
c/o J. P. Morgan & Co., N. Y. City.

Secretary
MISS LILLIE HAMILTON FRENCH
225 Fifth Avenue, N. Y. City.

MEDAL OF THE INSTITUTE

OBVERSE

DIG NVS
ORE

REVERSE

MEDALS AWARDED BY THE INSTITUTE

GOLD MEDALS

1913
ARCHER M. HUNTINGTON, LITT.D.
WILLIAM H. TAFT
SAMUEL L. PARRISH

1914
CHARLES W. ELIOT, LL.D.
MAJOR-GEN. GEO. W. GOETHALS
HENRY FAIRFIELD OSBORN, LL.D.
ABRAHAM JACOBI, M.D.

1915
LUTHER BURBANK, ESQ.
HON. ANDREW CARNEGIE

1916
HON. ADOLPH LEWISOHN
MRS. H. HARTLEY JENKINS
HON. ROBERT BACON

1917
SURGEON-GEN. WM. C. GORGAS
HON. JOHN PURROY MITCHEL
MICHAEL IDVORSKY PUPIN, SC.D.
GEORGE W. CRILE, M.D.

1918
HENRY P. DAVISON, LL.D.
HON. HERBERT C. HOOVER
WILLIAM J. MAYO, M.D.

1919
SAMUEL GOMPERS
WILLIAM HENRY WELCH, M.D.

PRESENTATION MEDALS

1913
CAPT. CLEMENT GREATOREX, M.V.O.
MARQUIS DE LA VEGA INCLAN
JANE ADDAMS, LL.D.
PROF. RUSSELL H. CHITTENDEN
MISS MALVINA HOFFMAN
MRS. FREDERICK NATHAN
VISCOUNT BRYCE
MABEL T. BOARDMAN, LL.D.
MISS LILLIAN D. WALD
SIR RICKMAN J. GODLEE

1914
HON. BRAND WHITLOCK
GENERAL LEONARD WOOD
WM. THOMAS COUNCILMAN, M.D.
MRS. ROSE HAWTHORNE LATHROP
EMORY R. JOHNSON, SC.D.
J. J. ALBRIGHT
EDWARD L. TRUDEAU, M.D.
MRS. ANNE DOUGLAS (SEDGWICK)
    DE SÈLINCOURT
A. L. METZ, M.D.
CHARLES H. DUVAL, M.D.
CHARLES C. BASS, M.D.
JOHN H. FINLEY, LL.D.
CORNELIA B. S. QUINTON, LITT.D.
MISS WINIFRED HOLT

1915
MONS. EUGÈNE BRIEUX
MISS ANNE MORGAN
HON. MYRON T. HERRICK
LOUISA LEE SCHUYLER, LL.D.

1916
MADAME MARCELLA SEMBRICH
HENRY M. LEIPZIGER, LL.D.
JOHN SEELY WARD
SAMUEL MATHER
PETER COOPER HEWITT, SC.D.

1917
HON. MADISON GRANT
MISS JANE A. DELANO
EDWARD H. SOTHERN

1918
FRANCIS GANO BENEDICT, SC.D.
HON. JOHN A. KINGSBURY
LEO S. ROWE, LL.D.
THOMAS W. SALMON, M.D.
PROF. CHARLES-E. A. WINSLOW

1919
RIGHT REV. CHARLES H. BRENT
RAYMOND B. FOSDICK
HARRY A. GARFIELD, LL.D.
CARL KOLLER, M.D.
FREDERICK LAYTON
HON. ROBERT SCOTT LOVETT
CHARLES M. SCHWAB
HARRY A. WHEELER, LL.D.

LIBERTY SERVICE MEDALS

1918–1919

EDWIN G. BAETGER
COL. JOSEPH A. BLAKE
LIEUT.-COL. GEORGE E. BREWER
MRS. JAMES STEWART CUSHMAN
LIVINGSTON FARRAND, LL.D.
EDWARD W. HINES
GOVERNOR MARCUS H. HOLCOMB
LIEUT.-COL. JAMES P. HUTCHINSON
MAJOR-GEN. M. W. IRELAND
MAJOR ALEXANDER LAMBERT
LIEUT.-COL. HENRY H. M. LYLE
HENRY NOBLE MACCRACKEN, LL.D.
MAJOR CLARENCE A. McWILLIAMS
GOVERNOR RICHARD I. MANNING
GOVERNOR SAMUEL W. McCALL
HENRY C. McELDOWNEY

PROF. JOHN C. MERRIAM
JOHN R. MOTT, LL.D.
MAJOR GRAYSON M. P. MURPHY
MISS M. ADELINE NUTTING
CHARLES L. PACK, LL.D.
HON. JOHN M. PARKER
W. FRANK PERSONS
MRS. WHITELAW REID
HENRY DAVIS SLEEPER
HORATIO R. STORER, M.D.
MAGNUS SWENSON
MRS. W. K. VANDERBILT
FREDERICK VOGEL, JR.
DANIEL WILLARD
PRESIDENT WOODROW WILSON
MRS. H. OTTO WITTPENN

PATRIOTIC SERVICE MEDALS

1918–1919

MRS. ROBERT BACON
CORNELIUS N. BLISS, JR.
HON. FRANK W. CARPENTER
WILLIAM D. COCHRAN
WILLIAM F. COCHRAN
MRS. NINA L. DURYEA
MRS. ROBERT A. FRANKS
MRS. CHARLES D. FREEMAN
MISS RAYMONDE GLAENZER
JOHN H. GOSS
MRS. ARTHUR CURTISS JAMES

MISS BEATRICE MACDONALD
MRS. STANLEY MORTIMER
MRS. HENRY R. REA
JOHN D. ROCKEFELLER, JR.
FREDERIC M. SACKETT
DR. PAUL H. SAUNDERS
MRS. CORNELIUS STEVENSON
MRS. E. T. STOTESBURY
MRS. FRENCH VANDERBILT
MISS MARY VANKLEECK
CHARLES WEINBERGER

TABLE OF CONTENTS

COMMUNICATION

ANNUAL DINNER

ARGUMENTS FOR AND AGAINST GOVERNMENT OWNERSHIP AND OPERATION OF RAILROADS

BY PROFESSOR EDWIN R. A. SELIGMAN

COLUMBIA UNIVERSITY, NEW YORK

In approaching the subject, it is important to bear in mind that, taking a broad view of the history of the railroads throughout the world, there have been three stages in the development. Not all countries have gone through all of the three stages, but all have gone through some of the stages, and some have gone through all the stages. At the beginning railways were regarded as the private business of the owners. Especially in England and in this country as well as in Canada, railways were placed under the regime of competition between the private corporations owning the railways. For in these nations, almost every part of the country was so anxious to secure railways that they fairly vied with each other in their efforts to grant inducements to the railways. There was no thought of restriction; there was thought only of persuasion.

After a time, for reasons that are obvious to all to-day, the disadvantages of various forms of competition between these private companies showed themselves and the small lines began to amalgamate and form larger groups, until before long in many countries, instead of private competition between separate railways, a condition supervened more and more approaching a series of private monopolies.

When that second stage developed, the evils of private monopoly began to disclose themselves and the demand for some form of government control became ever more insistent. We, therefore, find during this stage a growing and more drastic regulation of these private monopolies by government. Some countries indeed started out with the second stage, as they never entertained the idea of competition between private railways. In such countries we find from the very outset a system of private monopolies, carefully regulated by the government.

After the lapse of several more decades, the inadequacy of this system came gradually to be recognized and certain countries changed from the plan of government control of private monopolies to that of government ownership or operation. Thus the third and final stage was reached.

Some countries, again, started in with this third stage from the very beginning. Australia, for instance, never had any private railways, either competitive or monopolistic, but began with government railways; and a number of other countries followed the same plan.

Most countries, however, have gone through all of these three stages. Germany, for instance, started out with private railways, more or less uncontrolled; then changed to private monopolies, controlled by government and finally went over to government ownership. Italy also went through the three stages. Italy started out with private competition between a number of railways; then resorted to combination between two large monopolistic systems, and finally in 1907 accepted government ownership. France, which began with controlled private monopolies, has entered partly upon the last phase, having taken over with the last few decades two of the lines and having arranged to take over all the remainder within three or four decades.

Finally in federal countries, as in Switzerland, a still more interesting development has occurred. Switzerland, as is well known, is a federal state composed of separate commonwealths like our own. They started out with private railways, more or less uncontrolled, save by competition. Later on, when combinations developed, each state began to regulate her own railways. When that was found to interfere with interstate commerce, they reached the stage which we are beginning to attain, and the entire regulation was taken over by the central government, none being left to the separate states. Finally even that turned out to be inadequate, and over a decade ago the last of the railway systems was taken over by the federal government, so that there is now complete government ownership and operation.

It is clear then from this comparative survey that the generalization described above is applicable also to us. We also are in a definite stage of the same development, in that we have transcended the early stage of competition between private railways, and that our large railway combinations or groups which were first regulated by the separate states are now in part subject also to federal regulation. The question before us now is: shall we enter upon the third stage as reached by Switzerland, that of private monopolies controlled entirely by the central government, or shall we go over to the fourth and final stage of government ownership and operation?

In order to prepare the way for an answer to this question, let us analyze the reasons why this development has taken place, why almost all countries have proceeded from one stage to another, and why some have even ended with government ownership.

I

The first query then is: Why did private competitive lines give way to government regulated monopolies? Here the history of England is enlightening. In England all kinds of competition have been tried. First, as is well known, England attempted what is called competition of carriers on the line. It was supposed that the railways, like the canals and turnpikes, would be used by individuals owning not only their own cars but their own locomotives. Everybody was permitted to employ his own motor power and the tolls charged were fixed primarily for use of the way. This so-called competition of carriers on the line was, however, soon realized to be technically impossible and by the end of the thirties, not only were private locomotives abandoned, but even private cars now soon became the exception, rather than the rule.

Next came the idea of competition among the carriers themselves; that is to say, competition in rates and fares. For a long time everybody believed in this form of competition and thought that it would secure as adequate protection for the public, as was the case in private business through the operation of the general principle of competition. This, however, turned out to be completely unavailing by 1870, when the great amalgamations had been completed and when it was seen that competition between private railways could not be relied upon to assure either moderate or stable charges, and that competition inevitably gave way to combination. For competition in charges involved the dangers of what we call to-day "cutthroat" competition as well as the instability of rates so distasteful to the shipper.

There still remained, however, the idea of competition of service or competition in facilities. In 1871 the English instituted a great commission which sat for some time and made a special study of this topic. When they brought in their report in 1872 they stated that no reliance was to be placed upon competition. We quote the following paragraph from the report, because it is so germane to our present situation:

"The Commission and Commissioners carefully chosen for the last thirty years have clung to one form of competition after another. It has, nevertheless, become more and more evident that competition of all kinds must fail to do for railways what it does for ordinary trade, and that no means have yet been devised by which competition can be permanently maintained."

Furthermore, this Commission went carefully into the question not only of competition in general, but of competition in facilities or service, a point of which we hear so much to-day in this country. For although most of us have abandoned our earlier belief in competition in rates, many still cling to the idea that the solution of the problem lies in competition in facilities. As to this, let the Commission speak:

"It is impossible to say how far the facilities of modern England are due to competition. Still less is it possible to say whether greater facilities are not produced by amalgamation or monopoly and, above all, past experience leads to the inevitable conclusion that wherever competition is found to be adverse to the interests of the companies, it will in the long run be succeeded by combination. Competition cannot be relied upon to secure either fair prices or proper service."

We quote this in order to show that this particular contention was settled in England fifty years ago. Neither in England nor anywhere else except in this country has any further reliance since then been placed on the idea of competition in facilities, as the solution of the problem.

In England, therefore, as on the European continent, private competition gave way to combination. One form of competition followed the other into oblivion until there supervened monopoly, legal or actual. But with each weakening of the fact of competition, came a strengthening of government control and finally the control of private monopoly was succeeded by public monopoly or government ownership. Let us now proceed to discuss the causes of this final transition.

First, there was what may be termed the constructional argument. In many countries the needed capital was not available. That is the reason, for instance, why Australia started in with government ownership; and why we find government lines in some of the American dependencies and the British colonies. It explains the existence of the early government railways in some of the American states like Pennsylvania and North Carolina. If you cannot get people to invest their own capital, the government must step into the breach. With the evident profitableness, however, of the newer means of communication, this particular argument proved to be of slight consequence in the United States.

In the second place we find the military argument. This explains the construction of the trans-Siberian railway in Russia and the assumption of no small part of the Indian railway system by the government. The military argument has fortunately been unknown in this country; and let us hope that when the League of Nations comes to be realized, it will no longer play a rôle anywhere else.

The third is the political argument. When certain countries, for instance, adopted a definite trade policy, like protection, they found it desirable to nationalize the railway system as an adjunct to the new policy. This played a considerable rôle in the taking over of the Prussian railways by the government.

The fourth is the financial argument, based on the hope that the government will derive a clear profit from railway operation. In many of the smaller German states, for instance, the government railways have yielded large surpluses, which have operated to reduce taxation. This argument, however, would not apply in Anglo-Saxon countries. For if we ever take over the railways there is no doubt that we shall adopt the same principle as Australia and which we actually follow in the case of the post office; that is, the principle of fees, or the covering of cost, rather than the principle of profits. If the rates and fares were ever high enough to yield a net surplus, we should without doubt give the public the benefit of lower charges rather than the taxpayer the advantage of lighter burdens.

In the fifth place, we find the labor argument. The government, it has been claimed, is, on the whole, more apt to be a model employer, so that the workmen will fare better under government operation than under private management. This consideration played a not insignificant, although indeed not the unique, rôle in Italy, when government control was succeeded by government ownership in 1907.

The sixth and most important argument may be termed the economic argument. This is really a composite argument, consisting of several elements. A prominent place, for instance, has been occupied by the feeling that the abolition of private monopolies would lessen discrimination, both personal and local. In the next place came the expectation that charges would be reduced through the elimination of the profits of the stockholders. It was conceded, indeed, that there is often a coincidence between the private and the public interest; as when the private railway finds it profitable to build up the country, and thus increase both its own earnings and the public welfare. But when there is a divergence between private interests and public welfare, when there is danger that the interests of the stockholders will gain precedence over those of the public, the feeling was engendered that it might be better to eliminate the hazard once and for all. This has played no small rôle in some European countries.

There is another phase of this argument which is acquiring considerable importance here·as elsewhere. This is the feeling that public utilities should not be utilized to create large profits for private individuals. We know that in this country many huge fortunes have been amassed out of railways. Entirely irrespective of the fact whether they were honestly or dishonestly acquired, there is a growing conviction among many who believe in private property and even in the social advantages of large fortunes, that railways ought not to be utilized for this end and that no opportunity ought to be given to heap up immense fortunes out of what is primarily a public enterprise, even though it may be delegated for a time to private management.

Finally, we may advert to the last phase of the economic argument which plays a considerable rôle at present, *viz.,* that private management is inevitably attended by certain wastes of competition. For even though there may be a distinct tendency toward monopoly, there is apt to be, as at present in this country, a certain amount of competition at the fringes of the monopolies. It is difficult to achieve under private management unified control, standardized equipment, direct routing, joint use of terminals, and all these other results of which we have heard so much during the last few months under government operation. In other words, government ownership, it is claimed, is the one best calculated to bring about the economies of unity of operation.

While the above are the chief reasons that explain the strong trend in many countries toward government ownership, it is necessary to point out why the major part of the railways of the world are, nevertheless, still in private hands. What, in other words, are the chief arguments that may be advanced against government ownership?

II

These opposing arguments may be reduced to three in number: the political, the economic, and the fiscal.

The political argument may be approached from several angles. In the first place, it is pertinent to consider railway construction—an important matter in this country which does not yet begin to possess all the railway mileage which it will ultimately need. Will it be easy to keep politics out of the construction of new railways? Does not the picture presented to us every few years by the river-and-harbor bill show us the kind of interests that will be at work in the endeavor of each section to secure for itself new construction which may perhaps not be in the public interest? This is not lightly to be overlooked.

'Secondly, when we come to deal with the operation of existing lines, will it be feasible in a country like this to eliminate politics from the management of the railways? Entirely irrespective of the possibility, to be discussed later, of securing an efficient directing force, will it not be difficult to prevent the sectional interests of the country from influencing the central board? We all know what happens every time a new tariff bill is discussed, and how one section is played off against another. Yet the importance of railway tariffs to various industries and different sections is immensely greater than that of any customs tariff. Would there not be a serious danger of a reproduction on a great scale of the unseemly contests and the log rolling which are even now inseparable from the adoption of a new tariff?

Furthermore, consider the political aspect of the labor situation. We are all agreed that labor constitutes the first charge upon the railways; and that, whatever may be the solution of the problem, we must so arrange it that the laborers on the railways shall secure an adequate wage. But let us not minimize the difficulties that will be created by the addition of millions of men in the employ of the government. We shall either be compelled to take away from them the vote, which is unthinkable in this country, or we shall incur the risk of converting the railway employees into upholders of that party which is most lavish in promises. Until we settle the problem of trade unionism among government employees, with the general strike as the ultimate resource, will it not be hazardous to multiply government employees in enterprises which deal with primary necessities? We know how they attempt to solve this problem abroad. In Italy they were compelled, in the case of strikes of the railway employees against the government, to call every man to the colors and to shoot every one who did not respond. Would that method be practicable here? Are we really far enough along in our settlement of the labor problem to look forward with complacency to having millions of government employees? Have our friends on the labor side adequately considered this matter in the report which they have submitted in favor of government ownership? Is it not a fact they have succumbed to the danger of regarding the problem only from the point of view of their own particular interest. The railway executives have brought in a report which, although not designed primarily to do so, yet creates the impression of manifesting regard chiefly for the financial interests of the stockholders. The railway operatives have brought in a report which is frankly designed primarily to look after the interests of the laborers. They are both wrong because the real problem in this country is primarily to consider the interests of the public, and to give adequate service.

The political aspect of the problem therefore is a serious one. In a democracy like ours, where so many political problems have not even yet been approached, much less settled, it is a fair question whether government ownership may not involve, politically speaking, a jump from the frying pan into the fire. Are we ready for the jump at this time?

The second argument is the economic argument. This again has two aspects, that of discrimination and that of efficiency.

Personal discrimination may be passed over because it is now to a very large extent a thing of the past. We have been able virtually to get rid of personal discrimination through our system of government control. We hear nowadays but little complaint on that score.

As regards local discrimination, is it not a vain hope to expect that government operation will eliminate this? Is it not true that many forms of local discrimination must continue to exist under government ownership, because they are inherent in the very nature of the case? The question, *e. g.,* as to whether the rates to Reno, Nevada, should be lower than to San Francisco, is one which neither the government nor private individuals can answer in the affirmative, because it is settled by water competition. Again, export and import rates must continue, whether we have government railways or private railways. New York will continue to be a rival of Baltimore, the Twin Cities and of Omaha and Council Bluffs, government railways or private railways. We must not expect to get rid of local discriminations altogether; and we may diminish them as easily by government control as by government management.

Far more important, however, is the question of efficiency. It is notorious that in New York there has supervened a very perceptible decrease in the efficiency of the telephone service since the telephone has been operated by the government. Yet the telephone service is an exceedingly simple business compared with the railway. The railway is the most complex, the most subtle, the most delicate of all modern forms of enterprise. We can readily understand why some of our railway presidents receive more than the President of the United States. It is a difficult task—almost, I might be tempted to say, a more difficult task to run a big railway than it is, or at all events, than it was before the war, to run the government of the United States. We do not pay railway presidents those sums as mere gratuities. They are paid the market rate for their services because the sums in question are needed to secure the requisite ability.

How are we going to get the big brains of the country to remain in the service of the government railways? Do we find them to-day in our Interstate Commerce Commission? Do we find them in our Federal Trade Commission? Do we find them in our Tariff Commission? Do we find them in the management of the Post Office? Is it not more than probable, especially in a country like ours where huge salaries are most unlikely in government service, that the best brains will leave the government railways to enter private industry? And if they do, what will be the result upon the efficiency of the management?

But even if we could secure good men at the top, what is going to be the result of turning over to a government bureau, with its red tape and with its interminable delays, the management of a most complex enterprise, where immediate and decisive action is frequently necessary? Any one who is familiar with the way business affairs were handled at Washington before the war in almost every department knows the record of almost unbelievable slackness, of interminable delay, of outrageous duplication, of perpetual outside interference, of working at cross purposes, in short, of waste and inefficiency.

When we realize that the railway business is the most important of all our enterprises, that the present twenty billions of capital will before long be forty billions of capital and even ultimately fifty billions, can we contemplate with equanimity its control by a government board or by a secretary of railways? The only example we have had in this country in recent years of anything comparable to government operation of the railway business is the gas business in Philadelphia. When it was managed by the city we had poor gas, high charges and a large operating deficit. When the government turned it over to a private company, the result was good gas, lower charges, and profits to the government and private company alike.

Can we hope to do, under present political conditions, with this most complicated of all industries, what we were unable to do with a single industry in the city of Philadelphia? Have we yet reached the stage of political development when we can hope to eliminate all suspicion of politics from the government administration of business? And if not, will not government operation mean poor service, higher charges, and operating deficits to boot, which must ultimately be met by the taxpayer? Will not the profits of private management be dissipated into the losses of government inefficiency of operation? Will not, in short, the economic result be unsatisfactory?

We come finally to the fiscal argument.

The railway revenues last year were about five billions, or about five times as much as the government revenues before the war. In good years the railway revenues will continue to be large. But in poor years, whether due to bad crops or to business depression or to other emergencies, the revenues will fall off by the hundreds of millions of dollars. If the railways are run by the government, how will it be possible to provide for these sudden changes?

If we had, as in England, either an elastic revenue system or a budget which enables the Chancellor of the Exchequer every year to make his calculations within a few hundred thousand pounds and to balance his revenues and his expenditures, well and good. But how much chance have we of securing, in the immediate future, a real budget system at Washington, and how much prospect have we of introducing an elastic revenue system such as that which exists abroad? We know that this country has always been marked either by deficit financiering or by surplus financiering, and that the difficulties of our surpluses have often been greater than those of our deficits. Would not the taking over of the railways by the government with these billions of revenues and with these hundreds of millions of changes from year to year, constitute a hazardous fiscal policy? Are we ready for it yet? Is it not true, that government assumption of the railways must be preceded, as it was in Prussia, in Japan, and in Italy, by a reform in the fiscal policy which includes budgetary reform and elasticity of revenues? Shall we not otherwise be preparing for ourselves a fiscal chaos?

We have discussed the Federal fiscal problem. It remains to say a word about the state and local fiscal situation in relation to the railways. Almost everywhere at present there is a growing discontent with our system of state and local finance. In Ohio, in California, in New York, in the South, and in the West, our system of general property taxes is arousing increasing dissatisfaction. There is much unrest. There are demands for change. The coming of prohibition will make the situation still worse in those states and cities which depend upon high license for a substantial part of their revenue. In New York we shall lose some twenty millions of dollars. Yet how much thought have we given to the problem as to what is to be done by our states and cities if the Federal government takes over the railways? Much of our local revenues and a very substantial part of our state revenues almost everywhere in this country come from the public utilities and notably from the railways. Yet if the government should take over the railways, the states could no longer tax them, for they would then be an agency of the government and as such exempt from taxation. But if the states and localities should lose all the taxes that are paid by the railroads of this country to-day, the possible consequences are unpleasant to contemplate. Unless some comprehensive plan of tax reform, together with a really workable budget system, had been previously effected in all of our states and cities, would not the assumption of the railways by the Federal government engender untold difficulties and complications? This phase of the fiscal aspect of government ownership has not received the attention which it deserves.

If, then, we consider the political, the economic, and the fiscal arguments, is it not true that we have a combination of considerations which would impel us at the present time to go slow in adopting the program of government ownership? Government ownership may be ultimately unavoidable and even perhaps desirable, but the problem now before us is as to whether we have in this country yet reached the stage when this eventuality is to be welcomed. If there is any force in the above arguments, the time for that fiscal step is not yet at hand.

III

If, then, we decide for the present adversely to the project of government ownership, what conditions should be attached to their retention in private hands?

We should in the first place all agree that there must be at least a fourfold control, and that too of a more rigid character than we have yet had. This fourfold control would include the control first of rates and fares; second, of facilities and the mechanical side of operation; third, of railway accounts; and fourth, of railway securities. Some of these we have; others we must have. About this there is virtually no difference of opinion to-day. But assuming that we have secured them all, there still remain four additional objects which must be attained if the railways should be permitted to continue in private hands. What are these four objects?

The first point, I think, is that we must have assured, but limited, profits. We must have an assurance of an adequate return to the investors, or otherwise we shall not secure the capital. This assurance may take the form either of a direct government guarantee, or of a speedy and satisfactory adjustment of rates by the rate-fixing authority. On the other hand, we must have a limitation upon the profits in order to meet the argument adverted to above, that the profits which individuals can be allowed to make out of public utilities ought to be limited to the irreducible minimum.

Second, we must have an automatic adjustment of wages. There is no reason why the labor adjustment boards which have been such a pronounced success under our government operation should not be continued under private operation, provided it is recognized that any increase of wages granted by the adjustment board will at once be transferred to the public and not remain a charge on the railways. There is no conceivable reason why the private railway would then object to a satisfaction of all the legitimate demands of labor. What the railways formerly feared was that high wages would mean low profits. Remove this fear and you remove the great cause of friction.

Thirdly, we must seek to have regional operation with central control. Central control means the abandonment of state control. That is bound to come. We cannot have any adequate control of interstate commerce if there is a conflict between the state and the central authorities. We may indeed decide to grant to Cæsar the things that belong to Cæsar and leave a certain amount of control of strictly local matters to the state commissions. But in the essentials the nation must be supreme. Let us not forget the history of Switzerland.

When we come, however, to discuss the question of regional arrangement, there is room perhaps for more doubt. The question here at issue is as to whether there should be a complete monopoly within each region, or whether there should be competition between two or more railway groups in the same region. Here has emerged a decided difference of opinion. Not a few experts at present concede that competition in rates is undesirable, but pin their faith on competition in facilities. Is this a reasonable position? That competition in facilities has accomplished good results is indeed true. But so has competition in rates. Why then abandon reliance on competition in rates, and seek to retain competition in facilities?

The first has done good, but has also done evil, and we have discarded it. The second has done good, but has also done evil, and we are in process of discarding it. Has not the experience of England shown the futility of reliance on competition of any kind? If competition in facilities is good, why is it not equally good in the case of small lines? And yet the railway advocates quite properly demand the abolition of the anti-pooling law or the Sherman law as applied to railways. Why should competition be a bad thing between small lines and a good thing between large groups? If combination, which is the opposite of competition, is desirable in railways of hundreds of miles in length, why is it not desirable in railway systems of thousands of miles in length? There is obviously no logical halting place in the evolution from primitive competition to ultimate monopoly in the railway business. The sooner we recognize this fact, the better. As the experience of France has shown, competition within the regional groups is unnecessary. Perhaps the principal achievement of our present government operation is the proof of the wastes of competition—even of competition in facilities—as disclosed by the great relief afforded by the joint terminals, joint ticket offices and the abolition of indirect routing. Whatever may have been the benefits derived in the past from competition in facilities, it is questionable whether the benefits have not been outweighed by the defects. And why, it may be asked, may we be expected to remain the only country which does not discard this form of competition, as it has in common with the other countries discarded all other forms of competition—except, indeed, the two forms of competition which must continue to exist everywhere—namely, water competition and market competition or competition for the markets which may be reached directly or indirectly by the monopoly enterprises?

Above all, let us remember that the chief advantage supposed to be effected by competition of facilities may be attained equally well in another way. The argument of those who assert that we must still have competition of facilities is that without such competition we shall not have efficiency. What, however, is the real lure, the real stimulus to efficiency under private ownership? It obviously is profits; it is the money which we expect to make out of it. In private business competition brings about this result, because the successful competitor who puts his antagonist out of business makes the money. But if you have a system of monopoly and if you enable the monopolist to retain a part of the results of his good management, if you allow him to retain a substantial part of the profits due to efficiency, why should you weaken the desire to secure efficiency? And if this is true, cannot efficiency be predicated as well of monopoly as of competition? May we not in this way secure all the advantages of competition without any of its unquestioned evils?

This brings us to the fourth point, namely, that there

must be a division of the profits of operation. If we allow
the railways to keep all the surplus profits, we shall again
arouse the antagonism which is now in process of being
allayed. The rates which would be sufficient for a poorly
managed railway would obviously yield immense profits to the
well-managed railway; and immense profits will inevitably give
rise to suspicion. Furthermore, the division ought not—and
we say this with all due deference to our friends the labor people—go to the laborers. The laborers in general have always
consistently expressed their opposition to the idea of profit
sharing as a solution of the labor problem. The American
Federation of Labor and most of the workmen in this country
do not believe in profit sharing. What they contend for is a
wage adequate for decent living conditions, and one that will
rise with the standard of life. They do not believe in profit
sharing. Why then should we introduce profit sharing on the
railways? In fact we do not need it. If we secure the automatic adjustment of wages to which we have referred above,
the workman will get all the wages to which he is entitled.
Moreover, if there is to be a division of profits, why should it
go to the laborers rather than to the public? After all, it is the
general public which creates these profits by paying the rates
and fares. If we are to adopt the principle of a division of
profits between the owners and some other party, ought not
that other party to be the public?

But, you will ask, why then give any part of the profits
to the owners of the railways? Because that is the only way
of securing efficiency unless we have competition. And if we
no longer believe in competition, if we believe that the best
interests of the country demand unified management, joint use
of the terminals, direct routing and all these other achievements which have been brought about under government
operation—if, in short, we are to get on not only without
competition of rates, but also without competition of facilities we must secure the efficiency of which we all desire to
secure the advantage in some other way—and that other way
is not only to safeguard reasonable private profits, but to give
a stimulus to efficiency through the lure of greater profits.

Summing up the discussion, it seems clear then that the
solution of the problem at present is to be sought neither in

government operation nor in private competition, but in the strict government control of private monopoly, so devised as to safeguard primarily not the interest of the railroads, not primarily the interests of the employees, but primarily the interests of the community as a whole, that is, of the entire country.

OBJECTIONS TO GOVERNMENT OWNERSHIP OF RAILROADS

BY SAMUEL O. DUNN, EDITOR OF THE "RAILWAY AGE"

For many years we have had in this country much academic discussion of government ownership and operation of railroads. The question has now been transferred from the field of academic discussion to that of practical statesmanship. We have had a year of government operation. Therefore we need no longer base our consideration of its advantages and disadvantages solely on theoretical grounds and on the experience of other countries. Peace will be signed within a few months. Therefore, under the railroad control law, we must speedily decide whether government operation shall be continued or the railways shall be restored to private operation.

The former director general of the railroads, Mr. McAdoo, has proposed that the railways shall be retained by the government for five years, in order to make a thorough test of the existing system. But to propose five years more of the present system of government operation is almost equivalent to proposing permanent government ownership and operation. After five years more of the present system, the organizations of the individual railways would be so destroyed, and the financial relations of the government and companies would be so entangled, that to return the railways to private operation would be impracticable. Therefore, no matter what attempts may be made to camouflage it, the question actually confronting the people of the United States is whether they will soon return the railways to private operation, or adopt government ownership.

IS IT PRACTICABLE TO RETURN THE RAILWAYS TO PRIVATE OPERATION?

Increases of operating expenses are coming so fast that the large advances in rates which have been made within the past year are proving insufficient to cover them. The net earnings of many important railroads are such that if they should be immediately restored to their owners without guarantees of net income, they would be bankrupted. Some contend that this produces a condition which renders it impracticable to return the railways to private operation. But all that is needed to remedy this situation is to change the relation between the expenses and the earnings. This may be done by reductions of expenses or by advances of rates. If return to private operation is desirable, then obviously it is desirable to make such readjustments in expenses or rates as will render it possible for the railway companies to live. If there is not statesmanship enough in the country to devise means of safely returning the railways to their owners soon, it can hardly be assumed that there is statesmanship enough to devise measures under which government ownership and operation could be made a success.

Now, what are the principal questions to be settled in determining whether, from the standpoint of the public, government ownership is desirable? I think they are as follows:

First: Will government or private development and operation of the railways be more economical?

Second: Under which system will rates be lower?

Third: Under which system will the freight and passenger service rendered be better?

Fourth: Under which system will labor be treated more fairly, in respect of wages and working conditions?

Fifth: What are the comparative effects which the two alternative policies would have on the politics of the country?

The arguments which may be presented regarding these points are somewhat the same in the United States as in other countries. In one very important respect, however, our position is different from that of any other country. Our railway system, in point of mileage, is more than five times as large as that of any other country and, in fact, includes one-third of the entire mileage of the globe. Another important fact which must be borne in mind is that the country in which government operation has been most successful—that is, Germany

—has had a highly autocratic government, while we have a highly democratic government. Whether the results gained in Germany in future will be equally good, remains to be determined. In the study of the problem, we should give great weight to our own special conditions, or the conclusions we reach probably will prove far from correct.

COMPARATIVE CONSTRUCTION COST OF GOVERNMENT AND PRIVATE RAILWAYS

With respect to the cost of furnishing transportation, it is always contended that the government would have a great advantage because it can raise capital at a lower rate of interest than private companies. But it is doubtful whether there is a difference of more than one per cent between the rate which the government would have to pay and the average rate which private railway companies have to pay. Government bonds issued to carry on the war already are selling at prices which yield a return of 5 per cent, and purchase of the railways would almost double the government's debt. Besides, the total amount of return which must be paid upon the investment in railways is determined, not only by the rate of interest or dividends paid, but also by the amount of capital invested to provide any given amount of transportation capacity.

Now, the statistics of the world's railways demonstrate that under comparable conditions, governments almost invariably spend more in proportion to build and develop railroads than do private companies. It often has been charged that our railways are over-capitalized. As to some of them, this is undoubtedly true. But, whether measured by their book cost of road and equipment or their capitalization, our railways as a whole have cost less in proportion to their capacity for handling traffic and to the character of their facilities than any system of railways which has been built and developed under government ownership. It is possible in a brief paper to set forth only a very small part of the evidence which may be presented in proof of this statement. The wages paid by the railways in New South Wales, Australia, always have been substantially lower and in Canada slightly lower than in the United States. These, like the

United States, are new countries. In 1916, the cost of construction of the state railways of New South Wales was reported as $80,000 a mile, and that of the government-owned Intercolonial Railway of Canada as $76,000 a mile. The government of Canada recently built the National Transcontinental Railway at a cost, without equipment, exceeding $80,000 a mile. The average capitalization of the railways of the United States on June 30, 1916, was only $66,366 per mile. It need hardly be added that none of the government railways mentioned has facilities and capacity for handling traffic equal to those of the railways of the United States.

Interest of 4½ per cent on the cost of construction of the railways of New South Wales would be $3,600 per mile. Interest at 5½ per cent on the smaller capitalization of the railways of the United States would be only $3,650 per mile, and our railways never actually paid out this much in interest and dividends on their securities in any year in their history. The large savings which it is contended would be effected by the use of the credit of the government under government ownership are mainly fanciful.

COMPARATIVE EXPENSE OF OPERATION OF STATE AND PRIVATE RAILWAYS

A far more important question is that of the relative expenses which would be incurred in operating the railways. The cost of operation of our railways is now about four times as great as the total return which it would be necessary under private operation to pay upon their capital in order to cause prosperity and expansion in the railroad industry. Now, it has been the almost uniform experience of the world that, with comparable operating conditions and volumes of traffic, the operating expenses of state-managed railways have been greater than those of privately-managed railroads. The advocates of government ownership always have had much to say of the efficiency with which the German railways have been operated. No fairer comparison can be made than between them and the five large privately-owned railways of France. I have had experience with the service of both, and in most respects the service of the French railways before the war was superior to that of the German railways. Nevertheless, with lower average rates and a smaller volume of traffic, the expenses of the French railways were lower in proportion to their earnings than those of the German railways. The operating expenses of the private railways of Canada always have been relatively lower than either those of the state railways of Australia or those of the state-owned Intercolonial Railway of Canada. As to the railways of the United States, in spite of the fact that they have paid the highest wages in the world, their operating expenses have been lower in proportion to their volume of traffic than those of any other railways in the world.

INCREASE OF EXPENSES UNDER GOVERNMENT OPERATION

It is an even more significant fact that in almost every instance when railways have been transferred from private to government management, there has immediately been a large increase of operating expenses. In 1908 the French government assumed operation of the Western Railway, and in four years, while its earnings increased only 12 per cent, its operating expenses increased 50 per cent. Under private management the ratio of expenses of the Italian Railways to their earnings in the five years 1900-1905 inclusive was 67½ per cent, while after two years of government operation the ratio had increased to 83 per cent. Within three years after the government of the United States had acquired the Panama Railroad, its earnings increased 84 per cent, while its expenses increased 110 per cent.

We have recently had a year's experience with government operation of railroads closer to home. In the year 1917, when the railways of the United States were under private operation, the operating expenses of large roads having a mileage of 233,000 miles was $2,858,000,000. In the year 1918, under government operation, the expenses of the same roads were $4,007,000,000, an increase of $1,149,000,000, or over 40 per cent.

It may be said this increase in expenses was due principally to advances in wages made necessary by war conditions. But according to the latest statistics, the advances in wages actually charged into the year's accounts amounted to only $583,500,000. This leaves approximately $566,000,000 of the increase in expenses to be accounted for. In 1917 the increase in traffic handled was much larger than in 1918, and there were large advances in the prices of fuel and materials, as well as substantial advances in wages. And yet in 1917, under private operation, the *total* increase in operating expenses was less than $475,000,000. Furthermore, the increase in expenses in 1917 was much the largest that ever had occurred in one year under private operation; and I especially call attention to the fact that it occurred in a year during nine months of which the railways were operated under war conditions, while there were only ten months of war in 1918. The advances in wages I have referred to are not all that have been made, but merely those that were charged to expenses in 1918. It is estimated that the advances in wages made under government operation are now running at the rate of $1,000,000,-000 a year.

Are all the advances in wages which have been made justified? Owing to the policy which has been followed under government operation, the data for intelligently discussing that question have not been made available. Under private operation, when large bodies of railway employees made demands for advances in wages, the managements usually declined their demands. The controversies which resulted usually were aired in the press. They usually resulted in arbitration; and the public hearings held before, and the reports made by, the arbitration boards afforded information for judging of the merits of the points at issue. These matters, for the most part, have been handled differently under government operation. Last spring the director general of railroads appointed a Railroad Wage Commission to pass upon the claims of all classes of employees. It conducted investigations and public hearings and presented a report recommending advances in wages aggregating $300,000,000 a year. These were made. Many employees complained that the advances they received were not sufficient. Another board was constituted, composed of equal numbers of officers of the Railroad Administration and of the employees. The railway companies were not directly or indirectly represented. No public hearings have been held, so far as I know. No reports have been made setting forth fully for the information of the public the reasons for the findings made. And yet, on the recommendations of this board, additional advances in wages aggregating $700,000,000 a year have been made.

Now, we all know that large advances in wages should have been made. What I especially wish to call to your attention is the way in which these things have been done. The public must pay in freight and passenger rates these advances in wages. Under government operation the railways are supposed to be managed solely in the interest of the public. Nevertheless, while under private operation affairs were so managed that the public, to a large extent, knew what advances in wages were demanded and the arguments made for and against them; under government operation, it has not had this information, and has had no opportunity to bring its sentiment to bear in the determination of questions of such tremendous importance to it.

It may be said that matters of this kind would be handled differently under government operation in time of peace. But in order to get questions of importance settled intelligently and in the interest of the public, you must get the issues involved presented fully to the public. Under private management, this is done in railway wage controversies because the companies have an incentive to present one side of the case, while the employees have an incentive to present the other side. Under government operation it must always be vastly more difficult to get questions of this kind settled with due publicity and on their merits, because while there will be those who will have an incentive to present and press the claims of labor, there will be no one who will have the selfish incentive that the railway companies have had to oppose the claims of labor. The officers of the railways under government operation have not and never would have any such incentive. Obviously, public men who may be dependent upon the votes of railway labor for reëlection will not have it. Nobody will have it. Government operation renders it practically impossible to secure discussion and settlement of these important railway labor questions upon their merits.

Why was there a relatively larger increase in operating

expenses during the past year, in addition to advances in wages, than there was in 1917? The increase in the prices of fuel and materials has been relatively little greater. The explanation is that government operation has reduced the efficiency of officers and employees. This is not said in any spirit of criticism of the former director general of railroads, or of the railway officers who have composed his staff and have been directly in charge of the operation of the various lines. Director General McAdoo honestly adopted the system of consolidation and unification which the advocates of government ownership always have favored. He believed, as they did, that under it greatly improved results would be obtained. He did not estimate, as did an advocate of government ownership who testified before the Newlands Congressional Committee two weeks before government operation was adopted, that it would produce economies in operation amounting to $400,000,000 a year. Mr. McAdoo did, however, believe it would result in large economies. Testifying before the Senate Committee on Interstate Commerce on January 19, 1918, he said: "So I hope that large economies may be practised. How far they will be offset by increased cost of material and increased cost of labor, I do not know; but perhaps one hand will wash the other. . . . I hope that such economies can be effected as will prevent deficiencies, and I even hope that a surplus may result from government operation." He carried out his plan of unification with great energy and ability. He got most of the able railway men in the country to stay in his organization and render loyal support.

In spite of these things, almost every statistical unit which can be employed as a measure indicates that the railways were operated less efficiently in 1918 than in 1917. There was practically no increase in the amount of freight traffic handled. There was an increase in the ratio of empty car mileage to total car mileage. There was a reduction in the number of miles each locomotive and each car traveled daily. There was an increase in the number of tons per train but the increase was no larger than that which had taken place in previous years, and it was entirely due to heavier loading of cars. There was a decrease in the number of freight cars handled per train, although in the preceding five years, the railway companies had increased the average number of cars per train from 30 to 35. There was no improvement, but actual deterioration, in the general condition of track and equipment. It is a notable fact that this decline in efficiency occurred in spite of the fact that the Railroad Administration was not hampered by any of the restrictions by which the railway companies had been embarrassed. It was not subject to the laws empowering the shipper to route his own freight and prohibiting consolidations or agreements between parallel roads, or by government freight preference and priority orders. In order to expedite the loading and unloading of cars by shippers, it was able to and did make much higher demurrage charges than ever had been made before. It was able to, and did, appeal to the officers and employees, on the grounds of patriotism, to put forth their utmost efforts in order to help win the war.

A GOVERNMENT MANAGER ON GOVERNMENT OPERATION

Why, under these conditions, was there a decline of efficiency? It was due mainly to causes which always are present and the effects of which never can be avoided under government operation. You may say that is merely the conclusion of one who is biased against government operation. Permit me, then, to give to you some views expressed by a man with long experience as general manager of a system of state railways. The railways of South Africa are owned and operated by the government. Two years ago, a State Mining Commission was created to consider the question of the nationalization of the mines of that country. It called as its principal expert witness Sir William Wilson Hoy, General Manager of Railways and Harbors. Sir William presented an elaborate statement in which he reviewed the results of government operation of railways throughout the world. The following are some quotations from his testimony:

"There is undoubtedly a tendency toward over-centralization and rigid uniformity on state railways. . . . Over-centralization destroys initiative and resource, and if carried to excess, tends to cripple a large organization. . . . Staff control and discipline in a state concern are so bound up by regulations as to create greater difficulties in handling the staff (employees) than are experienced under private management. In state concerns, it is not easy to deal with the man who, while not doing an honest day's work, carefully steers a course which keeps him within the regulations. There is not in state concerns the same elasticity in the control of staff (employees) as in private organizations. . . . With regard to promotion and regard for good work, considerations of seniority play a greater part in a state than in a private concern. If seniority be made the sole factor in determining promotion, one of the main incentives to efficiency disappears, and the service suffers accordingly. . . . Where a large body of men, such as a railway staff, is employed directly by the state, there is a danger of their enlisting the efforts of legislators to secure better wages, shorter hours, improved conditions, etc. The enforcement on the management by parliamentary interference of changes in staff conditions demoralizes the entire railway service, impairs discipline, prevents good relations between the staff and the management, destroys economical operation and in every way is to be greatly deplored."

It would be difficult for anybody to give a better enumeration of the specific reasons for the decline of efficiency on our railroads than is contained in this summary of Sir William Hoy's several conclusions. We have had the very overcentralization of management and the consequent destruction of the initiative and resource of those in direct charge of the operation of the various lines which he mentions as being characteristic of government operation. How could the officers of the various railways engage in intense emulation with each other in getting good results when they were kept busy carrying out orders from Washington and when the incentive to put forth their best efforts had been largely destroyed by the knowledge that the good work they did would not inure to the advantage of the company that owned the property on which they were employed, and that therefore they would probably receive no substantial recognition or promotion for it?

Government operation has had the very effect of breaking down discipline among the employees to which Sir William Hoy refers. The federal manager of an individual railway under government operation is charged with the responsibility of getting results on it, but the effect of over-centralization is to cause all of the favors granted to employees to be bestowed at Washington. Furthermore, it has caused numerous inspectors to be sent out from Washington who have gone over the heads of the federal managers and the other high officers of the railways direct to subordinate officers and employees. These things undermine the respect of the men for their superiors and, as Sir William Hoy says of parliamentary interference with staff conditions, they demoralize the entire railway service, impair discipline, prevent good relations between the staff (employees) and the management, and destroy economical operation. There has been thus far almost none of the political interference on the part of the lawmakers that Sir William Hoy deprecates, but there is very good reason to believe that there would be under government operation in time of peace. If legislative political interference were added to the other influences which, even in time of war, have undermined efficiency, what would the operating conditions on our railways become in time of peace, and to what heights would their expenses increase?

Sir William Hoy said: "There is nothing inherent in state organization to prevent adequate decentralization, but the tendency certainly is toward over-centralization." Personally, I believe over-centralization is inevitable under government ownership. Under any system of management, differences will arise between the railways and their patrons and employees. When the railways are owned by several or numerous private companies, most of these differences will be settled locally. They may not be settled altogether satisfactorily, but they will be settled. On the other hand, when the railways are all operated by the government, every difference between them and their patrons or employees, however small, which is not settled entirely satisfactorily, will be appealed to the central governmental authority. If there were no central governmental authority to which to appeal, there would be an irresistible demand for one to be created. The central authority will pass upon most of these appeals. The more of them it hears and passes upon, the more appeals to it there will be; and every action it takes in an effort to remedy the conditions which cause the appeals will tend to cause centralization. The tendency toward over-centralization will, under government operation, always be irresistible; and over-centralization will always tend to produce inefficiency because, as Sir William Hoy says, it destroys the incentive and opportunity of those in direct charge of the operation of the various lines to exercise initiative and enterprise. The exercise of initiative and enterprise by the officers of the various lines is essential to efficient management, especially on a railway system so vast as ours.

Some advantage was derived during the past year from centralized control of operation. It rendered it possible to direct traffic over the lines and through the terminals best able to handle it. In consequence, it made it possible to move the freight in an orderly way, considering the volume of traffic. But even last year, when the roads were operated chiefly for war purposes, the advantages of centralized control were offset by disadvantages resulting from the destruction of the initiative and freedom of action of the officers of the various lines. The effects of these disadvantages would be much greater and more apparent under normal conditions in time of peace.

The conclusion from all the evidence must be that the operation and needed development of the railways would be much more expensive to the public under government ownership than under a policy of operation by a sufficient number of companies to maintain competition in service and emulation in efficiency of management. This additional burden of expense would have to be borne by the public either as relatively high freight and passenger rates, or as taxes levied to pay railway deficits.

DOES GOVERNMENT OWNERSHIP RESULT IN LOWER RATES?

Any fair comparison of the rates charged by the state and private railways of the world before the war must lead to the conclusion that under comparable conditions, the rates of private railways were, as a whole, lower than those of state railways. This was a direct result of their lower cost of operation. The average passenger rates of state railroads often have been lower than those of private railways; but these averages do not allow for differences in density of traffic and in the character of the service. The average passenger rate of the German state railways was much lower than that of the railways of the United States. But their average passenger rate was so low, first, because the density of passenger traffic was over five times as great as in the United States; and, second, because over 85 per cent of the passengers traveled third or fourth class in very poor cars in which many of them could not get seats, and in which there were only wooden benches for those who did sit. The average first-class passenger rate in Germany before the war was 2.9 cents. This was higher than the average passenger rate in this country, with the cost of a berth in a sleeping car or a seat in a parlor car added. The rates for all three classes of service on the private railways of France were lower than for the corresponding classes of service in Germany.

As to freight rates, it is indisputable that, under comparable conditions, they have almost invariably been lower on private railways than on state railways, and prior to the advances made last year, the average freight rate per mile in the United States, in spite of the higher wages paid here, was lower than in any other country in the world except India.

I do not criticise the advances in rates which have been made under government operation in this country. They were necessitated by increases in expenses and, in fact, are being found insufficient to cover the increases in expenses. Advances in rates would have been necessary under private operation. It is, however, proper and fair to emphasize the facts, that advocates of government operation have contended it would result in large reductions of railway expenses and rates; that these large advances in rates were made necessary by increases of expenses which occurred during government operation, in spite of the large economies which it has been claimed could be practised under that system; and that therefore it may be wise to look askance upon claims and predictions now being and which in future will be made, regarding the economies which could and would be effected and the reductions in rates which could and would be made under permanent operation. There never has been, and is not now, any basis in experience or reason for these claims and predictions.   They are now, they always have been, and they always will be the baseless fabric of a vision.

DEFICITS UNDER GOVERNMENT OPERATION

As I have remarked, the advances in rates which have been made have not proved sufficient to cover the increase in expenses.   The government incurred a deficit of $236,000,000 on the operation of the railroads in 1918.   In the first four months of 1919 it incurred a further deficit of $250,000,000.   The advocates of government ownership have contended that, under that policy, the profits earned by the railroads would go into the public treasury.   Opponents of that policy have pointed out that, although rates usually have been higher under state than under private operation, government ownership in most countries has resulted in deficits that the public has had to pay in taxes; and it has been predicted that this would be the result in the United States.   The very first year of government operation vindicated this prediction, in spite of larger advances in rates than the railway companies had ever asked for.   The former director general recently estimated that, on the basis of present expenses and rates, a surplus should be earned in 1919.   After having carefully studied the statistics of earnings and expenses for the last year, and especially the last six months, I confess I am unable even to conjecture upon what information he based this conclusion.   In my opinion, there is a far greater probability of a deficit of $500,000,000 being incurred in 1919, than of any surplus being earned.   In other words, with respect to deficits, the United States is having the same experience with state management that most countries do.

EFFECTS ON RAILWAY SERVICE

Is there any good ground for believing that, under government operation, the passenger and freight service rendered to the public would be better than under private operation? Certainly experience affords no grounds for any such belief. Our passenger service under private operation has had shortcomings, some of them serious; but, considering the conditions under which it has been rendered, it has been, on the whole, the best in the world.   The density of our passenger traffic has been only one-third to one-fifth as great as that of the railways of the leading countries of Europe; but you will seek in vain in Europe or elsewhere for comforts and luxuries equal to those our passenger service affords. As to freight service, how can anybody expect that a centralized government system, which would get all the business available, regardless of the kind of service it rendered, would try as hard to satisfy its customers as would a large number of privately-managed railways, each dependent for the amount of money it made upon the kind of satisfaction it gave its customers?

EFFECTS UPON RAILWAY EMPLOYEES

It may be contended that recent experience at least shows that railway employees will be better off under government than under private operation. The interest of the public as well as the employees must be considered, however. The developments of the last year have forcibly brought home to the public the fact that it is not the large capitalists that are mistakenly supposed to own the railways who bear most of the increased expenses caused by advances in railway wages. The average net operating income per year of the railway companies in the three years ended June 30, 1917, from which interest and dividends had to be paid, was only about $950,-000,000. The advances in wages made to railway labor under government operation now amount to $1,000,000,000 a year, or to over 5 per cent upon a sum equal to the total capitalization of the railways. Now, obviously, the bulk of the advances in wages are and must be paid by the "common people" of the United States. It is plainly to the interest of the public, not only that the employees shall be paid all they are entitled to, but that they shall not be paid more than they are entitled to. For reasons I have clearly indicated, it is easier to have the determination of what they are entitled to receive made in an orderly, public and fair way that will adequately safeguard the interests of the public, under private than under government operation.

Looking at the matter from the standpoint of the employees, it is very far from certain that they have more to hope from government than from private operation. They have received larger advances in wages within the last year, under war conditions, than ever before. But if we revert to the period before the war, we find the evidence shows that, while the state railways of the world usually employed more men to handle a given amount of traffic than did the private railways under comparable conditions, it was not true that state railways ordinarily paid higher wages than private railways. In respect of both wages and working conditions, the employees of our railways were better off than those of almost any system of state railways.

Looking to the future, if our railroads are to be returned to private operation, there should be, and probably will be, established some system for the adjudication of differences between railways and their employees under which the merits will be fully considered, and public opinion and representatives of the public will have the deciding voice. On the other hand, if government operation is continued, the entire subject of wages and working conditions is likely to be thrown into the maelstrom of political struggles. Now, as American citizens, would railway employees like to see their wages and working conditions become the subject of incessant political squabbling and fighting? Regarding the matter from the standpoint of their selfish interests, can they feel any confidence that in the long run they would gain more by having their wages and working conditions settled in this way than by having them settled by conferences with the managements of the railways, and, if the conferences failed, by orderly arbitration? The efficiency of railway labor and of railway operation under government operation undoubtedly would be lower than under private operation, and in consequence, expenses would be higher. Therefore, the resistance of the public to advances in wages might be greater in the long run under government than under private operation. Railway employees under government operation would be a strong political force, and they might be able to hold the balance of power between the great political parties. But if they carried matters with a high hand, they probably would find they would array a large majority of the public against them. In that event, they might find that, instead of government operation working to their advantage, it would be used to repress and even oppress them.

EFFECTS OF GOVERNMENT MANAGEMENT UPON POLITICS

These considerations bring us to what is probably the most important point to be determined in passing on the question of government ownership. What would be its effects upon our politics and government? No one familiar with our railway history needs to be reminded that the railway corporations once exercised a potent and malignant influence upon our state and national politics. But the political influence of the railway corporations has been almost completely destroyed. This is demonstrated by the many restrictive laws which have been enacted for their regulation. Under government ownership, not only would the question of the wages and working conditions of the employees be thrown into politics, but also questions affecting appointments and promotions to official positions, and expenditures for operation, maintenance, and improvements. Under the existing railroad control law, the President of the United States has autocratic authority over the operation of the railways. He delegates this to the director general. The President would not and probably should not be allowed to exercise such autocratic authority in time of peace. Congress could hardly be expected to go on indefinitely voting large railway appropriations over whose use, in spite of its responsibility to the public, Congress would have almost no control. Even though the director general should nominally be allowed to continue to possess his present autocratic authority, it would be but a short time until he would be subjected to enormous pressure to make appointments and expenditures for political rather than business reasons. This would be inevitable under our form of government. If part of his authority were tranferred to some other officer or body, there would result a division of responsibility for results, with the evil consequences to which this would lead. If Congress should begin to take more of a hand in railway affairs, the temptation of many of its members to use their power over the Railroad Administration to further local and sectional political purposes would be irresistible. Members of Congress might not wish to yield to this temptation, but they almost certainly would be forced to by the demands of constituencies which would think rather of the advantages that might accrue to their local or sectional interests from having certain things done than of the interests of the nation as a whole. In short, under government operation in time of peace, it would be impracticable to keep the railways out of politics or politics out of the railways; and it is impossible to exaggerate the seriousness of the effects upon our national life which might be produced.

The alternative policies which are available are not *unregulated* and *uncontrolled* private ownership and management, or government ownership and management. The alternatives are *regulated* private ownership and management, or government ownership and operation; for so long as we have private operation, we shall have government regulation. Let us hope that if private operation is restored, we shall have wise and fair regulation. If we do have, the results of private operation will be far more beneficial to the public than the results of government operation would be. If we cannot feel a reasonable confidence in our ability to devise and carry out a wise, constructive and successful policy of government regulation, on what basis of experience or reason can we found even a hope, much less an expectation, that we could and would perform the much more difficult task of devising and carrying out an intelligent and efficient policy of government management?

COÖRDINATED DEVELOPMENT OF WATERWAYS AND RAILROADS *

BY WALKER D. HINES, DIRECTOR GENERAL OF RAILROADS

The war has brought about some very unexpected changes to this country. I believe one of the highly important changes which the war has brought about is a change which is full of meaning for this city, and that change is that it has created an opportunity for the first time in the history of this country to make a really effective experiment in determining the value of our inland waterways. I take it you are all aware that the Railroad Administration has entered seriously upon the undertaking of establishing a transportation service on the Mississippi River between St. Louis and New Orleans. The service was entered upon last fall through the acquisition of the boats then available and a limited service has since been maintained. We are planning to spend approximately $7,000,000 in the aggregate through the addition to the existing equipment of about forty modern barges and six modern tug boats, so as to make a really effective test of the utility of the Mississippi River as a channel of commerce. Personally, I am a firm believer in the view that there are great possibilities in the development of the river. I shall count it as one of the most gratifying achievements of the Railroad Administration if we are able to realize the hopes that I have in that direction. I think in the nature of things a waterway of such extent and such capacity must have an important economic value in the development of the country. In addition to that the fact that the government has expended so much money in the improvement of the river makes it only common business sense to undertake to use what has been prepared and as long as the Railroad Administration continues I want to assure you that that use will be made in the most effective possible way.

Without any reflection upon the motives of the railroad companies, it is only natural to say and to perceive that any

* From an address before the St. Louis Chamber of Commerce, April 30, 1919.

one railroad company has no especial interest in developing the waterway. Each railroad company of course looked at its transportation problem from its own standpoint. It wanted to develop its own lines, it wanted to create feeders that would be exclusively feeders for its own lines and the Mississippi River, of course, could not be put into that class, and consequently under private management and under separate management of the railroad companies the motive never existed to develop the waterway. Temporarily the government has taken control of the railroads and has placed them in a unified system, and this great waterway is just as much a matter of national concern, it is just as much a matter for national development, as are any of the railroads which are under government control. So that the war, which brought about this unexpected result of government control of the railroads, has likewise brought about this unexpected opportunity for the development of the Mississippi.

I don't think there is any serious concern on the part of the people of this city and on the part of the people of the Mississippi Valley as to what will be the outcome of this experiment during federal control of the railroads. We all, however, have to recognize the strong probability that at a date in the not distant future some provision will be made for turning the railroads back to private management and when that times comes a very serious question will arise and perhaps that question is in your minds at the present time, as to what will become of this transportation system which the government has created upon the Mississippi River. As I see it, and I can speak only my personal view, because after all it is a matter upon which Congress will have to act, the thing that will be obviously in the public interest will be to retain this government transportation system on the Mississippi as a government transportation system after the railroads go back to private management, at least during an adequate experimental stage. My thought is that if, immediately upon the return of the railroads to private management, the government should sell its equipment on the Mississippi River, the strong probability is that the motive to make a success of that transportation system in the national interest might speedily disappear. At any rate I think it would be a serious risk to run.

My own judgment is that, however soon the railroads may be turned back to private management, this transportation system on the Mississippi ought to be retained, and earnestly pressed forward by the government so as to make a complete and lasting demonstration of the utility of the Mississippi as a channel of transportation. I suppose there is no community in the United States to which such a course will mean more than it will to the community of St. Louis. It will result in giving St. Louis in a lasting way the benefit of its magnificent geographical location. So long as the river was not used as it can be used St. Louis had little if any advantage over any other point which was a railroad center, but when the river shall be used as I believe we can use it, St. Louis, in addition to having this wonderful advantage as an exceptional railroad center, will have the benefit of the geographical advantage of its location on the Mississippi.

There are one or two points I wanted to impress upon all of you, because the success of this important experiment will be absolutely dependent upon the coöperation of the people for whose benefit the experiment is primarily made. In the first place, one of the great difficulties which has always existed in the satisfactory development of the inland waterways has been the lack of the necessary terminal facilities to effect the transfer of traffic from the river to factories and from the river to the railroads. The cost of making the transfer in many instances has been prohibitive. The situation existed where traffic could be loaded into a freight car and that freight car could be placed on the private track of the particular industry, or could be turned over to another railroad for further transportation with practically no additional cost for the transfer. But when we have a condition where the factories are not alongside of the wharves on the river, where the railroads which must carry the traffic the rest of its journey have not a track connection right on the wharf, there is an important transfer service to be performed at very large cost which would go far towards absorbing and offsetting any possible economy in the use of the river, and if that situation continues we cannot hope for the success which ought to be realized in carrying out our present endeavors.

This matter of providing the necessary terminals is in the nature of things to a large extent a matter for local initiative, and I want to urge all of you as far as it comes in your power to exercise any influence in the matter to bring about the proper development of the river terminals so that these boats, which are being operated by the government, can effect their transfers of freight as between factories and the river, as between the river and the railroads, so as to eliminate this prohibitive transfer cost which has existed in the past, and so as to put the waterway upon a reasonable parity with the advantages which are enjoyed by the all-rail lines. The effect of uncertainty as to the future of the waterway system may have a tendency to discourage immediate development of these terminals, but I want to impress on you that if you want the waterway transportation, and I am sure you do, the way to diminish to the vanishing point all uncertainty in regard to the matter is to improve these terminals as rapidly as possible. I believe if the local communities interested properly develop their terminals so that we can speedily demonstrate the economic value of the waterway there will not be any question whatever, but that Congress will see to it that adequate provision is made for the preservation of this national transportation system, and as a part of any legislation dealing with that subject it must, of course, be understood that Congress will provide for compelling the establishment of reasonable and proper through routes and through rates between the railroads and the transportation lines on the river, and in that way will require as a matter of law the interchange of traffic which perhaps is not in the separate interest of the railroads under private management. If you will only provide the terminals my judgment is that Congress will do the rest and that you will get in the completest measure the demonstration and the benefit of the great value of the waterway as a permanent part of the economic forces of this country.

In conclusion I want to say that in addition to doing all you can to bring about the proper development of these terminals along the river I want to ask all of you who have any interest in the matter of traffic to give your hearty support to this water line. You can feel that in doing so you are not only promoting your own interest for the time being but you are participating in an important national movement, because I cannot believe that a great waterway like the Mississippi can be left, consistently with the public interest, to practically the negligible amount of navigation that has taken place upon it in the past. I want to see this experiment succeed. I believe it is in the national interest that it should succeed and I appeal to you for your active support in the development of terminals and for your active support in the supplying of the traffic necessary.

PRIVATE OWNERSHIP, OPERATION AND FINANC-
ING OF THE RAILROADS

BY THOMAS DE WITT CUYLER, CHAIRMAN, ASSOCIATION OF
RAILWAY EXECUTIVES

No more important question is before the American people to-day than the final settlement of the railroad situation. By that is meant the ownership of the roads, the method of operation and the financing.

Four methods have been suggested:

First: Government ownership and operation.

Second: The continuation of government operation for a certain number of years under the present law.

Third: Government ownership and private operation.

Fourth: Private ownership and operation.

As to the first method:—

It may be regarded as settled for the present that the country is averse to public ownership. It has seen enough under government control to learn how impossible it is that efficient and proper management can be given to the railroads through such a method. The operation of private plants by public bodies generally tends to inefficiency, and especially when the operation is so vast in its character as is the operation of the railroads of this country. Aside from the inefficiency, there is also to be taken into consideration the political degeneracy that is sure to ensue from government operation of the railroads. There are many indications that the American people have drawn some shrewd conclusions from their experience of the past year and a half and I think it may therefore be assumed that when we come to settle the railroad question through legislation at the next Congress, government ownership and operation will not have to be seriously dealt with.

Second. It has been suggested by the late director general, and endorsed by the present director general, that for the purpose of testing the efficiency of government ownership and operation, the present government control should be extended, say for a period of five years from January 1, 1920.

It is difficult to understand upon what theory this suggestion is made. At best, it would be a test of simply one method of operation, namely, through government control, and the only question determined at the end of the period would be whether this had or had not been an efficient way of operating the roads. There is nothing to show in the period that has elapsed since the government took possession of the roads that the efficiency of the management will be improved or that all the ills that attend public ownership would be not only fostered but increased during the continuance of this control. The proposition has met with no real public support.

Third. Government ownership and private operation.

This has been suggested by Senator Cummins, who has given to the railroad question much study for many years, but it must be confessed that in the final analysis, the plan would seem to be impracticable. It is hard to believe that the American people would ever consent to own the properties and then lease them out to private capital for operation. If the ownership by the public were a good thing in itself, there is no reason why the people of the country should not receive the resultant benefits that would come from their operation. It is hard to conceive, on the other hand, that private capital would be willing to enlist in the organization of companies purely for operating purposes that must necessarily be strictly limited as to the return on their capital and also as to the tenure of private operation. Such a joint proposition would be sure to lead in the end to public operation as well as ownership, and there can be no question in my judgment that the public at the very outset, if such a proposition was made, would either reject it in toto or insist on public operation as well as ownership.

Fourth. Private ownership and operation.

This has been a tried method in the past and the results from the standpoint of the shipper and the people at large of the country have been satisfactory. There has been an unfortunate theory prevalent that the roads broke down at the beginning of the war and were unable from a physical and financial standpoint to render satisfactory service. It is true that great congestion ensued and that capital was wanting to provide necessary additions and betterments. But this came from no fault of the roads, no want of proper organization or ability to operate, but simply from the laws of the country as then existing, preventing combinations or the use of the roads as a whole. Therefore when the roads were taken over for war purposes, every existing law was set aside and the roads operated simply and wholly irrespective of law, from the standpoint of the country's needs. If the roads had been permitted to do that which the government has done, there can be no question but that the emergency would have been met and the operation been altogether more satisfactory from the standpoint of the public and the owners of the properties.

Now as to the future.

If the roads are to be returned to their owners, there must be sane and reasonable legislation enacted for the benefit of the public at large and the owners of the property. The public needs transportation. It is vital to the existence and success of the country. The owners must have a return upon their property which is fair and just if they are to advance the necessary capital to meet the demands of transportation. Additions and betterments must be provided for, wages must be protected and the return on the property investment must be safeguarded. In the past, the attitude of a shipper and to some extent of the public at large has been to get as much as possible out of the roads for the least possible payment. The shipper has not realized that his prosperity was dependent upon the proper maintenance and operation of the roads. The case is a good deal similar to the opposition of the farmer at first to the good roads movement. He could not see that the increased taxation brought better facilities for transportation of his goods and products, which more than overcame the increased cost. Where good roads have been built through rural communities, the farmer has at once recognized their benefit and no stronger or warmer supporters of good roads exist to-day than among the farming classes of the country. The shipper must come to realize that he must not only have the best of transportation but must be willing that there should be a return upon that transportation that will induce capital to provide for it.

The Association of Railway Executives, which I represent, believe in private ownership and private operation, but they are convinced that unless a fair return is assured upon the capital invested, the outlook for the country is extremely unsatisfactory. But they further believe that when the question is thoroughly understood by the country, the people at large will be willing that constructive legislation should be enacted. Such legislation would have for its basic foundation the recognized principle that the roads must be maintained at the very highest standard; must be ready to meet every demand for increased facilities and extensions; that the employees must receive a fair return for work performed; and that capital must receive a return that will make it feel safe not only in its present investment, but in all future financing that will be demanded from the roads.

As to the method of carrying out such a basic proposition there have been many suggestions. We do not believe that the country will consent either directly or indirectly to a guarantee by the government. That will savor too much of the people's bearing the cost. Nor do we think it desirable, if obtainable. The free operation of the roads under private ownership, with those safeguards that are essential, will, in the judgment of the executives, protect all parties in interest and preserve that independent spirit of private ownership that is so well recognized in this country. Whether these fundamental principles shall be carried out through the medium of the existing Interstate Commerce Commission or whether a body should be created who shall be empowered to see that the Interstate Commerce Commission carries out the rate basis in the spirit and letter of the Act is a question for consideration. But we cannot help but feel that, in view of the large burdens now resting upon the Interstate Commerce Commission, an independent body of men, say possibly three in number, who should enjoy a salary commensurate with the importance of their office, could better act in carrying out the law than a body that has already more than it can possibly carry on its shoulders. We believe that the fixing of all rates should be absolutely in this body or whatever other Federal agency may be provided, and that the state commissions should perform such proper police duties as are necessary for the safeguarding of the people of the states in which they operate.

It is believed that the coming Congress will approach this whole subject in a constructive and unbiased attitude and we are hopeful that out of all the confusion and distress that now exists sane and reasonable legislation will be enacted.

A PROGRAM OF RAILROAD LEGISLATION

BY THEODORE E. BURTON, FORMER U. S. SENATOR FROM OHIO

The primary need in solving problems relating to the railroads is a more intelligent comprehension of certain elementary facts and principles. We must abandon the idea that competition is helpful in the control of monopolies, like railways.

For many years it was the cherished policy of both state and national legislatures to do everything to promote the sharpest competition between the different agencies of transportation. In cases where sufficient facilities already existed, or could readily be furnished by additions to existing lines, new railways were encouraged and chartered. That resulted in much waste of capital in construction, and in very largely increased expenses of operation.

So long ago as the year 1842, there was a discussion on this subject in the House of Commons, in which Mr. Gladstone expressed himself. There was an existing line to the northwest of London, and it was proposed to charter another line paralleling it. Mr. Gladstone said he did not believe the public would be benefited thereby; that there was very much capital to invest, but that the principles applicable to industrial enterprise and to ordinary commercial operations would not apply to railroads; that after a brief period of competition, a combination would be the result; and he quoted as applicable to the management of railways a saying which he ascribed to Mr. Charles J. Fox: Breves inimicitiæ, amicitiæ sempiternæ (animosities brief, friendships lasting).

When the Inter-State Commerce Act was under consideration in the eighties, there was a proposition to authorize pooling. It was rejected by an overwhelming majority. Nevertheless, I think it is the conviction of those who have given the closest attention to this subject, that it would have been well had pooling been authorized at that time, because it would have prevented ruinous competition. One result of

46

the paralleling of lines was disastrous rate wars, which diminished very much the revenue of the railways, but did not confer any substantial or at least any general benefit upon the public. It was only the most wealthy and powerful shippers of freight who reaped advantages. They were able to mobilize their commodities and send them at a time when those freight wars were in vogue; not, however, passing on the cheapened cost to their customers, because with the restoration of normal charges the gain that they had acquired from the cutting of rates was credited to profit.

I do not say that competition will be entirely done away with, or should be. There at least will be competition in service. Railroad managers endeavor in every way to secure promptness, and the accommodation of the public, and these motives should have the fostering care of those officials who have to do with public regulation.

Nevertheless, it must be said that all this tendency to combination is not so much the result of a desire for monopoly as of developments which make for efficiency, for economy, and for the larger purposes which are necessary for the benefit of the public.

Every railway has certain duties and obligations to perform to the public. Reasonable facilities must be provided. Constant operation is required. In order that its work may be properly done, certain privileges must be granted, such as the right of eminent domain. Then again, there is a distinctive feature in the nature of railway property. Unlike banking capital, unlike merchandise, you cannot pick one up and carry it away somewhere else, it is fixed in a defined location.

These facts all lead to the conclusion that in their relation to the public railways are altogether different from other forms of property and that they should be accorded exceptional treatment, also that they should be subjected to an exceptional degree of supervision and regulation.

Twenty years ago, or more, there seemed to be danger that these powerful aggregations of capital would overshadow the government itself. They were influential in legislative halls; there was an opinion which was very widespread that their success and their possession of power were very desirable for the upbuilding and development of the country. But now the pendulum has swung the other way, and it is very difficult for the railways to maintain rates with public permission sufficient for their reasonable maintenance. The people are very loath to accept those higher charges which are necessary in order that the railways may meet their obligations.

On the question of the relation of the railway to the public, there have been three distinct phases or tendencies sharply defined. The first was one of favor to the roads. This was illustrated by numerous land grants, by an earnest desire for the development of transportation facilities in the country, and by the willingness of communities and states to grant subventions to railways and to give them various substantial concessions. The next, or second phase, was in favor of the shippers. This was in a measure contemporaneous with the Granger movement, beginning some five years after the Civil War, and had its initiative, as far as legislation is concerned, in state legislatures, but afterwards was manifested in the national Congress as well.

Perhaps the most notable illustration of this change in the popular attitude was in the apparent disposition of the Interstate Commerce Commission, in many of its rulings, to guard the interests of the shippers, without adequate regard for the requirements of the railways, or the necessary development of transportation facilities. The third tendency or phase has been one favorable to the railway employees. This commenced in humanitarian movements, in provisions relating to safety appliances, in the lessening of hours, and then recently —quite recently—in very substantial increases in wages. It is very evident that each of these three tendencies, or phases, has, and is likely to, run to serious excess. Indeed, there is a considerable number of very intelligent observers, made up of men who now believe in government ownership—not that they are naturally believers in the principle—who think the Federal government is the only body which has the authority and the prestige to stand in the way of excessive demands for wages and for taxes, and is the only institution that can gain popular support for such increases of charges as may be necessary.

It is maintained by them that so long as there is merely a controversy between private owners and the employees there will be an overwhelming sympathy for the employees; but if the weight of increased wages and higher taxation is felt in added rates and the payment of deficiencies from the public treasury, there will then be a popular movement, potent in its nature, against demands which are excessive.

If we can correctly interpret expressions of popular opinion, the people of the United States are by no means in favor of government ownership. What will happen in the future, no one can foretell. The considerations which will have greatest weight will be the convenience of the public, efficiency, and economy. Questions of public policy and of the relations of the state to business are too often mixed up with popular appeals which befog the real question, and there is a peculiar danger in that regard in the treatment of the railways. It must be said that the experiment of temporary governmental operation, though accepted as a necessity arising from the war, has by no means given general satisfaction.

Now, what are the immediate measures required for the solution of the railroad problem? In the first place, wipe off the statute, divorce from the popular thought, the idea that competition is a creative or helpful force in their management. We have had an object lesson in this war. We have learned that unified control and coöperation are essential. There were many object lessons before. I remember very distinctly an instance in northern Ohio. One of the best equipped trunk lines in the country, known as the Lake Shore and Michigan Southern, extended from Buffalo to Chicago. Some promoters came into the field and said: "We will build a parallel road." They went to the farmer and said: "Now, my friend, we will give you a competing line; you will have another way of getting to Buffalo and to Cleveland; we will charge cheaper rates; we will accommodate you; anyway, you will have competition and you ought to give us the right of way through your farm." The new railway was built so near that in some places you could flip a copper from the rails of the one to those of the other line.

Inside of two years they were both under the same owner-ship and virtually the same management, and there was nothing accomplished by the building of that road which could not have been accomplished by tripling or quadrupling the tracks of the other.

There have been many similar instances in the improvement of waterways. That delusion (for it is nothing less) has led to the expenditure of tens, even hundreds, of millions of dollars for the improvement of streams, which it was never intended should be used for navigation. Some years ago the most frequent argument for these improvements at Washington was, "Why, it will lower freight rates on the railroads." If a railway was built alongside a river that required locks and dams and expensive improvement to render it navigable and that railroad cost ten millions of dollars, the argument was, "Improve the waterway at an expense of another ten millions of dollars." For what? To make the railway behave itself and charge reasonable rates.

There was an instance in one of the Gulf states of a railway with very limited traffic paralleling a river of which you could say, "Nowhere such a devious stream, save in fancy or in dream," and there was no pretense that the stream would be used for navigation; but an official computation was made of how much the competing railway would have to abate from its charges because the potentiality of navigation could be afforded in the river. There were numerous recommendations for improvements in waterways, with no expectation that they would ever be utilized. So they went on, as it were, singing a song, "One million for this, one million for that, regulating freight rates, regulating freight rates." That delusion still has a strong hold on the popular mind, and is not absent in its influence on even members of Congress, and of Senators.

The next thing to be secured is an early readjustment of rates, so as to meet the additional cost of operation. Up till the beginning of this war, and the higher charges imposed by the government, there had been a very notable increase in the price of commodities and in the cost of living. That increase had not manifested itself in railway freight rates. The general average per ton per mile had kept down to the figure, and in some cases was less than, it had been when prices were at the very low level of 1890 to 1900. Indeed, while the average charges per mile for passenger traffic were a trifle less in 1916 than in 1896, and for freight substantially less, the index numbers show that the cost of food, clothing and the ordinary necessaries of life had increased 77 per cent. Again in 1917, while passenger and freight rates remained substantially the same as before, the cost of living went soaring. It was impossible that so great a disparity could continue. When we take into account the higher cost of wages, about $1,265,000,000 per annum more than it was in 1917, and the greater cost of material, there is an absolute necessity for increase, not that rates should soar to a point where they do not belong, but there should be a reasonable increase, and that now, with the assurance that it is to be permanent unless conditions very greatly change.

There have been arguments for a fixed minimum and maximum rate of return. I am not quite ready to give approval to that. Some propositions are to the effect that the return shall not fall below 4 per cent or rise above 7 per cent. The general objection to that is that at least if there is a government guaranty, it is in substance, if not in form, government ownership and if government ownership is to be adopted, let us adopt it purely and simply as an independent proposition. But there is the further argument that it takes away that initiative, that desire for skill and ability in management which is the very life-blood and the mainspring of all enterprises.

It might be a better plan to provide that the income over a fixed maximum shall be divided, say, one-half to the government and one-half to the owner, to be paid out in dividends, or let the employees share the surplus. But to say to the railroad managers, "Your income shall not go above a rigidly established percentage, no more than that" is to place discouragement on good management. Of course, the natural thing to be done when the return is unusually large is to lower the rates and give the public the benefit. And it must be always borne in mind in the relations of the public to the railways, that these great means of transportation require constant betterment and increase in facilities. Population increases with a certain rate of rapidity; fortunately wealth increases more rapidly than population; the volume of commodities consumed increases more rapidly than either, but transportation is at the head of the list. The general rate of increase in transportation is about two to three times—it is rather difficult to make an exact estimate—as great as the increase in population. That important fact means a great deal; it means that there is an unusual, sometimes excessive demand upon all the agencies of transportation for increasing their facilities.

There is another thing that must be done—consider this question as a national question. I should favor government incorporation of railways, or at least make it optional for them to incorporate with Federal charters. Why they do business—of course, I mean interstate railways—between the different states, and from one end of the country to the other in such manner that state lines are mere vanishing traces on the map. There may be a sign "Maryland Line," "Pennsylvania Line," but it is a mere gratification of the curiosity of the tourist. Unified control, unified operation, with as little recognition of state lines as possible, and with as little subjection as possible to the varying and sometimes inconsistent regulations of the different states, makes for the best adjustment of the railroad problem.

Again, in the matter of intrastate rates, some states have provided rates so low that if they were adopted as the general scale all along the line, they would be confiscatory. The Supreme Court has held, in a very able decision by Justice Hughes, that the Federal government, through its agencies, can control these intrastate rates, that is upon trunk lines. Louisiana should not make one set of rates and Texas or Oklahoma another.

It would be evidently disastrous to return the railways to the owners before a settlement of these great questions. I think, if I can judge the disposition in Congress, that it is much more appreciative of the requirements of the railways than it was five, ten, or fifteen years ago. There is a more intelligent comprehension of the general subject. I do not mean that careful consideration is not required. Do not leave the investigation to the railway magnates, or to the security holders alone, nor yet to unfriendly agitators, but let us in this country of ours do something new in this era for which we hope after the war, let all of us take an interest in matters of general concern and seek to make our influence felt, whether in or out of public life, outside the narrow sphere of our own personal interest.

I may say that the absence of that general interest on the part of the public is the most trying obstacle to the public man who seeks to do his duty. He comes to learn that the favor of a very limited number, who have obtained personal aid through his intervention, is far more valuable as a personal asset in politics than the good will of a multitude who pay little attention to public affairs. Such associations as this should do their part. If you don't do anything more, Dr. Johnson, make a well-considered report.*

Some of those who have to do with the decision of the question will read it. What is needed down at Washington and in the state legislatures is a careful and impartial presentation of intelligent views on these great questions from people whose interests are in the general welfare.

Thus I have hope that this problem will be settled, and I say again, settled properly; that the railroads will not be turned back to their owners until it is. It would be like sending them out on an uncharted and stormy sea if anything else were done. To my mind, it is in a measure immaterial whether the interval is one year, or three or five years, provided a definite policy is conclusively agreed upon under which the railroads after a fixed date shall be returned to their owners, and shall have such rights, in the way of charges, that they can live a profitable existence and perform their duties to the public. If this is done, the railroads will be able to respond to the demands upon them; they can safeguard the interests of investors; they can give fair, yet liberal compensation to their employees; they can keep pace with the ever growing requirements of commerce and of industry.

* This paper is the report of an address at a meeting of the National Institute of Social Sciences. The president of the Institute was in the chair.

A RAILROAD POLICY BRIEFLY OUTLINED *

BY GEORGE A. POST, CHAIRMAN OF THE RAILROAD COMMITTEE
OF THE CHAMBER OF COMMERCE OF THE UNITED STATES

As Chairman of the Railroad Committee of the Chamber of Commerce of the United States, I am charged, with my associates, with a responsibility which is very great, and which has called for an expenditure of time and energy and thought far beyond that which I could afford from my own business. But I have been impelled by the idea that somebody must try to make some contribution toward a sane and safe solution of this great question, of such vital importance to the people of our land. Therefore, for months, the days and the nights have been spent freely in listening to the proposals of many minds upon this subject, and there has been a great variety of opinion. All of the men and women are earnest in thought, possessed of different kinds of experiences, and all wanting to be helpful.

The Railroad Committee of the Chamber of Commerce, and also another body, of which I have had the honor to be a member, and of which your honored President has been a member (and I see in the audience that distinguished financier and student of public problems, Mr. Paul M. Warburg, who has been our associate), have come to certain conclusions as to what must be done by the Congress which is about to convene, toward the settlement of this railroad question. In framing up the recommendations to be made to those to whom we must report, and for the consideration of those whose attention we would attract, we have felt that it was necessary for us to take cognizance of certain outstanding facts, that need to be grappled with at the start, and which seem to be immediately responsible for public opinion as it is now formed. There is a very wide difference between public opinion as it exists to-day and public opinion as it existed before the railroads were taken over by the Government.

My associates have directed me, as their spokesman, to

* Report of an address at a meeting of the National Institute.

report to the body whose representatives we are, that public opinion requires that the railroads now under Federal control and operation shall be returned to their owners for operation just as quickly as such remedial legislation by Congress can be passed, as a necessary preliminary to their safe transfer from Federal to private control.

Many things which were matters of contention between the public and the carriers but a few short years ago are no longer matters of dispute. Railroad executives are now yearning for legislation which will bring about a situation which they earnestly and strenuously opposed before Federal control of railroads; which simply shows that the railroad executives, like all the rest of us, have learned a lot during this war period. We all agree now that the Government, through some agency established by it, must have a comprehensive supervision over the operations of the railroads, in order that there shall be estopped any possibility of the exploitation of the public by those who might plot against the public weal.

It is understood and agreed, again, that there should be brought about, as quickly as possible, a unification of our transportation facilities—steam and electric roads, inland waterways, hard surface highways, motor trucks—everything that is a means of transportation, so that they shall serve the public in the most economical way.

It was only a short time ago that railroad executives deemed it to be their duty to their stockholders and the owners of their securities to baffle any and all attempts that were made to build electric lines, or to establish waterway communications because of their supposed deleterious effects upon the railroads themselves. They were earnestly of the opinion that that was their duty at that time so to oppose, but they have changed their minds about that. In a recent conference upon the transportation question, Mr. Daniel Willard, President of the Baltimore and Ohio Railroad, who is recognized as a very distinguished railroad executive, a very thoughtful, fair-minded man, with vision, said upon this subject of the nationalization of our transportation systems: "We ought, for the development of transportation in this country of ours, with its magnificent distances, to so connect our steam railroads and our electric railroads and our waterways and our motor trucks, that a shipment may start anywhere, on any one of these agencies, and go to any place in the United States, over any or all of these agencies, or to any other place reached by any of these agencies. I should want it fixed, and believe it.should be fixed, so that through rates and through arrangements for shipments should be permissible from any place to any other place, over any and all agencies that may occur in between. There should be no putting up of a bar between any of the transportation agencies." Thus we see how far we have moved in that direction.

We have also come to a conclusion—and there is no dispute about it any more—about the joint use of terminals and the pooling of equipment in facilitating the movement of freight and passengers. That was forbidden by law before the war. The Director-General of Railroads of the United States proceeded to do it regardless of the law, because we couldn't win the war unless it was done. Because it was done during the war, the people find that it was well that it was done and that there is no reason on earth why it shouldn't continue to be done in the future, under any plan of reorganization. Legislation to effectuate that policy will be acquiesced in by everybody, and, in fact, is desired by everybody.

There seems to be a marked trend of public opinion also in the direction of providing for the consolidation of railroads into a limited number of strong, competing systems, such consolidation to be permitted, advised, or required by Federal authority, when it is deemed in the public interest.

Think of it! We have now had our minds clarified to the extent that we can see that in the consolidation of public service, there is the best service to the public. There is still ringing in our ears the denunciation by strident orators, seeking office, a little while ago, of all proposed consolidations— who thought the public welfare could be best served by compelling everybody to fight everybody. An office-hungry man who would face an audience in this day, and, under the developments of the war period, undertake to harangue a crowd with an appeal to send him to Congress upon that issue, would never draw a cent of mileage from the Federal Treasury as a public servant.

It is also pretty generally understood and agreed now that

State Commissions shall no longer interfere with rates that affect interstate commerce.* They are making a strong fight for the preservation of the powers they have, and they are a fine lot of men, but they are obsessed with a frenzied thirst for power they should not have, because they have not yet become sufficiently animated by the real purpose and desire of the people at large. They will come to it gradually, as the people at large have come to it conclusively.

I might go on and elaborate several more of the things that are now perfectly clear to us, about which we have fought in the past, to emphasize and effectuate which statutes have been piled up mountain high in the legislative tomes all over our country. Under the light of experience they are bound to melt and gradually fade away, and when reference shall be made to them in the future, it will only be to wonder in what state of mind the public were when they advocated, or acquiesced in the enactment of such legislation.

With all the millions, and hundreds of millions of dollars that have been ordained to be the right of the employees of the railroads to get more than they got on the first day of January, 1918, and the increased cost of railroad living for all the things which it is necessary to consume in the service of the public, there has not yet been a commensurate advance of that which the public pays for the service given. If such advance is not provided for before the roads go back to their owners, the government ought not to return them. The disbursements made necessary by governmental order must be not only equaled, but exceeded by the same government that ordered them, as an absolute condition precedent to ending Federal control.

What is the use of public sentiment saying: "Oh, put back the railroads into the hands of their owners! We thought them wicked and inefficient before the war, but now that we have had Federal control for fifteen months and suffered so seriously from poor service, *give them back!*" unless we are willing to pay the bill? The wages of the railroad employees cannot be kept up where they are, unless we are willing to pay over the funds that will meet them, in the shape of rates and fares. When the workmen have gotten all they want, or can get, with public approval, and everything else has been paid for, including coal, engines, cars, rails, taxes, and thousands of other necessities at high prices, the railroads must still have large sums of money so that they can constantly keep expanding their facilities. They must have a surplus so that if a devastating flood like that of Dayton, or an earthquake, like that on the Pacific Coast, or any other kind of disaster overtakes them, they can repair the havoc wrought and the public must have paid into their treasuries, or established their credit so that such extraordinary expenditures may be met.

What are we to do with the railroads? In the public interest we are, if we are wise and regardful of our own interest, going to give them a chance to live. If they are to be strong and adequate in service, not weak and impotent, more money will go out of our pockets for the service they render than ever before, because their living expenses are greater than ever.

COMPETITION AND PRIVATE INITIATIVE IN RAILROAD DEVELOPMENT AND MANAGEMENT

BY ROBERT SCOTT LOVETT, PRESIDENT UNION PACIFIC RAILROAD CO.

There is nothing so essential to the financial peace and the commercial and industrial welfare of this country as a definite governmental railroad policy. The time has arrived when Congress must grapple and effectually deal with the problem. It can no longer be evaded. Nor will it do to "pass the buck" from Federal to state governments, or to railroad managers or owners. That will not provide the transportation facilities which the people must have. The responsibility rests upon Congress, and happily there are indications that Congress intends to meet it.

The failure of the present dual and conflicting state and interstate commission system has been demonstrated. It satisfied neither investors nor shippers, and failed to provide the requisite transportation at the time of greatest need. To return to it inevitably means a renewal of the strife between shippers and carriers over rates; between employers and employees over wages; and between different communities over preferential rate adjustments, with each backed more or less by local regulating authorities; and failure finally to meet the growing needs of the country for transportation facilities, since the necessary capital will not be forthcoming. The necessity for exclusive national control as against conflicting state regulation seems now too obvious for serious discussion; and the debatable question is whether such control shall be through government ownership or by exclusive Federal regulation of private ownership.

It was the system of regulation and not private management of railroads that caused the breakdown in our transportation facilities during the war. The creation within the last ten years in the territory north of the Potomac and Ohio

59

Rivers and east of Chicago of state railroad commissions with power to fix rates and regulate the borrowing of railroad companies, and the power granted about the same time to the Interstate Commerce Commission to suspend rate increases hampered the financial operations and impaired the credit of the railroads to such an extent that railroad executives hesitated to increase fixed charges and investors were slow to provide the money necessary to continue the policy of improvement and expansion necessary to meet the great industrial and commercial development of this populous territory.

The breakdown of 1917 afforded an opportunity to contrast the non-competitive with the competitive system of railroad transportation. The prime object, and, indeed, the only legitimate object of government control during the war, was to provide the transportation necessary for the war; and this object was accomplished with very great success. Barring the first few months of the year, during extraordinarily severe winter weather, the traffic was moved and with a degree of order, regularity and efficiency that met every requirement of the war; and, in the matter of foodstuffs especially, probably prevented an Allied collapse. The object was accomplished in a manner that would not have been possible under the restrictive legislation resting upon the railroad companies. The non-war transportation was secondary and got only the service available after war needs were supplied. This service was necessarily inadequate for lack of facilities due to the previous lack of capital expenditures, and was of course unsatisfactory to the public. It was not, during the war, and has not since been, a fair test of non-competitive transportation. But it has been sufficient at least to give the public a greater appreciation than it ever had before of competition in transportation, and to suggest some of the evils that would attend government ownership, and has impressed Congress with the necessity of bravely meeting and endeavoring to solve the problem.

Consideration of any solution of the railroad problem involves the fundamental question whether there shall or shall not be competition. Answer to this determines very largely the kind of plan to be adopted.

All must realize that competition in railroad *rates* is unwise and practically impossible. Competition in rates cannot exist without rebates, secret rates and other kindred evils that make it intolerable. But competition in *service* and *facilities* always existed until the beginning of Federal control, and has really been responsible for the great advance in the quality of railroad service in this country, particularly in recent years. I believe strongly in competition in service and facilities as the dominant principle to govern our railroad policy. It means constant and persistent progress in improvements of roadway and equipment, in the comforts and convenience of transportation, in considerate treatment of the public, in the quantity and quality of service; and progress in every feature of transportation. Its elimination would mean comparative stagnation, would check enterprise and initiative, and would remove the inspiration for many of the conveniences and facilities which are most appreciated by our people. It would be a national misfortune to eliminate competition in service and facilities that exists between the trunk lines— the New York Central and the Pennsylvania Lines, for example—the great Middle West systems, the principal lines through the south, and the transcontinental systems. Where they run to extremes, as in duplicating passenger train service for instance, a government hand may and should be laid upon them. But this item of waste has been exaggerated. Of course, I am not advocating unregulated competition, but instead an enlarged regulation. Nearly everything characterized as "waste" in competition is for the benefit of the public. Therefore is it waste? Undoubtedly there is some actual waste. The unification of lines so as to send traffic along the lines of least resistance, the shifting of traffic according to the conditions for the time being on different lines, the shifting of engines from one line to another to serve the exigencies of the moment, and the consolidation of certain station facilities, etc. undoubtedly result in a saving of some expense and the freer movement of freight traffic during exceptional periods of extraordinary business. But the amount of expense thus saved is not relatively a great item, and the diversion of traffic from a line having more than it can handle to a line having less, in times of congestion, could be easily provided for through the creation of a proper governmental officer and agency, such, for example, as a Secretary of Transportation in the President's Cabinet. The unification of certain terminals would also result in some saving, but the government ought to take in hand this matter of terminals in the larger cities, whether competition or unified control be adopted It has grown entirely beyond municipal control and is national in importance in many places. Some saving, also, could be effected by the abolition of competitive traffic soliciting agencies, but the public would suffer great inconvenience thereby Moreover, the rigid economies enforced by keen supervision of details under private management as against the lax habits inherent in public management and the greater freedom and extravagance in methods of spending government money would much more than offset every year any possible saving from the elimination of expenses incident to competition Competition compels and enforces economies—requires attention to details for saving, obtainable in no other way. While the government may save expense in conducting certain kinds of business through its freedom in choosing methods and its non-accountability, no one claims that a government can conduct a business in the same way as a private corporation at the same expense. Cost in every department would mount and the savings would soon vanish.

But granting very large saving from the suppression of competition in service and facilities, what is the relative value and importance of it? Does it not mostly represent conveniences to the public, which railroad owners cheerfully furnish? And is the saving of expense the most important object to be attained? Where would that leave civilization? Are we not as a nation quite as much or even more interested in developing conveniences and service of our transportation facilities than we are in merely holding down transportation rates to the lowest possible level? Is this not more important as public policy than a few cents per hundred more or less in the freight rate? As for the greater efficiency resulting from unified control, there again arises the question of the relative importance of such efficiency as may thus be obtainable against the conveniences resulting from competition. Germany probably had the most efficient government in the world, but there are other things more desirable even than efficiency, and this is true in transportation. If we carefully analyze the relative merits of efficiency from unification and the advantages from competition in service and facilities, we will find that the latter will be very much better as a national policy.

These are only some of the reasons for the preservation of competition in *service* and *facilities*. Of course there should be thorough regulation by the national government of all such competition, with power to check it where it amounts to an evil. Consolidations subject to government approval should be permitted where the public benefit would plainly be promoted, particularly the absorption of financially weak lines of minor importance where by so doing the communities dependent thereon could be better served. But the government should steadily preserve competition between the large systems and pursue a policy of widening the competitive area between such large systems wherever practicable.

It follows that the advantages of competition in service and facilities would be sufficient reasons if there were no others for opposing the principle of government ownership of railroads. But another and perhaps the strongest reason against government ownership is because the opportunity it would afford to exploit railroads for promoting political ambitions would be a perpetual national scandal and expose the government to serious financial burdens. This danger in such circumstances is inherent in our government and in every other democracy. Autocratic governments which had no electoral constituency to propitiate could avoid the pressure. Every politician would be almost compelled to exert any political influence possessed by him to provide places for his supporters or improvements and facilities or rate adjustments desired by them. Each Congressman would be pressed by all the ambitious towns in his district for ornate passenger stations or other improvements, as he is now pressed for post offices, court houses and other public buildings; for additional and unnecessary trains to please particular communities, and for the construction of new railroads, extensions and branches to various ambitious towns and localities not fairly entitled to them. If the executive agents operating the railroads for the government should be strong enough not to respond to these calls, the Congressmen could and possibly might combine and "log roll" for these political projects, just as they are said to have combined in time past for the construction of public buildings, for river and harbor improvements, etc., etc. This is a very grave objection to permanent government ownership. It has not been apparent during the present system of government control, and therefore it may be underestimated. But that is because the present control was created during the war and for war purposes, and requests for special favors in the way of new construction, new stations, etc., etc. could be met by pointing out the necessity of conserving capital, labor and material for war purposes. In times of peace, however, the pressure would be enormous, and the railroad "pork barrel" would in time make the other "pork barrels" appear insignificant in comparison. What seems also a serious objection to government ownership is the very large financial undertaking that would be involved. On December 31, 1916, which is the latest date for which the Interstate Commerce Commission has complete figures, the total outstanding capitalization of all the railroads in the United States amounted to $20,679,350,501, of which $8,958,815,811 was stock and $11,720,534,690 was bonds. Many of these securities are worth less than par, and many, on the other hand, are worth more than par. The capitalization of the Class 1 roads included in the above total of $20,679,350,501 amounted to $16,523,449,283. The "standard return" of these same Class 1 roads and the switching and terminal companies under Federal control aggregates $905,202,388, which capitalized on a 5 per cent basis represents $18,104,045,706. Of course it would not be necessary for the government to provide the entire amount of this huge investment at once, if the government should be willing to acquire the property subject to existing mortgages, but this would undoubtedly add enormously to the value of the bonds outstanding, since buying subject to the mortgages, the bonds would in effect be guaranteed by the government.

There are other objections to government ownership, such as the political power of the employees to organize and control the railroads, the probable deterioration in the ability and efficiency of executive and administrative officers under the scale of government salaries in competition with private business, etc.

The present method of Federal control is the most efficient of any unified control because it puts complete power in the hands of one man, whereby direct and immediate and complete action is obtainable, but obviously it cannot be made permanent; and I am discussing only a permanent policy. Another plan is to divide the country into regions or zones and consolidate all the railroads in each region or zone into a single company. France has some such system as that, except that in some zones the roads are owned by the government and in others by private companies, there being a monopoly, however, in each zone or region. This has the fundamental objection, however, of eliminating all competition in service or facilities; and for reasons already pointed out, that objection is to my mind conclusive. Then of course there is in the United States the present system of dual and conflicting national and state regulation by various agencies, mostly commissions quasi-judicial in form and procedure, but legislative and administrative in functions; and this system has already proven a failure.

As stated at the outset, the fundamental question is whether the policy shall be regulated monopoly or regulated competition in service and facilities. If the decision should be in favor of the monopoly, then it should be through government ownership. If, however, the decision should be in favor of regulated competition, it should be under *exclusive Federal control* and regulation of *private* ownership. The choice lies between the two. The people of this country will not be satisfied with the private ownership of railroads with every vestige of competition eliminated through the zone system or otherwise. If private ownership is to be maintained, there must be the initiative and enterprise inspired by competition to the extent that competition is beneficial to the public: namely, in *service* and *facilities*.

But private management of railroads cannot be maintained if the new legislation is to require railroad investors and owners to take the risks and forego the profits of the business. If the return upon railroad capital is to be limited at best to a low, fixed return, even by the most successful and best managed roads, with no hope of any increase for wise selection, good judgment, successful management and other considerations ordinarily influencing values, while all misfortunes are to be borne by the investors, I fear the necessary capital will not be obtained. Hope must not be shut out from the railroad investor. If he has or is able to provide a transportation machine that will furnish the service the public requires at *reasonable* rates, and by good service and facilities and good management gets more business and makes more profit than his competitors, he should be allowed to enjoy the results of his effort. A "reasonable" rate to be fixed by a governmental agency in the light of all the circumstances, however multitudinous, is all that the public is constitutionally entitled to and is all that the vast majority of the public want, and any profits which the investor can realize under such a rate from good management and good business judgment and by attracting business through good service and adequate facilities, he should be allowed to enjoy. No legislation or system of regulation designed merely to discover what will be a confiscatory rate and then aim sufficiently above that rate to avoid difficulties with the Constitution will ever solve the railroad problem; and such unfortunately seems to be the character of some of the legislation recently proposed. If there is to be competition, the rewards of competitive effort must be allowed stockholders, since otherwise there is no inducement to compete; if the returns to successful stockholders are to be limited, then such returns must be guaranteed, since investors will not take all the risk with no hope of profit; and if the returns are guaranteed, then the incentive to competition is largely diminished. Therefore, unless stockholders of well located, well managed, successful railroads with established business are allowed the returns which they are able to earn under rates fixed by the government in the light of all the circumstances entering into the establishment of a "reasonable" rate, we might as well adopt government ownership at once, for that is the end to which any other scheme will lead.

NATIONALIZING RAILROAD CORPORATIONS BY STATUTE *

BY ALEXANDER W. SMITH
ATLANTA, GA.

Having no interest in any railroad corporation and no professional railroad connection, my viewpoint, as regards the questions before the conference, is that of an American citizen who is vitally interested, as all good Americans are, in the prosperity of his country. There are no other interests in the whole country so completely bound up with our peace and prosperity as are adequate transportation facilities. Transportation is related to the body politic as the circulation of the blood is related to the natural body, and anything that obstructs the flow of pure blood through the veins no more certainly interferes with the good health of the individual than does like interference with the flow of commerce through the arteries of transportation have a deleterious effect on the commercial and business health of the whole country.

Being a lawyer I have viewed the general subject from the legal angle. I have heard various suggestions made that we should do sundry things to improve the transportation systems of the United States. For instance, it is proposed that the United States government shall, under one plan, guarantee an income upon the securities of these corporations based upon the value of their property arrived at in some way not yet definitely fixed. It is proposed that the government shall authorize the consolidation of individual railroads into large systems, which necessarily involves interference with competition in local territory between lines that were previously competitive. If that is undertaken in some states, under the present corporate organization of railroads, it will run counter to constitutional inhibitions. Has the Federal government power to override the constitution of a state by undertaking

* Notes of a statement made at the Third Meeting of the National Transportation Conference, Washington, D. C., March 28th, 1919.

to authorize such railroads to consolidate, so long as the
are creatures of the state and subject to the provisions of it
constitution?

A corporation is a fictitious person. It has many attribute
of a living being. It contracts, incurs obligations, owes dutie
to the government that creates it, and is subject to the con
stitutional control of that government. When we conside
things desirable to be done in connection with our transporta
tion systems it is well to investigate some of the legal aspect
involved; take a view of the range lights and shoal-stakes, s
to speak, that mark out the legal channels through which w
can safely travel, else we may run on the rocks.

The National Association of Owners of Railroad Securitie
and their counsel appear to have considered the subject o
Federal incorporation solely on the basis of creating new Fed
eral corporations, and undertaking to transfer into them exist
ing state corporations, and their assets and liabilities. That i
practically impossible. Take the Southern Railway Compan
as a concrete example. It is a system made up of mor
than one hundred separate railroad corporations. It own
some of them; it controls others under long leases, and other
by majority stockholding. It has effected their merger by al
the known methods of putting one railroad under the operativ
control of another. Their obligations under the kaleidoscopi
arrangements it has made in bringing the system togethe
could not be transformed and lifted out of the several stat
corporations and set down in a new Federal corporation. A
a business proposition, it would be impractical.

In view of these difficulties, the railroad executives hav
thus far turned away from the proposition of Federal in
corporation. But there lies right on the surface a metho
to accomplish the same result in a perfectly simple way, viz
the passage by Congress of a general Federal incorporatio
act along lines parallel to the laws for incorporating nationa
banks, and nationalizing state banks. If a state bank desire
to become a national bank, it makes application to the Comp
troller of the Currency on certain forms supported by prope
vote of its stockholders and directors, and a certificate is issue
authorizing it to be thereafter a national bank. The Suprem
Court of the United States has decided that when a stat

bank is thus converted into a national bank, there is no change in its identity or corporate existence, and no interruption of the continuity of its business. Its allegiance by that act is transferred from the state to the nation, but the corporation is the same; its assets and liabilities are the same; and no transfer is necessary from the one to the other, because there never is but one corporate creature. (Metropolitan Bank v. Claggett, 141 U. S. 520.)

What a simple plan that would be if it is deemed necessary for the interstate railroad systems to become national corporations!

While Congress has no power to compel a state bank to become a national bank, because a state bank is no part of the fiscal machinery of the nation, it is submitted that it does have the power to compel a railroad system that is now engaged in interstate commerce to become a Federal corporation.

The power of Congress to create a bank at all was contested until it was settled by the Supreme Court that such power was implicit in the power delegated to Congress to issue money and handle its finances. Jurisdiction of Congress over a railroad engaged in interstate commerce is delegated in a specific, plain, explicit, all-inclusive, and plenary paragraph of the Constitution committing to it control over interstate commerce and all its instrumentalities.

If it be true that Congress has only implied power to charter a bank as a piece of machinery in its fiscal system it must be true that if Congress finds in the development of transportation that state lines have been wiped out, and that commerce disregards artificial obstructions, and that necessary machinery in carrying on interstate commerce is a railroad corporation, the express grant of exclusive jurisdiction over such commerce carries with it the power to create such a corporation.

If that is true, can it *compel* a state railroad company engaged in interstate commerce to become a Federal corporation? No one questions its power to create such corporations, ab initio.

It has been decided by the Supreme Court of the United States that no single state can create a railroad company

and endow it, as a matter of law, with the right to operate it
lines in any other state. Indiana and Ohio tried to do this cor
jointly. The legislatures of those two states, respectivel
created a railroad company, endowing each with the sam
name, and their identity, so far as natural persons were cor
cerned, was complete, the one created by the state of Ohi
and the other created by the state of Indiana. Their track
were located so they came together at the line between th
states. Every effort was made to create a single corporatio
with the dual right to do business in both states. The Su
preme Court held that there were two separate and distinc
corporations and that, in the very nature of the case, on
state could not give the power to its creature to go into th
domain of another sovereignty of equal dignity and do busi
ness there, except by permission of the other state. Henc
it is that all roads that cross state lines do business outsid
their native state by comity between the states. Comity is
privilege merely and not a legal right. (O. & M. R. R. C
v. Wheeler, 1st Black 286.)

The Southern Railway Company was able to merge it
constituent lines running through eleven states by reason o
the voluntary, but not necessarily concurrent, action of th
several states and their corporate creatures. First, the state
either by special acts or by general laws, gave statutory per
mission for the railroad corporations to combine. Second, a
constituent corporations had to take appropriate corporat
action, through stockholders and directors according to by
laws and charter provisions, authorizing the particular ste
necessary to a merger. So that each one of the constituent cor
porations was put into the combination by virtue of its ow
action taken by permission of its creator. Thus, by virtu
of the express consent of the several corporations and of th
express legislative sanction of the eleven states in whic
the Southern Railway system operates, something was create
different from the aggregate of corporate powers previousl
vested in the subsidiary companies. The Virginia corpora
tion known as the Southern Railway Company became an in
strumentality of interstate commerce, not by virtue of comit
among these eleven states, but it crosses the lines of sai
states and hauls interstate commerce through them as a singl

entity by virtue of the action of each of the states, and of the concurrent or supplemental action of the owners of each of the properties. Whether they intended it or not, it is a fact that every one of those states, and every one of those corporations, by such action, voluntarily submitted themselves to the jurisdiction of Congress through its exclusive control of interstate commerce, whenever it sees fit to act.

Congress has never exercised that power, but with all due respect to the eminent counsel who have raised legal objection to compulsory Federal incorporation, no satisfactory reply has yet been made to the legal conclusion involved, viz: that Congress has the power, if it chooses to exercise it, to say that every system of railroads engaged in interstate commerce by virtue of consolidating constituent lines (and no other such system can legally exist unless originally created by Congress): "You are now an instrumentality of interstate commerce, and in the development of the commerce of this country it has become necessary that full jurisdiction of your functions shall be vested in the Federal government. Therefore, you are required to transfer your allegiance from the state of your incorporation to the United States of America, in order that the Federal government may take such steps hereafter in the control of your business and in the promotion of the interests of interstate commerce as from time to time it sees fit." Congress could then establish consistent and uniform control of all systems of interstate carriers.

If Federal incorporation is made permissive only it is questionable whether Congress will not be embarrassed by some of the lines declining to accept Federal charters. Many of them have tax exemptions and special charter privileges which they would hesitate to imperil. Voluntary action would certainly destroy these privileges, while, under compulsory action, these property rights might be preserved under other provisions of the constitution not necessary to be here elaborated.

It should be repeated that this argument is confined to those lines which, by voluntary action, have been consolidated into interstate systems. They have thereby waived the right (if it exists) to object to Congress doing anything with them that it may desire to do if they expect to continue in interstate commerce.

As to the necessity of Federal incorporation, there does not seem to be any room for argument. If the Federal government is to visé and control the issuance of railroad securities, upon what principle, without the voluntary coöperation of the state corporation, can Congress interfere with its issue of stocks and bonds expressly authorized under its state charter? They may be not necessarily connected with its interstate commerce. Their proceeds may be needed for other purposes. Many railroad corporations engage in business other than transportation. The exercise of control over the securities of a state corporation by Congress is much harder to justify under existing law than the power to compel Federal incorporation by interstate systems. The basis of the securities, especially the original issues, is the charter of the constituent companies, and not of the holding or operating company. Rights in these are vested and protected by the Federal Constitution itself. But when the corporation operating the interstate system is compelled to transfer its allegiance to the Federal government, subsequent issues of its capital stock and bonds may be regulated as Congress directs.

The contractual relation between a state and its corporate creature presents no obstacle to compulsory Federal incorporation of interstate systems hereinbefore described, because the state has consented in advance that that may happen. When the state gave permission to its corporation to become a part of the instrumentalities of interstate commerce by virtue of its legal merger into an interstate system, it relinquished its right to object to any sort of control over that corporation which Congress might choose to exercise. Of course, until Congress exercises control the allegiance of the corporation remains with the state that created it. The argument is that both the states and the corporations, by virtue of the necessities of the consolidation that produced the interstate system, have contracted in advance that Congress may exercise jurisdiction over this legally established instrumentality of interstate commerce if, in its discretion, such action will promote the interests of interstate commerce. Such jurisdiction has been exercised in numberless ways. If, without destroying the corporation itself, it may be converted from a state corporation to a Federal corporation, there is no legal reason why Congress may not constitutionally require it to make the change.

STABILIZING RAILROAD INVESTMENTS

BY PAUL M. WARBURG

FORMER VICE-CHAIRMAN OF THE FEDERAL RESERVE BOARD

A government assurance of a reasonable return upon a fair value of the railroad property devoted to the public service forms a very important and much controverted phase of the railroad problem. In discussing it in a short and separate article, we must be permitted to presuppose a common accord with regard to the desirability of conserving private operation of railroads under strict government control, because it is for the very purpose of avoiding the two extremes of complete government operation, and unrestricted private operation, and in order to bring into a necessary union two incompatible partners, viz: private capital and drastic government control, that the assurance of return is being advocated. We must take, then, as conceded the following assumptions:

A. Unrestricted private operation must be dismissed as being incompatible with the public interest.

B. Government operation must be avoided:

1st—Because it is bound to pollute our political and social life, and

2nd—Because it makes for stagnation and inefficiency; it would mean unprogressive and costly operation, resulting in poor service to the public and high rates.

3rd—Because experience in foreign countries shows that the saving to be derived from the use of the government's credit is not likely to be sufficient to make up for the loss resulting from the higher cost of government operation, while the excessive use of the government's credit is hurtful to its standing and bound to increase the rate at which the government generally borrows.

C. Such advantages as the greater unification of operation produced under the U. S. Railroad Administration can be secured by proper amendment of the Sherman Act and the grant of a Federal franchise, without subjecting the country to the dangers and disadvantages of government operation.

The question before us is, then, why is it necessary for a minimum guarantee of return by the government to assure a reasonable return upon a fair value of railroad property in order to preserve private operation of railroads under government regulation?

Railroads have ceased to be purely private concerns. They are public utilities, and long before the war began the government to all intents and purposes had undertaken through its authorized agencies to fix the rates they may charge, the wages they must pay, and the service they must render. As a consequence, the net return upon railroad investments of to-day in effect is determined by the government. If private capital is to continue to finance the railroads and to provide the means necessary for their future growth, it must be assured of an "adequate return." If we can define what is an "adequate return" and if we can devise means to assure the railroad investor of an "adequate return" and if we can combine this assurance with a like assurance that private initiative and business methods will not thereby be destroyed, we shall have solved the real difficulty of the problem. If we fail in this, we must give up as hopeless our search for a thorough and permanent solution of private railroad operation.

The history of our railroads, with few exceptions, abounds with illustrations of excessive capitalization and of ill-advised construction or purchase of properties at exorbitant prices. In most cases the security owners have since paid the penalty for the errors of omission and commission of their directors, and through the process of painful reorganization, the "water" has been squeezed out. The present average capitalization of all railroads cannot be considered as excessive; but the process has been an uneven one, nor has it quite run its course. The Interstate and State Commissions, faced with the task of approving rates which affect alike the weak and the strong road, the looted property and the well conserved, the under-capitalized company and the one with a grossly watered capitalization, have therefore never been in a position to define what constitutes an "adequate return" because they never

were able to lay down what was the true investment or the
fairly accurate value upon which the return should be based.
On the other hand, both shipper and labor have constantly
rested their respective claims for lower rates and higher
wages upon the contention that it was the avidity of the
railroads to earn a return on an excessive capitalization that
stood in the way of a compliance with their just requests. Being uncertain of its ground, the Interstate Commerce Commission was unprepared or unwilling to grant prompt increases
in rates corresponding to the added cost of operation. While
wages and the cost of material were mounting rapidly, while
the war emergency called for prompt and bold treatment, they
refused to act, even though it was borne in on them from all
sides that to ruin the credit of the railroads would involve an
irretrievable national loss, and that, even in case they expected
the government ultimately to step in, its burdens in guaranteeing or financing would be greatly lightened if it had to deal
with solvent railroads earning a reasonable return. It was
pointed out to the Commissioners that it was easier to destroy
the credit of the railroads than to resurrect it, and that when
railroad stocks could no more be placed at par or above, the
inability of the railroads to finance further extensions and improvements was dangerously near at hand. The majority of
the Interstate Commerce Commission remained deaf to these
warnings. Speaking by and large, we must regretfully admit
the fact that railroad credit has now practically been destroyed. Only a few companies may feel confident of their
ability to sell their obligations in sufficiently large amounts
and on good enough terms to provide for a liberal further
development of their plants. Only about ten carriers of importance remain in a position to sell their stock at par or above.
With only a small margin of earnings no railroad can safely
finance indefinitely by a continuous addition to its fixed obligations. Conditions now prevailing mean, therefore, that, unless
something drastic be done, the end of private railroading is in
sight. Even though net earnings be temporarily improved—
by an increase in rates or decrease in expenses—the investor's
confidence that he may safely count upon an "adequate return"
has been shaken so seriously that a temporary improvement
would not restore the power of the railroads as a body to

finance themselves by the sale of stock upon favorable terms.

It is absolutely necessary, therefore, that both the Congress and the regulating bodies reach a clear understanding as to what is a fair and adequate return. In other words, we must reach a definite determination, once and for all, as to what shall be considered the uncontested intrinsic value of each railroad.

The interests of the shipper, the consumer and labor are so important, and at times so much opposed to one another, that no private corporation can assume the responsibility of acting as umpire between them. Government, in the circumstances, must shoulder the full responsibility for fixing transportation rates, for furnishing adequate service and for avoiding strikes, and, whether we like it or not, it must, therefore, be vested with practically plenary powers. But where these safeguards of government administration are to be combined with the advantages of private operation, the government's responsibility towards private capital must be considered as sacred as that towards shipper, consumer and labor. In other words, while the country must enjoy the full protection of practically unlimited government control of railroads, private capital is entitled to protection against confiscatory over-control; viz.: It must enjoy an unequivocal assurance that, in disregard of the law providing that the railways are entitled to earn a fair return on their invested capital, it shall not be deprived of a reasonably adequate return. Without such definite assurance, it is inconceivable to expect that private capital will show itself reckless enough to plunge into the further development of our transportation system. If history had created a tradition that such reasonableness could be assumed as a matter of course, or that it could be adequately defined by the courts, no such statutory assurance might have become necessary, but in the face of actual experience, I do not see how it can now be avoided.

Our governments, state and national, were negligent or shortsighted when they gave their first railroad charters without including a provision establishing a definite method of accounting and of maintaining a property account upon which both the net return to the owners and an eventual purchase by the government could be predicated. Unless we now provide such a basis, the old sore will be but superficially healed, bound to spring wide open afresh on the occasion of every new clash between the interests of the shipper and labor. The carriers would remain "the goat," sandwiched between these two contending forces, in the hands of helpless regulating bodies who would continue to flounder about without a solid ground under their feet upon which to rest their decisions.

There is no denying that the question of valuation offers grave difficulties. Original cost can hardly ever be ascertained; moreover, in some cases it would be far below to-day's reproduction value, while in others it might seem obscured in consequence of acquisitions, either by direct purchase or through stock control, of properties previously constructed by other corporations.

The replacement value, on the other hand, might offer a fair basis in case of a well-planned and well-maintained property; it would be unreasonable in the case of a poorly planned road such as no prudent business man or engineer would reproduce on its original basis. Moreover, the cost of replacement is subject to the drastic fluctuations of prices of real estate, raw materials and labor.

The average market price of securities has been urged by some, but bonds and stocks of recently reorganized properties would not offer any record of average prices over a number of years, and there are many other reasons why market prices would not offer a reliable basis.

A capitalization of net earnings has been suggested as a better test; but readjustments would have to be made in order to bring about a fairly equal basis of maintenance. Rules for establishing a fair standard return could, however, probably be laid down in a law, and the true average standard return when capitalized is likely in many cases to offer the most serviceable basis of valuation. Resulting from rates determined by Federal and state commissions, it could not in any case be considered excessive.

An enumeration of these difficulties leads us to the conclusion that no mathematical or technical rule could probably be devised that, if fair to one railroad, might not be doing violence, or be too favorable, to another. Shall we then throw up our hands and surrender to government operation because of our inability to agree upon a fair value of the railroads? Before we reach that conclusion let us remember that government operation cannot be brought about without condemnation proceedings, which again must be based upon a valuation. It is obvious then that we meet that difficulty in either case, and, instead of shirking it, we ought to face it squarely and overcome it as best we can. In order to cut the knot—as inevitably we must—it will be advisable, I believe, to place the duty of determining the fair value of the railroads in the hands of some expert and impartial body, laying down in the law the broad rules of approach, but leaving it within the discretion of the men to be appointed how to apply the tests; whether one or two of them, or all. It would be their duty not to attempt to drive the hardest possible bargain but, like a court of justice, to determine the fair value of the properties without the red tape or delays incidental to judicial proceedings and having due regard for all circumstances affecting the property and its prospective earning capacity, for which in some cases considerable sacrifices have been brought without as yet showing a visible return. I could imagine a "Valuation Board" of five, composed of members representing law, finance, business, labor and the railroads.

In order to have our thoughts travel along the same lines in our search for the guiding principles to be established, it is necessary to agree on some tentative means of approach. Let us assume, then, that a net return (available for interest charges and dividends after making ample provision for renewals and depreciation) of 6 per cent on the aggregate of the Federal valuations of the railroads constituting a traffic section shall be considered as the basis guiding the rate-making bodies; that, on the other hand, the railroads shall contribute to a general railroad contingent fund (to be drawn upon in lean years by all railroads on a pro rata basis) any earnings in excess of, say, 6 per cent on said valuation. Let us suppose that railroads signing such an agreement shall be freed from the restrictions of the Sherman Act with respect to the acquisition of parallel and competing lines, pooling, etc., which they may carry on under the supervision of a Federal regulating body. Such plan, if applied, would result in establish-

ing the securities of the railroads as a whole upon a basis
to which their actual intrinsic value entitles them.

There is no thought of guaranteeing dividends on existing
stocks or even interest on existing obligations, but only an assurance of a reasonable return on the actual value of the property of the railroad as a whole in each traffic section as determined by the Federal valuation: the "legitimized capital," as
it has been termed by a prominent financial writer.

No gift to the strong roads is contemplated, but the simple
and just application of the principle that a net return of 6
per cent (the excess to be divided) on what has been found
to be the real rock-bottom value of an industrial enterprise
is considered as fair and not excessive. The reëstablishment
of arbitrarily destroyed values would in some instances enable
certain companies to sell their stocks above par, but incidentally, in such cases it would add to our national strength and
taxable wealth, just as it would be to our national advantage
to have the Liberty Loan bonds go back to par.

On the other hand, the overcapitalized roads would find
themselves in a position where, in order to finance their future
growth, they would either have to revamp and scale down
their capitalization, so as to bring it well within the limits of
the Federal valuation (that is, bring it within the sound
limits of actual valuation) ; or they would have to enter into
negotiation with stronger railroads, operating under Federal
franchise, particularly those whose stocks would sell above
par, in order to merge their property on the basis of an exchange of securities to be approved by the Valuation Board.
This would lead to a consolidation of railroads—eliminating
some uneconomic duplication and operation of too many small
units—and would work towards greater unification, a development, apparently, generally desired by the country. Competition would, however, be preserved between the large systems.

In our eagerness to secure greater unification, let us remain
ever conscious, however, of the fact that it is most important
that unification does not go too far. The advantages of a
unified system can be secured through proper coöperation
under the direction of governmental regulating agencies, even
though a reasonable number of strong and competing lines be
preserved. For the continued intensive and free development

of a country whose resources we have only begun to unfold, we need an aggressive spirit of enterprise—not the lazy and arbitrary bureaucratic and autocratic atmosphere that with us would be certain to follow if one great regional railroad company should cover each section of the country as has been proposed by others. A business spirit of rivalry must be kept alive by the preservation of a number of large units of railroads competing on broad lines—not in rates, but in service.

If, for the sake of an illustration, we agreed to accept as the temporary Federal valuation the average "standard return" capitalized on a 6 per cent basis, which we might term the "earning valuation," that, in effect, would mean that carriers as a whole and by natural traffic sections in fixing their transportation rates, and in pleading with the rate-making bodies or with the courts, from now on would have a definite basis upon which to rest their claims for schedules producing 6 per cent net on these aggregate "earning valuations." The railroads, under the law, are entitled to an adequate return on their property. It may be advisable, therefore, to let the physical valuations proceed and let the aggregate of the final valuations, plus future additions, serve as the basis for rate-making purposes, and as the limit for the issue of securities.

If legislation as here proposed were enacted, the return of 6 per cent on the aggregate valuation of the carriers as a whole would constitute a clear and, for the first time, well-defined right which the carriers could enforce before the courts, while heretofore no such definite basis existed. There would be ample room for the stronger roads, by energetic efforts in promoting new business or greater efficiency, to increase to 6 per cent or more the net earnings accruing to their security holders. Moreover, with the absorption of the smaller or unprofitable roads by the stronger ones, the rate-making problem would be greatly simplified.

It is claimed that statutory government assurance of a reasonable return on a fair value of railroad property as a whole would prove to be a step towards government ownership and operation. If we are correct in assuming that the assurance here contemplated would have the effect of sustaining railroad credit, and if ample government supervision and control is likely to secure for the country substantially all the advantages that complete government ownership and operation might be expected to bring about, there would hardly be any inducement left for the country to take the disastrous plunge into government ownership and operation, with all its well known dangers, while no equivalent advantages might still remain to be secured by such a step. The surrender to government operation would appear much more likely if railroad credit should remain insufficiently protected, and if the proponents of government operation were left in a position to press the argument that greater economy and cheaper rates might be secured by the direct and free use of the government's credit.

Some writers contend that it would be cowardly and unwise to barter away private initiative and freedom of action and earnings for a statutory assurance of a limited return. It is not in order to obtain the government assurance here recommended that I am in favor of submission to far-reaching government control. It is because I consider far-reaching government control an unavoidable element of any future plan of private operation that I deem it necessary to insist on assuring the railroads as a whole a reasonable return that unrestricted government control will by law be bound to observe. I deem this protection necessary like a war risk insurance policy, without which private capital would not have ventured to brave the dangers of mines and submarines.

A profit-sharing arrangement upon a definite understanding as to what is to constitute an "adequate" return, would appear to offer for those in charge of railroad operations a more attractive basis, and, therefore, would develop more readily a spirit of enterprise, than what they have had in the past.

I strongly believe in the idea that capital and labor must consider themselves partners, a conception which is bound more and more to lead to the full recognition on the part of labor that, in return for the enjoyment of short hours and the highest possible wages, labor must give its maximum in work, not the minimum, in order to enable the country successfully to compete and to maintain these high standards. Where government regulates business I strongly believe in creating a basis that establishes a common interest between them. It brings about a fair and constructive spirit of progressive development on the part of the regulating bodies instead of the pernicious attitude of commissions that merely seek to restrict, prosecute, punish, and destroy. Any regulating body that does not perceive that it has constructive functions as well as restrictive duties is doomed to fail and to become more of a curse than a blessing.

To require the railroads to turn over to a general fund a share of their profits in excess of 6 per cent on a fair value of their property would, to my mind, not only offer a great protection for the railroads themselves, but, if proper provisions are inserted, they might greatly benefit the country at large.

The work of the Federal Reserve Board was greatly facilitated by the provision in the Federal Reserve Act restricting the member banks' net return from their holdings of Federal Reserve bank stocks to 6 per cent per annum, the balance going half to the government, and half, with certain limitations, to the surplus or reserve accounts, ultimately reverting to the government. The Federal Reserve banks in 1918 earned about 75 per cent net on their stock. If this profit had accrued to the benefit of the member banks it would have been considered a public scandal. It is safe to expect that in that case the present attorney for the shippers, appearing on behalf of the farmers and business men of the country, would have raised a protest against such extortion, urging the Federal Reserve Board to reduce interest rates. If these vast profits had gone to the member banks, it is doubtful whether the Board could have withstood such a demand, even though it might have entailed further disastrous inflation and increased burdens to the whole country. Inasmuch as anything earned in excess of 6 per cent, directly or indirectly, belonged to the United States government, any such pressure or misconstruction was, however, excluded, and it was readily understood, and willingly admitted by all, that the enormous profits were not due to extortionate interest charges, but to the vast quantity of services rendered at very moderate rates. In consequence of this limitation of profits the Federal Reserve Board, when deciding what are the interest rates best serving the whole country, finds itself free from the uncertainties which have so fatally affected the deliberations of the Interstate Commerce Commission in this respect. The Federal Reserve Board knows that the country has decided once and for all that 6 per cent is the fair return to the Federal Reserve bank stockholder, and that the balance belongs to the government.*

If the Interstate Commerce Commission, or whoever may fix transportation rates in the future, were certain that no serious harm or abuse could result from permitting "adequate rates," they would find their task greatly facilitated. They could no more be alarmed by the possibility of excessive railroad profits and, on the other hand, they would be less apt to overreach themselves in imposing excessive burdens upon the carriers.

It would lead too far to discuss in detail how to organize and render effective these contingent funds. It may not be amiss, however, to touch upon the very important question of granting directors and officers a certain share in the net returns of the railroads. I do not believe in fixed executive salaries, or directors' fees, without a definite relation to the success of their work. In this respect I am wedded to a system that has directors and officers find their main remuneration in a certain share of the profits earned in excess of a given minimum return to the stockholders. In our case it is obvious that such a provision would have the effect of preserving in the management of the roads a genuine live and active spirit of business efficiency, enterprise, and rivalry. Incidentally it would indicate the way to solve the puzzling problem of dealing with negligent or dummy directors, or securing "directors that direct," and protect the stockholders. If the pocketbook of every director (and officer) would be vitally affected by any mistaken action on the part of the company (instead of his collecting a fee, no matter how poorly the stockholders fare) they would be bound to keep their eyes wide open; and the simple device here proposed would go further in remedying what shortcomings still may exist in this respect than the clumsy and ill-advised Clayton Act. Incidentally, we might consider whether the Federal Reserve Act in having the regu-

* It must be borne in mind, however, that the Federal Reserve System is dealing with a large number of involuntary stockholders, and only with a capital stock of about $80,000,000. If it had to raise billions of dollars in the open market a maximum of 6 per cent would be considered too narrow a limit for a return upon an industrial venture.

lating body appoint one-third of the directors of the Federal Reserve banks does not possibly offer a useful analogy for railroads taking out a Federal franchise.

May I emphasize as strongly as I can that in presenting these views I do not wish to appear dogmatic with respect to any particular detail. It is the end that I hold dear, not the means of approaching it. If the end can be achieved in any better or simpler way, I shall welcome that other method, provided it reaches our aim finally and conclusively and does not bridge the problem by a palliative bringing only temporary relief. The principles that, in planning for future private operation of railroads under government control, I deem essential are:

That practically plenary powers of regulation must be given to the government's regulating agencies, but that a clear and definite basis must be established upon which regulating boards will base their rates;

That this basis must give an unqualified assurance to the railroad industry as a whole of a minimum return;

That there must be an honest and substantial chance for private capital to earn more than a minimum, so as to preserve a spirit of enterprise which should permeate the entire staff from top to bottom;

That the owners of the railroads should share profits above a reasonable minimum with the country at large;

That consolidation should be encouraged so as to bring about a smaller number of railway systems, of which the strongest existing roads would form the natural backbone, but that this unification should not go far enough to destroy a healthy and reasonable competition in efficiency, in service, and in opening new fields of enterprise;

And, finally, that preference should be given to a plan which at this time would disturb as little as possible outstanding well-established and well-protected railroad securities, and which would avoid to the largest possible degree the direct use of the government's credit.

OBJECTIONS TO GOVERNMENT GUARANTEE OF RETURN ON RAILROAD CAPITAL *

BY SAMUEL REA, PRESIDENT OF THE PENNSYLVANIA RAILROAD COMPANY

While the trend of public opinion is now unmistakably opposed to government ownership as a solution of the railroad problem, there is much discussion of the possibilities of a government guarantee of railroad income, and if the income is guaranteed in substance, the principal of bonds must be paid at maturity, if not previously scaled down through government valuation. The railroad investor—so badly frightened by punitive laws and regulations and small profits—is willing to listen to any reasonable plan, whereby he can have a guarantee, hoping that he will have no more serious fluctuations in the price of his securities, and will be assured of a fixed income. He is not given the value to be placed on his individual investment on which the guarantee is to be based, nor the income to be guaranteed. He knows nothing of the division that is to be made between the various classes of securities of his railroad, nor the standing that is to be given to the various liens on his railroad property, and consequently does not know what is to be the final value of his securities, or whether he will finally get any return thereon at all. That knowledge, if it had to be conveyed beforehand, would be a serious eye-opener to the railroad investor. He should know it beforehand or he is taking a step in the dark. A governmental guarantee would plunge the country into a wholesale financial reorganization of the railroads extending over a period of years, and would ultimately mean government ownership. But to temporarily palliate the situation, the guarantee is to be coupled with private operation. What is to be the capitalization of these private operating corporations? Are they to be mere shells with no large financial stake in the properties

* From an address before the Chamber of Commerce of the United States, St. Louis, Mo., April 30, 1919.

they operate and administer? Is there any business man present who would recommend the government to guarantee returns on property having a value of about eighteen billion of dollars and turn it over to six, or even eighteen, private operating companies without demanding the power to thereafter define its financial and operating policy? Can any stock or bondholder imagine that our government will guarantee railroad stocks and bonds, and charge nothing for that guarantee? Should capital improvements thereafter be made according to the business necessities or on the political judgment of each administration? Would political favoritism as to new improvements, branches and extensions, and orders for supplies be inevitable in the government guarantee plan? Should we then employ officers and men who have political influence? Should we impose this guarantee plan on the country in the midst of the great struggle she must meet to reconstruct her industries and put national affairs and taxation on a peace basis? What period do you think it would take to work out the financial reconstruction of all the railroad systems of the country, and all their leaseholds, guarantees and other obligations, and what is to occur meanwhile? These questions open up some of the problems of a guarantee. Why even the Railroad Administration's Federal Control contracts, that deal only with the parent companies, and are based on the earnings for the three years ending June 30th, 1917, remain in large part still unexecuted, and many vital questions and settlements thereunder, are still untouched, although it is the ardent wish of the administration to dispose of them.

Now, selfishly, the investor might take a 4½ per cent guarantee for his railroad security, and let the country take over his problem, but he must look further and realize that as a citizen and taxpayer he would be called upon to pay, in taxes and in the greater transportation costs upon production, his share of the extra cost of the government guarantee and administration, so that the net result to him of the guarantee plan would not better his condition.

What is the advantage of the guarantee plan to the private citizen who is not a railroad security holder? Those who support it admit that private ownership and initiative under equitable regulation produce the most efficient and economical

operating results. The contrary obtains under governmenta
direction, and the citizen pays the cost in higher rates and
higher taxes.

On top of that annual guarantee on about eighteen billion
of dollars of existing railroad property, from six hundred
million to one billion dollars more would be required annually
for additions and betterments to the roadbed and equipment

Now the chief advantage emphasized for the guarantee
plan is that the government could raise new capital cheaper
than private corporations, and that by various schemes o
regional unification the weak roads could be tied to the strong
further economies effected, and some element of competition
left. Now we know that reasonable competition as to servic
and attracting traffic is the best method of keeping up th
standards and accommodating the public and enforcing econo
mies, but there must be some appealing force to assure suc
reasonable competition, and the guarantee plan on its fac
does not seem to possess that force. I agree that the govern
ment could probably raise new capital much cheaper for
time than the majority of the railroads, but the savings ob
tained in that way would be easily obliterated by extravaganc
and lack of concentrated and continued responsibility unde
the government guarantee plan with our form of governmen

Under the Federal Control Contracts the government a
lows 5 per cent on deferred rental payments, and 6 per cer
on new capital expenditures. This, in substance, shows tha
the government financing can become just as costly as tha
of the conservative corporations. We have also seen th
strongest nations selling bonds at rates as high as those allowe
by private corporations. Mr. Paul M. Warburg has this t
say upon the subject as the result of his long experience, bot
in private and government finance:

"It has been argued that through the use of the Goveri
ment's credit, railroads would procure the necessary fund
at a lower rate of interest. As against that, we must rememb<
that the excessive use of the Government's credit tends to ii
crease the rate at which a Government borrows. With us
would not only affect the rate of the Government bonds to l
issued in re-financing the outstanding railroad securities, est
mated at $17,000,000,000, but it would add to the rate to l
paid by our Government when some of our Liberty Bonds

due course will mature and come up for renewal. Moreover, the incessant use of Government bonds, in order to finance the annual requirements for future railroad developments and improvements, would have a disastrous effect upon the price and standing of our Government securities. Granting, however, that some economy could be secured by substituting the Government borrowing power for that of the railroads, it would be insignificant when compared with the increase in cost of operation and waste and inefficiency that inevitably would follow Government operation."

Shall we, therefore, in order to save some small difference between the rate which the railroads would pay and the rate the government would pay on new capital, incur the risks of a guarantee plan? Shall we try to effect a saving in that part of the railroad dollar used to pay interest and dividends that represents less than 20 per cent of the whole dollar and at the ' outset admit that expenses of operating and other expenses (already requiring 80 per cent of that railroad dollar) when subject to government dictation, would increase rapidly?

Let us try to depict the situation in any year when the income earned was less than the guarantee, how would the deficit be made up? Congress would have to appropriate the money out of the public treasury and raise the funds by public taxation. If the deficiency ran through several years Congress would be obliged to make repeated appropriations from the public funds to the railroad companies. Instead of getting the railroads out of politics we would probably be making them the major issue in national politics. It is difficult now for the Government Railroad Administration to get from Congress the funds needed to meet the government obligations to the roads when the government is in complete charge of operations and is collecting and disbursing the revenues. What would be the situation with eighteen railroad companies in full charge of the operations and the revenues, and the government called upon to make good their operating deficit? Bitter partisan attacks would be made on the corporate management for their failure to earn their minimum standard income, and demands in Congress for investigation of alleged extravagance and inefficient management and waste of the peoples' money given to the railroad bondholders and stockholders.

The French railways have had a guarantee of income by

the government for many years, and the French experience
has been by no means a happy one, and it is acknowledged
that it is ultimate government ownership. But in France the
government keeps a string on every dollar advanced to the
private companies on account of the guarantees. When the
French treasury advances funds to a railway to enable it to
meet its capital charges, it is in the form of a loan at interest,
and the loan must be repaid. When a French company becomes hopelessly in debt to the government on account of
advances on the guarantee, the government is obliged to protect its interest by buying in the property, and that would occur
promptly with our weak roads. This is what happened to the
Western Railway of France that was taken by the government
in 1908, after years of continuous appeals to the treasury
to make up the annual deficit. But those who have suggested
a government guarantee for American railroads want an out
and out guarantee—a payment of government funds to the
private companies whenever they fail to earn their standard
return. Such an arrangement might work out fairly well
with roads not in need of a guarantee, but I think it is plain
to see what would happen to roads or regions that did not
earn their guarantee.

To my mind the guarantee of railroad income by the government would inevitably lead to government ownership—first
of the weak lines, and later of all the lines. It might be
argued that the government, instead of paying funds out of
the treasury to the less prosperous companies, would advance
the rates. But this again, it seems to me, would lead to the
same sort of bitter political debate and attacks on the corporate
management. It would probably be alleged that these weaker
roads, knowing that their income would be provided by the
government in any event, were purposely failing to do their
best.

American industry has made its wonderful progress because the industries, and the men conducting them, have been
rewarded for efficiency and penalized for inefficiency. It
is the fear of failure as well as the hope of reward or commendation that incites men to do their best. A government
guarantee on private capital invested in transportation would
to a large extent remove the fear of failure, but would it

be for the public welfare, or be helpful to our industries, which pay freight rates? If the government could keep rates at a level that would provide sufficient revenues for all roads to earn their guaranteed income and operating expenses, why can we not equally assume that the government will allow such adequate rates under a system of government regulation, stimulated to economy and efficiency by private ownership and initiative, and without the blight of a government guarantee?

The guarantee is not a solution of this great economic question, but a patch upon it.

But we are told that weak roads are one of the barriers to a constructive policy, and some are near bankruptcy. They are to be regionalized and, ignoring trade routes or commercial necessities, are to be attached to the strong roads under a guarantee plan; but the basis no man has worked out even for a single large railroad system. What is the benefit of this experiment in furnishing a more efficient transportation service? We are testing regionalization under Federal control. The total estimated rental guaranteed the railroads in the first class was $900,904,000 and the net railway operating income in the calendar year 1917 was $974,778,937. This existing margin of over $73,000,000 in excess of the guaranteed rental to be allowed the railroads was in favor of Federal control, and later the expense of corporate officers and their staffs, and the extra war taxes, were thrust upon the corporations and the government was relieved. But that was not all, regionalization and unification, with savings of advertising, use of short routes, permit system of moving traffic, mobilization and pooling of equipment, elimination of outside agencies, ticket and freight offices, elimination of selfish competition, full train loads, and no empty cars, were to save hundreds of millions more, and all of this was further assisted by higher rates. You all know the result. I don't criticise it; I appreciate that we have had abnormal business conditions since the war began, but these are facts. The result could not have been prevented under government control of policies and management. Maybe the experiment was worth paying the price, although I doubt whether the full price is yet realized.

Don't let us get frightened about the task of rehabilitating railroad credit or imagine that it is an impossible task. It is entirely possible if we approach it with the proper methods and with equitable legislation. We had a Civil War—its cost was heavy. Compared with the aggregate wealth and position of our country, each citizen had more national debt per capita than we now face. We met the cost and it was our pride to steadily reduce our national debt. Following the war period the railroads and the country expanded, and laid the foundation for the greatest progress the world ever saw. It had some pains and sacrifices, and we cannot escape similar experiences. It is the price of liberty and progress. We had weak railroads after the Civil War, but we had a fair chance to conduct the railroad business and other industries. The Pennsylvania Railroad had ton mile revenues of about 2½ cents, so that it could pay its taxes, expand its property, and lease or acquire weak roads even in the war period. It did this, and gradually reduced the rates as its business justified, and its solvency was assured. If the roads are allowed reasonable rates to properly support the railroad investment and service, and these rates are accompanied by constructive regulation, the credit of weak roads will like so many weak roads in the past, be built up gradually by the growth of the country without taxing the public treasury or breaking down the few fairly strong roads. They will also be helped by ability to co-operate in the use of service and facilities with the strong roads, and adapt their capital and operating outlays to their necessities.

The root of our difficulty lies in weak railroad credit, and Congress must by legislation place the welfare of the public, which is so intimately intertwined with the transportation systems, beyond the powers of any state or Federal commission to disrupt the entire transportation system and investment. The way to do this is by a statutory rule that will insure adequate rates, and responsible regulation. Without such action there can be no railroad financial rehabilitation.

I suggest that the first step in the program of having the roads produce an adequate return upon the investment should be taken by the government itself which now has control of the railroads. There is no justification in throwing the railroad deficiencies on the backs of the taxpayers through a congressional appropriation, and if the government itself, in the control of the properties, has not sufficient courage to deal with the rate situation as it has dealt with wages and material costs, then from what source can we expect the requisite courage to deal with this great business and financial question? While wages and material costs are high, that adjustment of the rate structure to existing conditions should be the first constructive step in railroad financial rehabilitation, and constitutes a necessary preparation for the return of the railroads to their owners after appropriate legislation. The railroads of most countries face huge rate increases compared with the ante-war period, and our necessary increases being smaller than theirs will not place our industries at any disadvantage compared with those of other war-burdened countries. That the United States Railroad Administration, and Congress, had determined to deal equitably with one of the largest investments, and probably the greatest consumer of supplies and one of the greatest employers of labor, would invoke widespread confidence in our war reconstruction plans.

CONCLUSION

Politics and business have not mixed so far in any country, and even in the countries under autocratic institutions, government guarantees or direct government ownership have not brought initiative, low rates, or anything to commend them to us here. That is why the railway executives held fast to the essentials requisite to continue public regulation and make it effective. I conclude that the immediate remedy for the railroad situation is

1. Adequate revenues on which the railroad credit may be strengthened and the new capital attracted;

2. Concentrated, responsible national regulation, separated as between its executive and administrative functions, and its judicial functions, and founded on equitable legislation, that will require our regulators to insure strong transportation systems, and not weak railroads;

3. All railroads under public regulation to be authorized to lease, acquire or consolidate with any other railroad corpora-

tions, and reasonable coöperation permitted in facilities, equipment, and train service;

4. Regulation of security issues;

5. Regulation of wages, with the employee, the employer and the consumer represented;

6. Funding of the capital debts incurred during government control;

7. Rehabilitation of revenues of the existing railroads should begin immediately while they are under government control.

Neither government ownership nor a government guarantee confronts us unless we have reached the conclusion that the American people so undervalue the public service of their railroads, and are so determined not to allow fair returns on the railroad investment, that their legislators, their regulators, and their courts, expressing their will, can no longer be trusted to deal equitably with the railroad investment, which affects the welfare of fully one-half of our citizens by direct ownership, or ownership through their participation in the savings, insurance, trust, educational and charitable corporations and institutions: that the states will continue to increase taxation on railroad gross and net results and will not concede adequate railroad rates: that labor will demand the highest wages, and give the least return and take no interest in the success or failure of their employers: that the producers will insist upon their prices and profits, and with the consumers will decide that transportation results concern no one but railroad investors. Then I am willing to admit that private ownership and initiative cannot exist. Then let the railroads go to a guarantee plan to be consistent with the rest of the country, but call it by its real name, gradual but sure government ownership and operation. I cannot accept the proposition that the public interests will be so well served or so continuously guarded under government ownership or government guarantee. Our history, and the experience here and abroad, is conclusive that bureaucracy, increased expenses, lack of enterprise and failure of initiative will inevitably follow either government ownership or guarantee. Nobody has a deeper financial interest in the proper solution of this question than the men conducting the industries represented in the United States Chamber of

Commerce, and they should decide for themselves whether rates or service will be better under a system of private ownership and initiative, or under governmental ownership or guarantees. I have faith in the ability and integrity of our business men, financiers and wage earners; but the country wants protection against those imported, costly, so-called socializing experiments, that breed uncertainty and timidity, that paralyze private initiative, and endanger liberty in our personal, business and political life. Convinced that the American people, when they know the real situation, will deal fairly with the railroads, let us hold fast to the well tried experience of individual initiative and management of the railroad lines owned, not by the government, but by the people and their institutions, subject to equitable, responsible regulation.

THE GREATER EFFICIENCY OF PRIVATE OPERA-
TION OF RAILROADS

BY A. J. COUNTY, VICE-PRESIDENT, PENNSYLVANIA RAILROAD
COMPANY

GOVERNMENTAL VS. PRIVATE OPERATION

Without a doubt the welfare of the country demands that
the government should permanently operate the railroads (and
that means it should own them as well), provided it can be
demonstrated from experience here or abroad that they could
be operated more efficiently by the government than under
our "so-called" private ownership. That legal term, largely
of English origin, is used to indicate that ownership is not
concentrated in the state or municipality but in the private
citizen. At the threshold of this paper I would point out
that such legal designation is frequently misunderstood, because it does not state the facts of the present situation respecting railroad ownership. Our type of ownership is a
genuine public ownership, i.e., ownership by millions of our
citizens and through their savings, insurance, educational, philanthropic, and other institutions, contra-distinguished from
government ownership by the nation or by a state, municipal
ownership by a city or a county, or private ownership where
one or a few individuals often own an industrial or recreational railroad in the operation of, and profits from, which they
are practically solely concerned. But let me return to the
subject. England probably faces the same question of governmental operation, but with the disadvantage that wages
were adjusted to war conditions, while the freight rates were
not, although compared to our average ton mile revenue they
already seem fairly high.* Therefore, it is difficult to escape
some governmental guarantee, or regional plan of operation in
England to insure a fair return on the railroad investment.

---

* Since 1915 it is estimated that the average annual earnings of English
Railroad workers were increased from $350 to about $900, and in the United
States from $800 to about $1,400.

Indeed, as England has a much smaller country thickly populated, already well developed with numerous railroads, and
many of them parallel or serving the same general territory,
and having duplicate competitive service, amalgamation and
merger of railroad corporations of England seems a more
simple proposition than the one which would face the United
States, which still requires much more new mileage to develop
its large area. It can scarcely be done even in England without
the loss of much traditional pride and competition in service
that in all might seriously outweigh the estimated benefit of
any unification scheme, and the better course may still be for
Parliament to authorize the companies to effect such corporate
amalgamations and unify such service and facilities as the
Board of Trade may deem to be in the public interest, and
grant adequate rates to sustain the investment under the
changed conditions.

GOVERNMENTAL OPERATION IN 1918

Fortunately in our own country, as well as in foreign
countries, we have the results of government operation as a
guide to our conclusions in considering the important question
of governmental vs. private operation. We should not hesitate
to utilize the experience of Federal operation in our own
country for the year 1918, if beneficial. The roads were then
formed into non-competing operating regions, directed by
regional directors, acting with and for the Director General
and his staff of departmental directors covering every department of railroad activities. There existed a unification of
roads, routes, offices, agencies, facilities and equipment, including coöperation with the waterways, and a similar unification of accounting, finance and purchases. The powers of
the Director General over rates and traffic were practically
without limitation, and the approved capital budget for additions and betterments to the roadbed and equipment was for
items which would increase operating efficiency, and help carry
a larger volume of business. The government had the most
sympathetic help from the entire nation, and the officers and
employees of the railroads, and the citizens had the impetus
of war and patriotism to stir them to the best endeavors. The

luxuries of traveling were eliminated, and the anti-trust and other restrictive Federal and state measures were held in abeyance. Hire of equipment and insurance and other charges were also eliminated, and other accounting short-cuts, applicable only to a unified system, were used to save expenses. Railroad administration expenses were further saved by requiring the railroad corporations to appoint and compensate their own officers and employees, pay for their own offices and maintain their own fiscal, accounting, inspection and executive organizations without any allowance from the government, although the corporate organizations were essential to assist the administration to carry on railroad affairs, make financial and accounting settlements, and carry out the terms of the Federal control contract and see that their property and equipment were suitably maintained. Even the hundreds of millions of working capital consisting of materials and supplies on hand and in the possession of the railroads were taken over by the government as a feature of Federal control. Every working element was adapted and unified by Federal orders to obtain the best results as a single railroad system, and the public rarely winced. There was one serious obstacle to achieving the greatest transportation record the country has ever known, and that was the increased number of inexperienced men in the railroad service compared with preceding years.

The final operating results for the year 1918 and the accompanying costs and statistics are not yet available, but the year 1918 closed with expenses increased $1,148,000,000 over 1917, or 40 per cent, and a deficit of over $200,000,000 to the Railroad Administration in earning the standard compensation required to be paid to the railroads. That compensation being based on the three-year test period ending June 30, 1917, was regarded as moderate for it amounted to only about 5.2 per cent on the total investment on December 31, 1917, of the railroads in their roadbed and equipment provided for public use. Questions of cost and efficiency cannot be swept aside in deciding a permanent railroad policy, and will continue basic to the citizens of the country who wish to preserve its commercial and financial standing, and buy and sell in the markets of other countries, unless we are to have a national policy like many of the foreign nations which, for military or other national purposes, own and operate their railroads largely to effectuate that policy and throw higher costs into general taxation. One serious element of cost in 1918 was the increase in wages authorized by the Federal government. An increase was equitably due the railroad men, but that granted equalled the total annual compensation to be paid by the government to all of the railroads for the possession and use of twenty billion dollars of property and equipment. That railroad employees should be adequately paid is beyond question, but the annual wage increase was equal to about 150 per cent of the total capital expenditures for additions and betterments to the railroads and their equipment in 1918, and it was equal to about 4½ per cent on the total railroad investment of the country. Quite a notable wage increase was made without much reference to whether living costs in New York City exceeded Maine or Alabama. But increased wages were not the only increased costs over 1917, the employment on the railroads of larger numbers of employees to produce the same amount of transportation service, and, I think, the transfer of administrative and operating questions in large part from the local railroad officers to the central administration at Washington, or to the regional officers, and the creation of numerous bureaus requiring service and information of all kinds to the great detriment of the regular work, proved a large factor. All things considered, with a new and different organization, it is a wonder things went as well as they did. A trained and disciplined organization and final responsibility directly centered on the home ground are great factors in retaining railroad efficiency, and these were lacking.

As I have friends on both the corporate and Federal side of the railroad question, I must be rather circumspect but I judge from the recent testimony by the users of railroads before the Senate Committee on Interstate Commerce and expressions in the public press, and from those who ship and travel, that neither the railroad men, the shippers nor the general public were satisfied, and the little additional traffic carried, compared to the performance by the individual companies with all legal restrictions and confusion, did not apparently justify the taking over of the railroads from an economic standpoint. However, the government in a war period required a free hand to deal with labor and material prices, and with financing, as it proposed to monopolize the markets for liberty bonds and other government financing. Summed up for one year it did not justify itself as a permanent railroad policy on the score of either service, low costs, or political benefits. Compromise and delay could not be kept out of the situation, notwithstanding the good intentions and patriotism of all concerned; and the concentration of a large number of railroads into non-competitive operating regions did not point any royal road to great savings or efficiency. Instead, it to a large extent disrupted the trained organizations and orderly traffic movement and use of facilities already existing on the various roads, and left open many questions and settlements as to the maintenance and improvement of the properties that it will take years to adjust. Fifteen months following the effective date of Federal control finds the larger number of contracts for the possession and use of the railroads still incomplete, and the government is largely indebted to the railroad owners and to those furnishing railroad supplies and carrying on contract work. This operating experience does not differ very much from the government control of other industries, but the railroads probably fared better because so many experienced men were asked to assist in the conduct of their affairs, although others directed the policy they were to carry out. Congress adjourned without making the appropriation essential for carrying on the work of the railroads. We saw the humiliating spectacle of the United States failing in the punctual performance of its financial and other obligations, and the railroad question became the football of party expediency. Similarly in five months' operation by the government of the American telephone service a deficit of $4,000,000 is reported, and something like a general increase in wire rates will be essential to wipe out the deficit, and hide future deficits by that process, but the public pays the deficit just the same.

The truth is that many of the programs and policies of 1918 now appear to have been too novel and too ambitious compared with the means and organization available to carry them to success, and such ordinary features as upkeep of properties and output of service, show the results. Many of the men who started them have resigned, and the results must be assumed by their successors who may, or may not, have a different policy. But would these results change in peace conditions under government operation? Would the changing party officers and conditions be able to formulate and adhere to a continuous constructive policy covering the whole country? If the government were supreme as an owner or guarantor, could we change the effects of the war period into efficiency as great as that of the privately operated companies subject to reasonable governmental regulation? We have reached practically a peace condition now, and we are supposed to keep politics out of the railroads, yet, as above stated, Congress adjourned without providing the appropriation to pay administration debts and railroad rental already overdue, and unless the railroad corporations had assisted the government by the use of their individual credit, or the War Finance Corporation had come to the rescue, it would have been humiliated by inability to pay its railroad debts and must have economized at the expense of the road and equipment, if not of the workers, and have relied on the railroad corporations assisting themselves instead of the government carrying out its obligations written and implied as features of Federal control.

STATE AND MUNICIPAL OPERATIONS

A negative answer comes to the foregoing questions from our own state railroads and public improvements in the past. Political management, political capital expenditures to favorite districts and favorite schemes were prevalent, political appointments, and political purchasing and pass favors were the records that the privately operated roads inherited from these past experiences. The story of the Federal government's ownership and control of the Union Pacific furnishes another record, with representatives of the political parties serving on its board, and the long period during which the United States dictated its management, while the great fertile empire west of the Mississippi languished for transportation facilities and enterprise. Private ownership, initiative and enterprise changed this. Governmental operations on Canadian roads versus the privately operated roads in that country confirm the inefficiency and higher costs of the governmental roads. Even to-day with all of our progress the present experiment in Massachusetts of "transportation at cost" by state regulated transit in Boston tells the tale of poor service with costs exceeding the seven cent fare and still rising; and in New York City the subway municipal ownership still retains the five cent fare, but the city must force the taxpayers to sustain its rapid transit investment of probably two hundred millions or more through general taxation.

FOREIGN EXPERIENCE

Appreciating that while the railroads of almost every country, except England and the United States, are operated as government owned roads (although only one-third of the total world mileage is government owned), we must refer to the experience of other countries in recent years for proof as to the inefficiency of government owned vs. privately owned roads, and we must use 1913, before the war, largely, as the most trustworthy comparative basis. French lines although worked under the guarantee plan, have in many features become government operated roads, and in 40 years all lines will be government owned roads.

HIGHER RATES ON FOREIGN ROADS

From reliable sources we find that in 1913 the ton mile revenue of Germany was 1.24 cents; France 1.16 cents, and the United States only 0.72 cents, notwithstanding higher wages and other costs and the heavy tax payments the railroads of the United States made to the national, state and municipal governments. Attempts are made to explain away these low freight rates in the United States as against the most efficient of government owned or government guaranteed roads of Europe. At the request of the Senate Committee on Interstate and Foreign Commerce, Professor Adams, then in charge of the railroad accounts of the Interstate Commerce Commission, prepared in 1905 a table of specific freight rates on chief commodities for each country—bituminous coal for 300 to 600 miles the American rate was .33 of a cent to .52 of a cent per ton mile as against the Prussian rate of .72 of a cent to .82 of a cent per ton mile; woolen and cotton yarns, coffee, tobacco, etc., showed a marked difference in favor of American railroad rates. Later the Bureau of Railway Economics made studies of average ton mile rates on bituminous coal, iron ore, lumber, grain, stone, fertilizer, etc., with those charged in England, France and Germany, which verified the very reasonable freight rates we enjoyed under private operation in this country. Whether the country can have such low rates in the future depends on the enterprise of our railroad men in coöperating with our business men, and on the efficiency and loyalty of our labor, and also upon the freedom of the railroads from conflicting and meddlesome regulation, and seriously growing taxation, often the product of wild appropriations for useless waterways and other projects intended to compete with the railroads.

Government ownership and operation can promise no reduction in rates. Have we been able to obtain lower rates permanently on any government operated public utility that is charged with the necessity of earning a return on the investment? From Panama to Alaska the answer is "No."

HIGHER CONSTRUCTION COSTS ON FOREIGN ROADS

Can we gain anything from employing the construction and capitalizing methods of government-owned lines of Europe? Our cost per mile of main track is about $56,000; France, $104,000; and Germany, $86,000. Some persons attempt to explain away this substantial difference by claiming higher real estate cost for Europe, but they ignore the higher labor costs here, and also that American railroad capitalization has been shaken down by successive reorganizations, foreclosures, etc., so that the charge of watered capital has little or no foundation any longer, and American construction methods have been more effective than those of Europe.

LOWER WAGES ON FOREIGN ROADS

Is there any working man that can claim he can benefit in wages by the government-owned and operated system? The average yearly compensation of railway employees in the

United States and foreign countries whose railway systems were owned and operated by the government were, in the year 1913: United States, $756.83; Austria, $335.90; Germany, $408.97; Hungary, $300.41; and Italy, $376.81. On this wage basis railroad charges in the United States would, of necessity, have to be much higher except for the greater efficiency.

TAXES

If the roads are operated by the government the general taxation must be increased to raise about $200,000,000 to $225,000,000 per annum for our state, municipal and Federal governments, heretofore paid by our privately owned railroads. Generally the government owned and operated roads in foreign countries escape the necessity of paying taxes and earning interest on the cost, and the capital accounts are used liberally for all betterments, and yet they are compared with our railroads. There is no comparison that should convince us to adopt government operation or ownership.

EFFICIENCY

Shall we go to the government operated railroads to learn efficiency? "No" is the answer if we look keenly into the situation. So far as passengers are concerned there are many countries with much lower fares, but the accommodations are also much lower, and when we reach equality of accommodations and convenience with the standard of this country there is nothing to attract us. In the matter of freight train loading, the average load on our roads, taking the country as a whole, is more than twice that of a country like Germany. The German railroad system before the war was regarded as practically free from changing political control, but in actual experience, leaving aside construction costs, higher rates, freedom from state taxes, and other charges imposed on our roads, the system is not adapted to America. The charge for baggage is very much more excessive. Often to the freight rates are added special charges for loading and unloading. Less than carload lots are at practically prohibitive rates compared with carload lots, and in fact collection agencies to obtain full carloads are a necessity of the situation, to obtain rates upon which smaller quantities may move, and the collecting agencies are compensated by charging the shipper a rate ranging between the rates on carload and less than carload lots. Germany has not been free from increased rates when the needs of the government treasury require them. Fast freight service is generally charged double rates. Notwithstanding the use of autocratic powers the complaints of car congestion, high rates, high operating ratios, and low wages are made. American railroads have revolutionized their equipment and methods of operation but Prussia clings to old equipment and old methods. Mr. Acworth, the English authority, stated this and added: "It would be difficult to point to a single important invention or improvement, the introduction of which the world owes to the state railway." Austria, France, Belgium, Italy and Australia, tell pretty much the same story of unification but with increased offices, increased personnel and increased cost and often bad service. They do not differ much in experience from our own roads when operated by the states. If this were an extensive economic treatise I could fill it with figures that would abundantly demonstrate that the United States under ownership by its citizens, and operation under competitive conditions and individual initiative, has provided the most efficient as well as the most economical transportation system of the world. That position was not achieved by magic, but by an ownership individually by millions of our citizens and through their savings, insurance and other institutions; by individual initiative and enterprise to reach the natural resources of mines, forests, and agriculture, and, unlike other countries, opened up the country to be populated rather than to follow the population; and they also spread out to and from the important ports, cities and commercial routes. They risked their capital and gave a service that could prosper only by accommodating the public, and by improving tracks, equipment, and facilities that increased the train loads and freight traffic volume above any other country of the world. What our railroad system may do in the future when returned to their owners depends largely upon the effects of Federal control and future governmental regulation of rates, and the condition of their working organizations and the property and equipment.

SUMMARY OF FOREIGN EXPERIENCE

The men on whose shoulders the commercial and social prosperity of the country rests, no matter what political party is in power, should study these results. Their enterprise would be compelled to carry the burden of governmental operating costs. For their benefit I add that W. M. Acworth, Esq., English economist above referred to, concluded his testimony before our joint sub-committee of the House and Senate on Interstate and Foreign Commerce in May, 1917, as to the experience in foreign countries with government-owned and operated roads, in this way:

"President Hadley (of Yale) has summed up the conclusions of the Italian railway commission, based on the railway experience of the world as it existed 35 years ago, as follows:

"(1) Most of the pleas for State management are based upon the idea that the State would perform many services much cheaper than they are performed by private companies. This is a mistake. The tendency is decidedly the other way. . . . The State is much more likely to attempt to tax industry than to foster it.

"(2) State management is more costly than private management. . . .

"(3) The political dangers would be very great. Politics would corrupt the railroad management, and the railroad management would corrupt politics.

"The essential lesson of the history may be said to be this: It is impossible to obtain satisfactory results on Government railways in a democratic State unless the management is cut loose from direct political control. Neither Australia nor any other country with a democratic constitution—perhaps an exception ought to be made of Switzerland—has succeeded in maintaining a permanent severance. The Australian Parliaments have loosened their hold for a few years, but only for a few years. In France, in Belgium, in Italy parliamentary interference has never been abandoned for a moment. Without imputing a double dose of original sin to politicians, it is easy to see why this happens. The railways belong to the people. It seems therefore to the ordinary citizen only right and natural that parliament should control the management of the people's railways. And yet facts are stubborn things; and the facts show that parliamentary interference has meant running the railways, not for the benefit of the people at large, but to satisfy local and sectional or even personal interests. They show further that, under parliamentary management, it is easier to get money for big schemes of new construction than for inconspicuous day-to-day betterments and improvements which probably would produce much greater public benefit. Some day, perhaps, having learned wisdom by experience, a parliament and a people may recognize that management for the people is not necessarily management by the people."

His experience is supported by the views of other eminent foreign economists.

IS GOVERNMENT FINANCING A SUFFICIENT OFFSET TO HIGHER OPERATING COSTS?

The policy of government ownership and operation has received a rude shock in the United States, but its advocates are by no means asleep. They still cling to the idea that in some fashion even if the government could not permanently operate as cheaply as the private management it could finance the roads cheaper. They are very solicitous about our weak roads, and urge unification with the strong roads and a government guaranty of about 4 per cent. Our present and past experiences should be enough to bury these ideas. Anything providing an opening wedge for governmental interference and control tends to an ultimate ownership. It is frequently stated that the United States could finance the roads on a 4 per cent or 4½ per cent basis, whereas the private companies would average about 6 per cent for new capital money. Now as to this, the war has proven, first, that most of the financing connected with the railroad control both for the corporations and the government will cost 6 per cent in interest charges, that is, for the large addition and betterment program of capital expenditures, the government charged 6 per cent to the corporations until the work was finished and then it allowed the companies 6 per cent on the total capital cost of such improvements; second, the war period demonstrated that when any country undertakes a financial responsibility of twenty billions, to be increased probably three-quarters of a billion to one billion per annum for capital improvements and investments, it naturally creates such increased obligations as to materially affect the interest rates and market prices of its own securities. Citizens bought many Liberty Bonds on the basis that a dollar invested in our government securities would be worth its face value only to learn by experience that government bond prices were affected by supply and demand, and sold for several dollars below par. Governmental cost of financing in England during the war was not, I believe, any cheaper than that of its best railroads. Even if the government could finance somewhat cheaper the new railroad capital requirements, they are small compared with the annual operating expenses. But it is clear from past experience that whatever saving might be effected through lower interest rates would be easily wiped out by loss of operating initiative, costly political operation, by increased number of bureaus and employees, and log-rolling improvements that in time would arise in our form of democratic and changing party government.

WEAK AND STRONG RAILROADS

Further, even a guarantee by the government increases its fixed charges, and with the loss of taxes now paid to the government—state and Federal—by the railroads would mean a resort to higher taxation of business. Higher transportation rates would be, in part, the cure. We must never expect to have all roads equally strong financially and physically, and we must not expect the government to underwrite the bad policy of poor location or inefficient management. The best way to strengthen weak roads in time is to allow all roads in each traffic territory rates that as a whole are adequate and will produce fair returns on the investment in that territory. That, and the prevention of the construction of unnecessary lines and facilities, will improve weak roads, and also make the better established roads in the same territory able to have sound credit, and in time probably purchase and merge these weaker lines. Heretofore neither weak nor strong roads have been equitably dealt with in the rate situation for many years, and the result has been lack of development; our railroad investors in either weak or strong roads cannot expect a government guarantee without paying for such a guarantee by reducing the value of their properties or the volume of their securities, or the return thereon. A guarantee in substance means an all around reorganization which the country should not be compelled to face in the war reconstruction period. Instead, the business necessity of adequate rates should be faced, so that those who got the benefits of the railroads should pay reasonably to support them. In addition, the multiplicity of detailed regulation should be modified—it is costly and saps the vitality of individual initiative, because the regulators have assumed the position of general managers without any corresponding financial or other responsibility for future results.

CAN THE FEDERAL RESERVE SYSTEM BE APPLIED TO RAILROADS?

The Federal Reserve System, with its regional banks, has made our banking so sound and elastic that it is often referred to as applicable to adjust the railroad situation. I think there is some force in that suggestion, but my estimate of the success of our banking system is this—it has had the benefit of concentrated Federal control, and state banks often take out Federal charters to carry on state and interstate banking business. Each bank has its local management, and the government allows it the right of private initiative and management to carry on a most active banking business in competition with other institutions of the same and other territory, so long as its methods are honest and legal. The regulatory powers exercised through the Federal Reserve Boards and the District Federal Reserve Banks are so constituted that they cannot become purely political. The boards are required to be directed by representatives of the banking business, commerce, agricultural, or other industrial pursuits, in addition to representatives of the government, and in the case of the Federal Reserve banks the stockholders are also represented. Theoretically we have enough machinery for railroad regulation but we need the mandate of constructive railroad laws. We need the concentration of responsibility on some central regulatory body for not only revenues, but outgo and final railroad results and credits, and we need to add to the railroad regulatory bodies experienced business men with interests strong enough to enforce a national policy to insure the development of the transportation facilities and the credit of the railroads. This can be done without placing the burden of financing and management upon the government, and if it is done we can avoid the politicalization of railroad ownership, management, employees, railroad capital expenditures and service. It is a time to speak plainly and act promptly, for in a reconstruction period, such as we are now facing, it would be a great impetus to steady employment and industrial and commercial conditions if a stable constructive railroad policy that would keep alive individual initiative could be promptly enacted by the Federal government.

CONCLUSION

In conclusion, we have large territory and extensive natural resources still requiring development by the railroads, the existing railroads must be regularly improved and expanded, terminals, yards, warehouses, shops, etc., must be improved and kept modernized, and in many places electrification should be undertaken to cheapen and increase the transportation output. Initiative, enterprise and finance must have free play under constructive public regulation, or these necessities will not be forthcoming. I cannot gather from our experience at home or abroad anything that justifies the substitution of a government owned or operated railroad system, or even governmental regional non-competitive systems worked by private railroads with government guarantee, unless we are convinced that the railroads cannot expect adequate rates and a fair return on the investment from the regulatory and judicial authorities, and that American business men are willing to bury personal initiative and competition in railroad service, and that America's working men have determined that all railroad profits shall go to them and little or none to the capital of their fellow citizens on which the whole railroad enterprise of the past is based and who must provide the capital for future expansion. If we have reached that deplorable condition then government ownership and operation with all its economic and political evils and waste is the only refuge. I am convinced that American citizens have not reached that state of mind; there was no evidence in the recent Senate committee inquiry on the railroad situation to indicate that any large part of the citizens who depend on railroad service demanded government operation or ownership, but rather, as a whole, they desired private initiative and operation continued, with the railroads owned by the public and their institutions. The quicker we get back to that condition under reasonable and not punitive regulation, and allow adequate returns to be earned, will we terminate a very artificial situation, and hasten readjustment to normal conditions without jolting business, finance or the wage earner. What is now required to restore confidence in Federal control of railroads and remove some financial uncertainty, is for the government to promptly conclude the contracts for the possession and use of the railroads since January 1, 1918, make regular quarterly payments of the standard compensation, provide a means to finance capital expenditures, and by all means to pay its own railroad current supply bills, and provide working capital essential to carry on such a widespread national instrument as the railroads.

ADDENDA—CONDITIONS IN JUNE, 1919

Since the foregoing paper was prepared several important events have taken place which seem to strengthen the position outlined.

1. The War Finance Corporation has been utilized to assist in financing the railroads since the failure of Congress to pass an appropriation in the last session.

2. The President of the United States has convened Congress by a special message from France in which he advocates:

(a) The return of the wire system to private operation, and that has now been accomplished in part.

(b) Preparation for the return of the railroads to the owners not later than January 1st, 1920.

3. The Director General requested Congress to approve an appropriation of $1,200,000,000 for railroad purposes. Congress declined to make any appropriation at present of a figure beyond $750,000,000, although there is no doubt that the $1,200,000,000 is necessary.

The Director General's statement to Congress indicates that for requirements of 1918, including improvements, etc., over $941,000,000 was required, less $500,000,000 heretofore appropriated by Congress, leaving a balance of $441,000,000. This with $758,000,000 estimated requirements for 1919 made up the total appropriation of $1,200,000,000 desired from Congress. The Federal control estimated requirements for 1919 include an operating deficit for the first four months of that year of $250,000,000, while the similar deficit for the year 1918 was over $236,000,000.

The question of an increase of rates to place the railroads on a self-sustaining basis is recognized as imperative, but the Director General has taken no action in the matter because he believes it would tend to increase the cost of living, and that if the government should undertake to raise three or four hundred million dollars through increased rates to take care of the situation, it would probably be found that the increase in prices resulting from railroad rates would cause the ultimate consumer to pay three or four times that amount in the last analysis. Legislation has also been introduced which would take from the Director General power to increase rates, and restore these powers to the Interstate Commerce Commission.

The suggestion that fewer systems of railroads should be evolved, and that the strong roads are getting enough to support the weak has had a rather bad shock by the discovery that out of eighty-six systems, which have about 94% of the total railroad revenues of the country, only eighteen of them during the test period of three years ending June 30th, 1917, had earnings equivalent to over 6% on their property investment, representing 35½% of the total operating revenues of the entire eighty-six systems, thus leaving about sixty-eight of the systems with returns of less than 6%, and these sixty-eight systems had 64½% of the operating revenues of the eighty-six systems. To attach the weak to the strong systems without an increase of rates would mean that both would break down. There is also an insistent public demand that the railroads be returned to private ownership at the earliest possible date. Unless the public are content to continue to make up railroad deficits from the public treasury, this raises the practical question of how the railroads are going to be rehabilitated unless the rates are first increased to meet increased costs and restore railroad credit, and unless the properties and equipment are returned in first-class operating condition. So far no allowance has been made in the railroad accounts for deferred maintenance due to the lack of men and materials in 1918, and the policy is apparently being practised of cutting maintenance to the bare bone so as to enforce economies. Provision must also be made for the funding of amounts due to the government by the various railroads on account of capital expenditures made during the period of government control in 1918 and 1919. The necessity for the closest coöperation between the Railroad Administration and the Railroad Corporations is, therefore, evident to avoid future claims and controversies, and to insure the return of the railroads in a condition to properly serve the public and possess the ability to finance themselves without government support.

EFFECTS OF GOVERNMENT OWNERSHIP ON DEVELOPMENT AND EFFICIENCY OF RAILROADS

BY JOHN J. ESCH, CHAIRMAN, COMMITTEE ON INTERSTATE AND
FOREIGN COMMERCE OF THE HOUSE OF REPRESENTATIVES

As a premise to the consideration of this subject the financial burden which could be imposed upon the government were it to acquire ownership of the railroads ought to be first considered.

On December 31, 1918, the outstanding obligations of the government amounted to $21,000,000,000 with an annual interest charge of about $1,000,000,000. About $18,000,000,000 will be required for the fiscal year of 1919, and possibly $10,000,000,000 for the fiscal year of 1920. Notwithstanding many of these billions will be raised by heavy taxes the remainder must be raised by sale of bonds, the interest on which will be added to the interest charges we must already pay. The total capitalization of the railroads is about $20,000,000,000, of which $8,755,000,000 is stock. If, as many predict, the physical valuation of the roads should equal their capitalization the government to acquire title and possession would have to pay the $8,755,000,000 for the stock and assume the bonded indebtedness and interest thereon or on its own bonds issued in exchange. This would mean more debt and more interest and raise the total to staggering proportions.

Government ownership following upon the heels of a world's war and adding to the billions of indebtedness which that war has entailed, billions more, would have a deterrent effect upon transportation development for a time at least. After the Saturnalia of these last two years Congress would be influenced by the demand for lower tax burdens and a greater economy in the expenditure of money. With the railroads restored to private ownership and control with the prompt recuperation of the nation's business attendant upon peace there would return to the railroads that initiative, that enterprise and spirit of development which have characterized them from the beginning and made of them the greatest system in the world.

The motive for government ownership in some countries like Germany is military necessity, in others like Canada political necessity, in others like Australia financial necessity, and in still others a combination of these. In small countries like Belgium, Switzerland and Japan the fear of domination of business interests by foreign capital was the impelling motive. In the United States none of these reasons can be claimed as sufficient justification. Relief from burdensome regulations, strikes, excessive rates, Wall Street control it is urged will result from government ownership. Government ownership will not obviate the necessity of government control. On the contrary, as in the case of Germany, it will enlarge it. Strikes have occurred on the government-owned roads in Australia, New Zealand, Italy and Canada. As to rates no country, prior to the war, enjoyed such low rates as the United States. Wall Street, or the so-called bankers' control, can and ought to be eliminated by giving to the Interstate Commerce Commission authority to regulate stock and bond issues.

In the matter of development the government cannot secure as good results as its citizens who are actuated by the laudable desire to secure a fair return upon a fair investment even when rigidly regulated by the government. If our railroad construction had been the function of the government from the beginning the roads might have been better and more strategically located, but there would have been fewer of them and we would not to-day have a population of over 100,000,000. If the experience of some of our own states and of Canada be recalled we may even doubt the superior wisdom of governments in locating and constructing their own lines. When in the fifties North Carolina started her state railroad she built it in the shape of the letter U, yielding to political pressure and the wishes of high state officials. The Intercolonial of Canada, which for the fifty years of its operation has netted a loss of many millions to the taxpayers, is government owned and operated and so located as to make it impossible to compete with its privately owned competitors, the Grand Trunk and the Canadian Pacific.

Railroads exercised a baneful influence in politics for many years but due to state and Federal laws this influence has been largely eliminated. With government ownership and the necessity of submitting an annual budget to Congress to provide for new lines, additions, extensions and betterments would not all manner of political pressure be brought to bear upon Congress to secure an apportionment of the appropriations for such purposes by districts and states as now obtains in the matter of public buildings and river and harbor improvements? No matter what agency might be created by law to expend money for such purposes Congress, by controlling the purse strings, could have its way. Transportation development under such circumstances would be sectional, uneconomical, and often not in the public interest. In many states large sections are still without railroads, in others it would be claimed that existing lines should be double tracked, in others costly terminals should be supplied. To attain these ends log-rolling and other questionable legislative practices might be resorted to. Even an enormous war debt and the debt imposed by government ownership might be insufficient to suppress the voting of many questionable appropriations. Under private ownership these evil temptations would be impossible. France through political pressure a few years ago was forced to take over the Western, a weak and struggling road, and has found it a burden ever since. In Germany members of the Reichstag have clamored for the construction of costly depots on lines in their several districts. The same is true as to members of the Canadian Parliament through whose districts the Intercolonial runs.

Under government ownership transportation of commodities from place to place, from point of production to point of consumption, on one road or another road might become aggravated political issues in comparison with which the making of a tariff bill would be the task of an infant class. Under the existing order such far reaching problems as the shipment of grain from the mid-west to the Atlantic or Gulf ports, or the proper differential on shipments from Chicago to the ports of Boston, New York, Philadelphia and Baltimore are left to the untrammeled judgment of the Interstate Commerce Commission. Ownership in such matters would incite a desire to control through Congressional action and lead to sectional controversies. What a temptation there would be to win favor by securing a reduction of rates to one's constituents by joining with others having a like purpose! Enforcement of rates sufficiently high to meet all expenditures on the part of the commission might be rendered difficult because of the attitude, which long has been maintained as to the Post Office Department, that being owned and operated by the government it was not to be run for profit but for the general good.

Government control under the existing Federal Control Act would be the control in all essentials under government ownership. Has such control met expectations and promoted the demand for government ownership? We believe it has not. The few economies that have been effected do not compensate for lessened freight and passenger service. Notwithstanding the zeal and the ability of the Director General and his staff and the great difficulties arising out of the exigencies of the war the character of the Federal control and the extent and manner of its exercise have caused many former advocates to doubt the efficacy of government ownership. There has been no transportation development during the fifteen months of Federal control and there of course has been no construction of new lines. Nor has there been the normal increase of rolling stock, nor, in many instances, the proper maintenance of way and equipment.

A state of war and the prime necessity of subordinating everything to the movement of men and munitions may be urged in extenuation and yet our people had hoped that under unified control with limitless power and financial resources a better showing might and ought to have been made. With full control under government ownership in time of peace we are not sanguine that there would be better results. Delay, higher costs and greater waste and extravagance which seem to inhere in all government activities would inevitably follow. The bureaucracy, which ownership would result in, deadens initiative, dulls ambition and retards development. An apt illustration is at hand in the building of the Alaskan Railroad. Under the act approved March 12, 1914, $35,000,000 was authorized for the construction of the main line at an estimated cost of $50,000 per mile. Although five years have elapsed only 228 miles have been constructed and at a cost of $141,441 per mile. The appropriation authorized has already been expended with over 100 miles uncompleted. The overhead expenses, as is characteristic of all government work, were excessively high. The National Transcontinental of Canada, estimated to cost $34,083 per mile, was constructed by government commissioners at a final cost of $99,000 per mile, competing private roads being capitalized at from one-third to one-half that amount. Such examples would make Congress hesitate to vote appropriations for any extended development or if, yielding to pressure, it made the appropriation, the development would be at too great a price to insure even operating expenses.

THE EFFECT ON EFFICIENCY

It has been a fundamental doctrine in the two greatest democracies in the world, England and the United States, to leave to the individual fullest scope for his activities without encroachment by the government. Hope for reward stimulates inventive genius; the certainty of tenure in office at a fixed salary deadens it. Herbert Spencer says:

"We did not get from the State the multitudinous useful inventions from *the spade to the telephone;* it was not the State which made possible extended navigation by a developed astronomy; it was not the State which made the discoveries in physics, chemistry, and the rest which guide modern manufacturers; it was not the State which devised the machinery for producing fabrics of every kind, for transferring men and things from place to place, and for ministering in a thousand ways to our comforts. The world-wide transactions conducted in merchants' offices, the rush of traffic filling our streets, the retail distributing system which brings everything within easy reach and delivers the necessaries of life daily at our doors, are not of governmental origin."

Our most successful railroad managers and presidents have come from the ranks with promotion based on merit and not merely length of service. Their skill, fitness and executive capacity met with prompt recognition and suitable recompense. They were not handicapped by the dull monotony and hopeless

/

state of employees in the classified service. It was because our railroads were developed under private initiative, the spur of reward with an open field, that they have become the most efficient in the world. This is true of whatever test may be applied. If financial, our capitalization is less per mile than that of any other country having the same standard gauge and with passenger rates first class and freight rates the lowest. If economical, our average freight train load is the greatest and more units of traffic are moved per employee while at the same time paying the highest wages. We have the best passenger service open to all on equal terms. We have not as yet felt inclined to demand second, third and fourth class accommodations with correspondingly lower rates although this may be necessary with the increase in population and desire for travel.

As a rule, higher efficiency in both administration and operation is found in private industry than under government. The necessity of making expenses and a reasonable profit compel strictest economy and avoidance of waste. Government in industry, whether it be transportation or otherwise, is not embarrassed by fear of a deficit. Salaries and number of employees are not made to bear so close a relationship to output. In Germany, where efficiency in the operation of railroads is higher than in other countries having government ownership, there are 2,077 employees to each 100 miles of road as compared with only 624 in the United States.

President Elliott of the Northern Pacific in a recent address stated:

"The Pennsylvania system furnishes 12.2 per cent of the total ton mileage and 14½ per cent of the total passenger mileage of the steam roads of this country. On Dec. 31, 1917, that system had 233,600 employees, and on Dec. 31, 1918, it had 273,101 employees. Although the ton mileage handled in 1918 was less than in 1917 (the railways being in the year 1917 under private control) nearly 40,000 more employees were required to handle the smaller volume of business."

While this result is doubtless due in some measure to war conditions, it is suggestive of an inevitable tendency to increase costs of transportation under government control and ownership. Such increased costs must be paid out of increased rates or out of the public treasury. The organization of the two million railroad employees of the country into an efficient, workable force is an undertaking of such great magnitude and fraught with such possibilities of failure as to give us pause.

Secretary Lane in 1912, while a member of the Interstate Commerce Commission, declared:

"No one who has had experience in Government affairs would be bold enough to say that the Government of the United States could now operate the 250,000 miles of railway with as much satisfaction to the people as the railways themselves are now being administered."

The late James J. Hill has stated:

"Paternalism and extravagance have lived in conjugal union since governments began. No decree of divorce can ever be pronounced between them, and their offspring, inefficiency, is the perpetual disturber of wholesome business life."

Under the Federal Control Act, approved March 21, 1918, authority was given to the President to initiate rates, fares and charges. The Director General, Mr. McAdoo, under this authority, ordered an increase of 25 per cent on freight and 50 per cent on passenger rates, resulting in an increased transportation cost for the calendar year 1918 of approximately $800,000,000. In addition to this vast increase of revenue the above mentioned act appropriated $500,000,000 as a revolving fund "for the purpose of paying the expenses of the Federal control, and so far as necessary the amount of just compensation, and to provide terminals, motive power, cars, and other necessary equipment." Mr. McAdoo, in his testimony given a year ago before the House Committee on Interstate and Foreign Commerce, stated that because of the economies he hoped to effect, the amount of this revolving fund would be sufficient. Owing to the vastly increased cost of operation, due mainly to increase of wages, his successor, Mr. Hines, has been compelled to apply to Congress for a deficiency appropriation of $750,000,000 to pay the debts of the last calendar year and provide funds for the current year. In other words, notwithstanding the fact that the government collected from the people $800,000,000 more for transportation than was collected in 1917, the net operating income of the railroad properties was more than $200,000,000 less than in the year 1917.

These results of a year's experience with Federal control and operation are not such as to encourage the hope that with further control and operation under government ownership there will be any marked increase in efficiency and certainly no reduction in rates.

ADJUSTMENT OF WAGES AND CONDITIONS OF SERVICE UNDER GOVERNMENT AND COR-PORATE OWNERSHIP OF RAILROADS

BY W. N. DOAK, VICE-PRESIDENT, BROTHERHOOD OF RAILROAD TRAINMEN

In approaching this subject we necessarily must do so from a purely American viewpoint which, on account of the nature of our transportation lines and the varied conditions under which they operate, precludes comparison with other countries. No country can be compared with ours, neither can the transportation conditions of other countries be measured by ours. We, then, must be guided by our experience and our conditions, which again present problems in making an estimate as to advantages, either one over the other, of corporate ownership or public ownership, because we have had corporate ownership only in the past with no experience with public ownership, except a brief period of government control. This period of control was under such extraordinary conditions that it precludes a fair estimate of the advantages or disadvantages under normal conditions. We are accordingly brought to the point of having to weigh possibilities and circumstances for a balance of our past experiences.

Of the many plans tentatively suggested as a solution of the transportation problems, I am of the opinion that some form of public ownership, independent of partisan politics, operated as a strictly business proposition is the best. My reasons are based upon past experience and observations. We have tried unrestricted private or corporate operation, governmental regulation as to rates and service and government control, also for a brief period an experiment in unification under corporate ownership. Now all seem to be agreed that some other plan must be resorted to and the question is before the people in a most serious aspect. Finances must be had, rates must be adjusted and the service must be brought up to the highest efficiency.

In order to stabilize the finances we certainly must remove the element of doubt and uncertainty and capital must be furnished in such amounts that extensions and betterments may be made, adequate wages paid and prompt service rendered.   Government ownership surely would overcome this obstacle more promptly and effectively than any other plan. Rates could, in my opinion, be adjusted more promptly under a system of public ownership than under any form of private or corporate ownership by treating the transportation systems as a unit, providing a more uniform rate for the country as a whole.   By a combined unified system, I believe more prompt and efficient service could be had under normal conditions.

As to the adjustment of wages and conditions of employment, we have reached the point where it has been recognized that there should be a uniform wage rate and that fair conditions of employment should alike be applied to the employees on the small lines as well as on the large ones.   This principle is recognized by our laws and likewise a general tendency has been to standardize wages by sections, and now it has become nation wide or shortly will be.   Why should not the man employed on the small line receive for the same service as much pay as the man on the large line, and the same is true of the man on the Pacific Coast as the one on the Atlantic Coast.   Also this is the fact as to safeguards in his employment and his general conditions of service.   This feature, therefore, is easy of accomplishment under government ownership.

The adjustment of disputes is no longer a question of speculation as to methods on the railroads, as a real solution has been found, and while it can be handled under any form of operation of the railroads, it unquestionably can be handled effectively under public ownership.   Probably this plan can be worked more effectively and with fewer elements of doubt under public ownership than under any other plan.   Government control has made it possible to demonstrate to a greater degree the practicability of a plan of adjustments of wage and other disputes between transportation lines and transportation employees.

We have had comparatively few minor strikes on the railroads in many years, and no major strikes.   However, there always has been and probably always will be more public alarm over threatened suspension of transportation than over any other one question that may come up, because under our transportation system and the dependency of the people on these arteries of commerce rests to the greatest degree the national life. This has caused considerable agitation and uneasiness in the past. However, under our past and present laws we have really had more accommodations than have been secured under any other law in any other country in the civilized world, and far less suspension of traffic on the American railroads than probably in any other country in the civilized world. But each time this question has come up it has caused great concern and has been widely and generally discussed. In the year of 1916 in a general movement by the transportation men for a shorter work day, the question of a method of adjusting disputes became a national topic, with the result that it was more or less one of the leading questions in a presidential election. Compulsory investigation, mediation, conciliation and arbitration in their various phases were discussed by the American public, and there was almost a demand for some form of compulsory legislation; but no such legislation has as yet been passed. The reason that some action has not been taken is due to the fact that after a careful study of this question from a fair and impartial standpoint one is invariably led to believe that no plan of this kind is feasible, and the history of experiments in other countries clearly demonstrates that our past plans of voluntary arbitration have been more effective than any plan in any other country has been, so far as is known. There is a reason for this conclusion, it being based upon observation and experience in the application of the so-called compulsory methods resorted to in other countries, when the constitutions, laws and customs of other countries are compared with the constitution, laws and customs of this country. As every individual in the United States is guaranteed his freedom of speech and action, accordingly the individual could not be restrained from leaving his employment; and such being the case, there is no power that could compel him to remain with his employer if his conditions were not satisfactory to him. Therefore, if an individual could not be estopped, it is equally true of all the individuals employed in a given occupation.

Following the passage of the so-called Adamson Law, which had for its purpose the granting of a basic eight-hour day for transportation employees, it was found that the law was not applied and eventually the employees in order to make effective the principle were compelled to adopt other methods, with the result that a settlement was reached independent of the Act, to be applied in one way if the Act was declared constitutional and in another way if declared unconstitutional. The application of the basic principle having been agreed to, it was found, however, even with the basic principle disposed of, that the method of application and interpretation had to be determined upon in another manner. Accordingly it was agreed that a commission would be appointed equal in number from each side, and such commission immediately began functioning and continued in existence for a period of more than a year, during which time they handled more than 30,000 questions arising under the basic principles agreed upon. It is singularly strange and worthy of note that in all these questions handled by the commission, composed as it was of an equal number of representatives of the employers and employees, the conclusions were unanimously arrived at. This demonstrated the practicability of a plan for the settlement of disputes by a commission of practical men.

Commencing with the period of government control, the question arose as to how disputes on the railroads could be disposed of, which finally resulted in the creation of a board consisting of eight men, four from the operating officials of the railroads and four from representatives of the employees, to which board all disputes must be referred and its decisions to be final. This board has been in existence for nearly a year and has handled all kinds of disputes between the transportation employees and the railroads, and up to the present time has handled more than 600 disputes without a single dissenting vote in the decisions on these questions. This demonstrates that this is the real solution of the labor question on the railroads. Following the creation of the board to deal with disputes arising among those engaged in conducting transportation, other boards have been created to handle the shop men's disputes, and a third board to handle all the other classes employed on the railroads, and the net results have been that these boards have likewise been able to agree.

These boards were created by voluntary arrangements, and are functioning to-day under voluntary agreements. Their decisions are final and binding upon the parties concerned, and there are no labor disputes on the railroads at the present time. During the period of the war there has been no alarm or uneasiness caused by the railroad employees arising out of labor disputes, it being the one industry that has been free from trouble during the war. It is therefore fair to assume that such can be as effectively handled in peace times and under normal conditions.

The transportation employees are not adverse to the principle of arbitration, but they are adverse to having their matters handled by men who are not familiar with the real question involved. And it argues that there is a reason why they are adverse to the past practice in arbitration matters, as we have found in a great many instances, due to unfamiliarity with the question at issue, that instead of settling the dispute the award has tended to create more controversies arising therefrom than were involved in the original question. I believe the present plan in effect is the real solution of the question, and when once a matter is settled by practical men it eliminates the possibility of subsequent controversies arising from the settlement.

As to the operation of a plan of this kind, it could be worked under government control, corporate ownership or public ownership, but there will be certain drawbacks, probably, that could be more easily overcome under some form of government ownership. But in no instance will compulsory investigation, conciliation or arbitration effectively settle disputes on the railroads, and if this plan is carried out under any form of government control, private control or otherwise, it must be done as a purely voluntary method; and the board created to handle these disputes must not be hampered by restrictions of any nature. It should be required to settle these controversies only on the basis of equity and in accordance with the knowledge gained through the experience in handling these questions as an employer or an employee.

I have always been opposed to government ownership of railroads, and would still be adverse to such a plan if it were to be conducted as a governmental, political system. It would be bad if the transportation systems of our country were to become a part of the partisan, political organizations. But if the government will handle the transportation question as a business proposition, providing means for financing the roads, making provision for extensions and improvements, adjustments of rates and service on a high plane with a view of accommodating the public and at the same time developing the transportation lines to the needs of the country, as well as providing for fair and reasonable wages and working conditions of employment to the employees by affording fair tribunals for the adjustment of complaints and grievances and the settlement of a fair basis of wages and hours of service, government ownership will be the real solution of the many complex questions that have seriously confronted the transportation lines and likewise the American public for a number of years. This is not only possible, but is reasonable and can be accomplished if this subject is approached from the standpoint of the good of the American public and without regard to any one particular interest, but with due regard to all interests involved. The operating officials of the railroads and the railroad employees will make a success out of the transportation lines if they are given a fair opportunity to do so, and the question of disputes will eventually disappear if this subject is approached in a fair and reasonable manner. All elements of doubt and suspicion will be removed and we will enter upon an era of prosperity the like of which has never been seen. On the other hand, if the railroad question is to become a partisan matter and is not approached with a view of the solution of these problems, or is viewed from a financial or money making viewpoint, we may be confronted with a disastrous situation on our railroads. I therefore hope that while this opportunity is presented, when this question is before the people, the situation will be viewed from the standpoint of what is the best for the people as a whole, and in so doing I am led to believe that the time has come when we should take some steps looking to some form of public ownership in the interest of the American public; and, if so, it is fair to assume that the wages and conditions of service of the employees will be adjusted in the end without the slightest difficulty.

PUBLIC CONTROL OF RAILROAD WAGES

BY WM. CHURCH OSBORN

It is generally believed that the government took control of the transportation organization of the United States on the 1st of January, 1918. Such is not the case. The Control Bill gave the government real control of only a part of the organization. It is true that the government assumed control of the physical property and the money of the railroads; the right to change rates, etc., at its pleasure. The government freed itself completely from the restrictions of the Sherman Act and the Hepburn Bill as to pooling, consolidations, etc., including the regulations of the Interstate Commerce Commission, all of which had for years been the accepted policy of the country in managing the transportation interests, but the government did not assume control of railroad labor.

A transportation system is a living organism. It gets its life from the men who run it and it works well or ill according as the men constituting the organization conduct themselves. It is a mistake to think of a railroad as the right of way, the rail, the engines, the cars, the terminals and the financial management with the bonds, stocks and balances in bank. As a fact, these things are less than half of a railroad. The other half is the working organization of men—from the president to the gate tender, from the traffic manager to the advertising agent—which runs the road. The flight of the Twentieth Century from New York to Chicago is made possible because each one of some thousand men performs his appointed duties at the stated minute. The people of the country will get good or bad transportation; will pay more or less for it, as the two million or more of ordinary railroad employees perform their duties well or ill.

The total operating revenues of the railroads for 1918 were $4,800,000,000; of this $2,400,000,000 was paid to labor, the rest went in materials, taxes and the rental. The dominating fact of government operation is therefore, that although the government took actual control of about 50 per cent cost value of the transportation organization of the country it remained in the position of a private employer with reference to the remaining 50 per cent of the transportation business, i. e., the human organization of the system. Mr. Kruttschnitt, president of the Southern Pacific lines, is reported to have said that if he had to choose between the return of a railroad without an organization, or of an organization without a railroad, he would take the organization. The Control Bill granted to the government no special powers of arbitration of differences with the railroad employees. It made no prohibition upon leaving the government railroad service without notice and without cause; it granted no coercive authority such as enlistment or the fixing of a penalty for failure in duties. It left the "right to strike" in full effect. It is, therefore, a misstatement to say that we have had government control of the railroads since January 1, 1918.

The cost of materials and supplies, the maintenance of the organization and the necessary payments for capital and taxes absorb to-day about 50 per cent of the gross annual revenues. The remaining 50 per cent is paid directly to labor. We have, therefore, about 50 per cent of the railroad business under regulation and control and about 50 per cent free. The question is whether an organization half regulated and half unregulated can endure.

The problem before the American people in settling our transportation question is no longer to check the rapacity of capital, or to control the autocratic tendencies of the operating officials, or to fix the nature of the facilities to be given to the public. Capital no longer regards a railroad investment as a profit maker and will be thankful if its existing investments shall return a moderate income. The once haughty managers of railroads now know their masters and agree to requests of national and state commissions on all sorts of details, from placing unnecessary brakemen on a train, down to the character of drinking cups permitted in the cars. They are ready to install steel equipment, terminals, block signals and any other desirable railroad facilities, provided they can obtain the money to pay for them. The great body of financial sentiment approves government supervision of the issues of railroad securities and is prepared fully to endorse the government making of rates, provided they will make a return upon the existing investment. The people may therefore feel that as to 50 per cent of their transportation no serious obstacle stands in the way of a full control; as to the remaining 50 per cent of transportation the situation is different. From the passage of the Adamson Law, raising wages by Congress, under threat of a nation-wide strike, in the month of January, 1917, down to the settlement of the harbor strike in New York City in 1919 by the acceptance of the strikers' terms by the railroad administration, there has not been an instance where the demand for increased pay and reduced hours by the railroad employees has not been granted.

Since the passage of the Adamson Law, viz.: the period from January 1, 1917, to date, the pay of railroad men has been increased by successive stages so that the actual increase in pay in the year 1918 over the year 1916 would amount to over $900,000,000 and the estimated increase in 1919 over 1916 would be approximately $1,000,000,000. In order to understand these figures they may be contrasted with various other railroad items; for instance, the increase in freight and passenger rates in 1918 produced the sum of approximately $800,000,000. It is estimated that these excess rates, 25 per cent on freight and 50 per cent on passenger, will produce in the fiscal year from July 1, 1918, to June 30, 1919, the sum of $1,000,000,000. In other words, practically all of the increase in rates has been absorbed by the increased labor charges on the roads. Contrast again the payments to labor with the payments on account of capital and we find that the increase alone in labor is equal to the entire annual rental of the properties. That rental is fixed under the Control Bill at approximately $920,000,000 a year.

There is no mystery about who pays the railroad freight rates. They are paid first by the farmers, the manufacturers and the dealers, but they are passed on to the consumers and make part of the cost of living. The people pay the freight. The people pay excess labor charges just as they pay excess capital charges. A general railroad strike is therefore a strike to make the people pay more or grant easier conditions. A railroad strike stops industry and the food supply. Hence we are all afraid of it.

One great result of government operation has been to make it clear to the public that they have not to deal with an ordinary conflict between capital and labor. Capital is not at present involved or interested in the subject. It is probable that the readjustment will give capital little or no voice in rates or management. The question before the country is a larger one, viz., whether the 50 per cent of railroad earnings going to labor shall be subject to regulation and control as is the remaining 50 per cent, or whether it shall be left to the laws of supply and demand and subject to the "right to strike." The government management has shown itself to be helpless in the face of an organized demand by a large number of voters and that tendency of government, being equally apparent both in England and France, may be taken to be a general characteristic and we must consider any plans for the future management of transportation with that feature in mind.

It is the general statement in Washington by Senators and others in interest, that the roads may be turned back to private management but under far greater control than has existed heretofore. The labor question is an inconvenient question, certain to stir up trouble and arouse anger, but if the people are to have satisfactory transportation conditions, they must face the problem of the control of railroad labor as well as that of the control of railroad capital and operation. This is not a question for capital. As I have pointed out, capital for railroad enterprise has ceased to be speculative and profit making and is merely interest bearing. New capital can be had at market rates by making it secure. The subject of future capital requirements is not germane to this paper.

There is a common assumption that the roads will be turned back to private owners without action upon the labor problem. As the roads are operated at a heavy loss under the existing conditions that proposal would mean placing upon private management the burden of exacting efficient service from labor and reducing payrolls to a point at least of transportation solvency. The result would be uncoördinated efforts of a great number of different railroad managers, some strong, some weak, some vindictive, some easy, each considering his business as a separate problem and solving it as a special railroad problem without reference to the general labor requirements and conditions of the country. Doubtless, such a readjustment would be accompanied by costly and exasperating strikes. The public would be inflamed against the railroad management and much injustice and suffering would result to the men and to their families. A more ideal way, and one more consonant with the views of an idealistic administration, would be to require the Interstate Commerce Commission to inquire into and regulate the surroundings and proper compensation of railroad labor, both wages and hours, as compared with the general labor conditions in the country. Upon that commission should sit men familiar with the conditions of railroad labor and also men familiar with the interests of the shippers using the railroads, such as members of Chambers of Commerce and the agricultural industry of the country. If possible, some members should be found who really represented the consuming public upon whose broad shoulders ultimately rests the burden of supporting the transportation of the country. Indeed, the balance of power on the commission should rest with those who have no interest except to second the general welfare, who can carry a just proportion between the special interest of the railroad employees and the general interest of the farmers, the laboring classes and the salaried people throughout the country. If the public desires to control its transportation interests, and has determined through the Commission what is a fair return for railroad labor in its different classes, and has made provision for a just revision of the scale from time to time as may be required by general conditions in the country and in the industry, the public must then face the question of how the award of the Commission shall be enforced.

Shall railroad labor be considered to be "affected with a public interest" as is railroad capital? Shall entry into the service be made subject to certain fixed conditions with regard to leaving the service, such as thirty days' notice, the refusal of reëngagement in case service is terminated without adequate cause? Shall compulsory arbitration be adopted? Shall it be a misdemeanor to leave the service in a strike against an award adopted fairly and after due consideration? How can the railroad service be made attractive by way of old age pensions, better facilities for living, etc.? Such are the problems which the American people face in settling their transportation question. If we attempt to turn over the management of the 50 per cent of the problem to private control, we must face difficulties of a character far more serious since the changes brought about by the war, than those which existed previously. The owners of the railroads do not wish to take them back under existing conditions. There are many who think that the proposal to leave the readjustment of these matters to private control would bring about a general bankruptcy of the transportation systems of the country. As a matter of fact, the government control is bankrupt to-day. In spite of the fact that it has raised railroad receipts a billion dollars, its management is a half billion dollars behind its obligations. Government operation will require a billion appropriation by July. About a quarter of the war tax levy for this year besides another billion in transportation tax are thus due to government operation. Were it not for the taxing power, the government administration would have to seek refuge in a receivership. This condition is largely caused by the increased cost and the growing inefficiency of labor under government control, and makes plain the necessity of attacking with moderation and fairness but determinedly the problem of securing effective regulation of railroad labor in the United States.

The problem is not one of labor and capital. It is one of the relation of one branch of labor to the other labor, industries and interests of the country, for railroad rates touch everyone in the United States. There is no work in which men take such an intense and loyal interest as the railroad men take in their jobs. There is no class from whom loyal service is so essential to the public interest, because of their direct touch with the public both in passenger and freight transportation. There is no class of labor for which the strike is so tempting and so potent a weapon. A transportation strike is a blow at the food supply of the country and paralyzes all industry by withholding material and shipments. It would be an indictment of our courage and our collective intelligence to leave this desperate remedy of a transportation strike as a temptation to the railroad workers and as a menace to the general public.

The discussions in Congress and in the press have avoided the subject of railroad labor. There is a general readiness to let some one else bell the cat.

Railroad operatives are a very fine body of men. Their work takes them away from home and involves some risk. They are well entitled to good pay and good hours. But in the interest of the public they must submit to steady discipline and be held to it. The same interest requires that its food and material supply be not interrupted, and that its freight charges be not unduly raised.

Surely some method can be found, fair alike to the railroad employees and to the general public, which will solve the question indicated in the foregoing pages, upon the grounds of absolute justice and equitable treatment relatively to other industries and interests in the country.

COMMUNICATION

THE WORK OF THE PUBLIC HEALTH SERVICE DURING THE WAR

BY RUPERT BLUE, SURGEON GENERAL, U. S. A.,
PUBLIC HEALTH SERVICE

The following résumé of the activities of the United States Public Health Service during the European War of necessity can only sketch the prominent activities of the service during that period.

To fully appreciate the present-day activities of the service it is highly desirable that a short historical outline of its growth be set forth as a preliminary to any discussion of its work during the war.

The Public Health Service of to-day is the growth of a series of legal enactments extending as far back as 1798. Numerous laws passed by Congress from time to time in the years intervening have increased its powers and functions, perfected its organization, and changed its name, to keep pace with the progress of the medical and sanitary sciences and to afford better protection to the public health of the nation under changing conditions.

The primary function of the service in the early days of its existence consisted chiefly in affording medical relief to seamen of the merchant marine and other designated beneficiaries. In the proper administration of this function, however, the field of endeavor of the service was gradually widened into activities of a strictly public health character. In fact, by later enactment of Congress the service was specifically charged with certain public health duties. Although the service had thus engaged in public health work for many years with legal sanction, it was not until 1902 that Congress changed its name by incorporating in it the words "public health." The act of July 1st of that year changed the name of the Marine Hospital Service to the "Public Health and Marine Hospital Service." By the terms of this same enactment the President was authorized in his discretion to "utilize the Public Health and Marine Hospital Service in times of threatened or actual war to such extent and in such manner as shall in his judgment promote the public interest without, however, in anywise impairing the efficiency of the service for the purposes for which the same was created and is maintained."

In 1912 the name of the service was changed to the "Public Health Service" and broad authority conferred upon it to "study and investigate diseases of man and conditions influencing the propagation and spread thereof, including sanitation and sewage and the pollution either directly or indirectly of the navigable streams and lakes of the United States."

WAR ACTIVITIES OF THE PUBLIC HEALTH SERVICE

With the declaration of war the activities of the Public Health Service, like those of other Federal establishments, were immediately directed toward the successful prosecution of the war. Its peace-time activities, beneficial though they were to the nation, were perforce curtailed in order that its personnel and facilities might be thrown into the war-time balance. Accordingly the first step taken toward directing its energies to the work at hand was the promulgation by the President on April 3, 1917, of an executive order constituting the Public Health Service "a part of the military forces of the United States" and making available all stations of the service "for the reception of sick and wounded officers and men."

With the mobilization of large bodies of troops in training camps and other concentration points, which followed the declaration of war with gratifying rapidity, it became immediately necessary to enforce strict measures for the protection of the health of the soldier and the sailor. The military authorities fully realized the necessity of this protection within the camp and cantonment and adequate provision was immediately made to reduce disease to the minimum. But it was just as essential to establish and maintain proper sanitary conditions in the areas surrounding the camps as within the reservation itself. The soldier and sailor had access to this territory, and if his body was to be kept fit to fight democracy's battle this contiguous territory had also to be sanitated. The obligation to protect the health of the military forces in this civilian territory was therefore placed upon the Public Health Service.

To secure the reduction of disease hazards which menaced the uniformed man involved the establishment of an efficient health department or organization around almost every camp and cantonment. A brief description of the extent of the work required to achieve what might be called a sanitated area will suffice to show the enormity of the task and the great sanitary good actually achieved by the work performed. In each cantonment area the work involved the proper supervision over water, food, and milk supplies; the proper disposal of human excreta, and the elimination of breeding places of flies and mosquitoes. In fact, the operations of the service, expressed in a sentence, had for their object the control and reduction to a minimum of all communicable diseases. In carrying forward this great work, the Public Health Service never failed to utilize to the fullest possible extent the existing local and state organizations. In some instances, however, in order that prompt protection be afforded it was necesary to perform much work which the state and local authorities were eventually able to perform themselves.

Of all the problems encountered in sanitating these extra-cantonment areas, the elimination of malaria presented the most troublesome. Theoretically the control of malaria presents no difficulties from the standpoint of public health officials. In perhaps no other disease is so much exact scientific knowledge available. Practically, however, the problem of malaria control often presents great difficulties because of the financial outlay involved, the extensiveness of the operations necessary and the time taken to eliminate the mosquito and its breeding place. This is what is meant when it is said that the service encountered difficulties in eradicating this disease. Nevertheless these seemingly insurmountable obstacles were overcome.

In those cantonment areas whose normal growth had been seriously retarded by malaria, the community witnessed thousands of American soldiers living among them with practically no malaria. The total amount of malaria contracted by our troops at southern cantonment cities during the recent war was practically nil as compared to that of our previous war period in 1898.

It is not to be thought, however, that malaria and its eradication constituted the sole problem in disease prevention encountered by the service in its extra-cantonment sanitation. As stated above, every communicable disease was brought within the range of the operations of the service.

This was particularly true of venereal infections. Statistics showed that a far greater number of men are infected before joining the military forces than contract the disease after entering the camp, and it soon became apparent that the reduction of this disease was largely a civilian problem. Accordingly Congress, on July 9, 1918, gave' legal recognition to the need for controlling this disease in civilian areas by enacting legislation which created in the Bureau of the Public Health Service a Division of Venereal Diseases.

In addition there were established in and near the cantonment areas some 46 clinics for the free diagnosis and treatment of venereally infected persons. These clinics were operated in conjunction with the American Red Cross and local authorities. Remarkable advances in the control of social diseases have been made during the past year as a result of the work performed along this line.

In concluding this necessarily brief account of the extra-cantonment work of the Public Health Service during the war, it must be remembered that although these areas are designated for convenience as "extra-cantonment," the area often also comprised many war industries of vast importance in the war program of the government. It was the aim of the Public Health Service to protect the workers of these factories as well as the soldiers and an equal degree of success has followed its operations within these establishments.

The extra-cantonment work of the Public Health Service during the war may well be considered the greatest sanitary achievement or demonstration ever undertaken by any government.

The lack of coördination of Federal public health activities especially concerned in the prosecution of the existing war resulted in the signing by the President on July 1, 1918, of an executive order which placed under the supervision and control of the Treasury Department, to be administered through the Public Health Service, of all civil public health activities of the character above mentioned. As a result of this executive order the Public Health Service assumed charge of the work connected with the sanitation of the 170 shipyards of the country, which work had been previously under the direction of the United States Shipping Board. Medical supervision was also exercised over various government nitrate plants located at various points within the United States.

A long step forward in national public health administration was taken on October 27, when the President signed the act of Congress establishing in the Public Health Service a sanitary reserve corps.

With this enactment on the statute books the public health activities of the country can be properly expanded to meet acute situations and coördinated under the direction of the Federal government in meeting national emergencies.

Any statement of the duties devolving on the Public Health Service because of the war would be incomplete without mention of the highly important work recently imposed upon the service by Congress when it authorized the construction of a number of hospitals for the institutional care of returning soldiers and sailors, beneficiaries of the government under the provisions of the War Risk Insurance Act.

The annual dinner of the Institute, followed by an address, "The League of Nations and Labor," which was delivered by the Honorable George W. Wickersham, LL.D., and the awarding of medals, was held on the evening of April 25, 1919, at the Hotel Astor, New York City. The president, Emory R. Johnson, Sc.D., presided.

Gold medals were awarded to Mr. Samuel Gompers and William Henry Welch, M.D.

Presentation medals were awarded to Right Rev. Charles H. Brent, Mr. Raymond B. Fosdick, Harry A. Garfield, LL.D., Carl Koller, M.D., Mr. Frederick Layton, Honorable Robert Scott Lovett, Mr. Charles M. Schwab, and Harry A. Wheeler, LL.D.

OPENING REMARKS BY DR. EMORY R. JOHNSON

Members and guests of the National Institute: You are representatives of approximately one thousand men and women, members of the Institute. Each member of the Institute is a person who has accomplished some important work. At the head of our list of members stands William Howard Taft, the Honorary President of the Society.

It seemed to the officers of the Institute that the President of the United States should also be an Honorary Member of the National Institute. I was therefore authorized by the officers, this winter, to notify President Wilson of his election as an Honorary Member of the Institute, and I was also authorized by the appropriate committee of the Institute to confer upon the President a special gold medal, in recognition of the work he was doing to bring about enduring international peace. The President accepted membership and the special medal that was struck in his honor. In accepting the medal he wrote:

"May I not beg you to express to the members of the National Institute of Social Sciences the deep appreciation with which I have received the Liberty Service Medal, which they were generous enough to confer upon me? I consider this a very delightful evidence of their support."

It happens that one of my courses at the University of Pennsylvania deals with the subject of the regulation of corporations under the Anti-Trust Law. I remember looking up, some few years ago, the number of cases against the trusts that had been settled in Mr. Roosevelt's administration. We, of course, recognize Mr. Roosevelt to have been some trust "buster," but during the seven and a half years that he was President, there were only 44 cases against the trusts brought to final determination, an average of less than six per annum; whereas during the four years of President Taft's administration, under the leadership of the Attorney General of the United States, who is to be our principal speaker this evening, there were 80 cases against the trusts brought to final determination, an average of twenty per year.

I have often wondered how it was that Mr. Wickersham was so successful in dealing with the trusts. I recall that as I looked out of his office windows one day, I looked down upon Wall Street, and possibly the fact that Mr. Wickersham looks down upon Wall Street more or less frequently may account for his knowing what the trusts are and how to deal with them.

I shall not, however, introduce Mr. Wickersham to talk about the trusts to-night—he is to speak upon one phase of the question of The League of Nations. Fortunately, he has selected for his topic, "The League of Nations and Labor."

I am seated between Mr. Wickersham and the representative of the largest number of organized laborers that any man in the history of the world has ever represented; and it will interest you to know that just beyond him sits the largest individual employer of labor in the history of the world. So Mr. Wickersham will speak to men who are able to check him up.

I do not need to tell people of New York, or people of this country of Mr. Wickersham's work as Attorney General or in connection with labor questions and the international problems associated with the Panama Canal. He occupies an envied position as one of the leaders of the American bar. I shall content myself with presenting the Honorable George W. Wickersham as the principal speaker of the evening.

THE LEAGUE OF NATIONS AND LABOR

BY GEORGE W. WICKERSHAM

FORMER ATTORNEY GENERAL OF THE UNITED STATES

I am to speak to you to-night on one phase of the League of Nations which has not been so much discussed as many other phases, namely: the provisions affecting labor.

Almost exactly a century ago, in October, 1818, Robert Owen, an idealistic and practical Scotch manufacturer, addressed a memorial to the representatives of the powers which had united in the overthrow of Napoleon, then sitting at Aix-la-Chapelle, in which he said:

"That the period is arrived when the means are become obvious by which, without force or fraud, or disorder of any kind, riches may be created in such abundance and so advantageously for all, that the wants and desires of every human being may be satisfied."

And, he added:

"It is the grand interest of society to adopt practical measures by which the largest amount of useful and valuable productions may be obtained at the least expense of manual labor and with the most comfort to the producers."

Strange to relate, that invitation not only was declined by the statesmen gathered at Aix-la-Chapelle, but it received no recognition whatever from them. Yet, despite the Utopian nature of this alluring picture, Owen was no mere visionary. He was able to point to a very practical success in the application of his theories in his model establishment at New Lamark. What he had there accomplished well justified his confidence in the practical benefits to the world which the extension of his system would have secured. But the time for its favorable reception by the governments of Europe had not yet arrived.

The Czar Alexander's dream of a world league of nations already was fading away; the treaty of Chaumont, with its idealism, had been merged into the practical Alliance of 1815, between the sovereigns of Russia, Austria, Prussia and England. Castlereagh's distrust of a general union of large and small powers had found expression in a memorandum stating:

"The problem of a universal alliance for the peace and happiness of the world has always been one of speculation and hope. But it has never yet been reduced to practice, and if an opinion may be hazarded from its difficulty it never can."

The conferees at Aix-la-Chapelle were absorbed in the consideration of political problems of a dynastic nature. They were not in the least interested in the conditions under which men, women and children in the different countries were compelled to toil for their daily bread. They displayed even less interest in the proposals of Robert Owen than did the British Parliament when, in June, 1815, he caused a bill to be introduced providing

"for the preservation of the health and morals of apprentices and others in cotton mills."

This measure was to be applicable to all mills in which twenty or more persons were employed. It forbade the employment of children under ten years of age, limited the period of work for all persons under eighteen to ten and one-half hours per day, exclusive of one-half hour's instruction in reading, writing and arithmetic, and forbade all such persons working between the hours of nine p. m. and eight a. m. During the first four years of their service, employees under eighteen years of age were also to be instructed in the elementary subjects mentioned for half an hour every day, at the expense of the employer.

The proposed measure was dismissed by the Committee of the House of Commons as revolutionary, impracticable and utterly wanting in common sense. But the inherent social justice embodied in its moderate provisions slowly but surely won aid and progress in England and it proved to be the precursor of an ever widening program of governmental regulations for the protection and betterment of the working peoples of Great Britain.

It would far exceed the limitations of this occasion to attempt to trace the history of international efforts in the same direction. Every measure adopted for the benefit of the workers in one country more or less has affected conditions in other countries. High wages and opportunity for advancement in America served to stimulate immigration from countries where conditions were less favorable, and the great influx of cheap labor from Europe operated to keep down wages and retard improvements in conditions under which men, women and children were employed in industry in the new world. These conditions stimulated the formation of organizations of workers, and the resultant struggle for improved conditions developed and intensified a class consciousness both here and abroad. Meantime, various international associations were formed for the consideration of questions especially affecting industrial workers, which held meetings and congresses for the exchange of views and the formation of opinions which should influence governmental action. The Socialist *Internationale* was one type of such organization, the Trades Unions another. International conferences on social insurance and on unemployment also were held, and in 1900, the International Association for Labor Legislation was organized in Paris by a group of statesmen, economists and professional men, which now has a membership representing twenty-five countries. In 1901, that association set up an International Labor Office at Basle, towards the support of which fourteen governments have contributed. It was through the labors of this organization in studying and ascertaining the effect upon the health of women and children of the use of white phosphorus in the manufacture of matches, and the conference to consider that subject, held by it at Basle in 1904, that a treaty was secured among the principal European nations, and legislation by the Congress of the United States, which, in effect, prohibited the use of that deleterious substance. International governmental conferences respecting labor questions practically began with the conference held at the instance of William II at Berlin in 1890, at which fourteen governments were represented—a conference which, however, took no action beyond the adoption of a few resolutions. Between 1882 and 1914, some thirty agreements between governments were made, some of them extending to alien workmen the advantages and safeguards of industrial legislation in the countries where they were employed, and some providing for the adoption of a common labor standard in two or more countries. Just before the war, in 1912, the conference held at Zurich, under the auspices of the International Association for Labor Legislation, called attention to the necessity for international action in dealing with such subjects as the administration of international labor treaties and labor laws, child labor, relations between employers and workmen, the regulation of home work, hours of labor in continuous industries, the protection of workmen from accident and industrial disease, workmen's holidays, and the length of the working day.

A few months after the outbreak of the war (February 14, 1915), an interallied labor and socialist conference was held in London, at which resolutions were adopted dealing with the conditions of peace, including the recommendation of a league or association of nations for its preservation. Similar meetings for like purposes were held in May and July, 1916, in February and August, 1917, and in February, 1918. At almost all of these conferences, resolutions were adopted recommending specific provisions in the peace treaty, when it should be made, including particularly the right of small nations to self-determination, limitation of armaments and the abolition of secret diplomacy. The labor standards recommended for all nations by these various conferences, almost uniformly included such subjects as the protection of women and children, social insurance, prohibition of night work, the eight-hour day, and safe and sanitary working conditions. Some of those provisions which Mr. Wilson embodied in his fourteen points, were formulated and recommended by one or the other of these conferences months before the delivery of his address to the Congress of January 8, 1918.

The most detailed and specific statement of the Allied war aims was embodied in a memorandum originally presented to the Interallied Labor and Socialist Conference in London in August, 1917, and, after revision, approved by the National Committees of the Labor Party in January, and by the labor representatives of the Allied nations in February, 1918, and presented to the Prime Minister as the opinion of the organized workers of Great Britain.

"Whatever may have been the objects for which the war was begun," sets forth this memorandum, "the fundamental purpose of the interallied conference in supporting the continuance of the struggle is that the world may henceforth be made safe for democracy. . . . Whoever triumphs, the peoples will have lost, unless an international system is established which will prevent war."

This end was proposed to be secured through the authority of a League of Nations. The memorandum contemplates the creation of a supersovereignty over the existing nations, international legislation, compulsory arbitration, the abolition of compulsory military service, disarmament, governmental control of private munitions manufactories, and it declares that the League of Nations must be included in the peace treaty. It further urges an agreement

"for the enforcement in all countries of legislation on factory conditions, a maximum eight-hour day, and prevention of sweating and unhealthy trades necessary to protect the workers against exploitation and oppression and the prohibition of night work for women and children."

It further emphasizes the duty of the governments to provide against unemployment resulting from the discharge of the very large number of men which would follow after the treaty of peace.

Almost all of these plans proposed by the various labor conferences advocate a League of Nations for the purpose of securing the application to all the countries uniting in the treaty, of the program of international and industrial labor standards and conditions recommended.

The League of Nations proposed to be organized under the Paris Covenant does not, however, follow the lines of these recommendations. It provides, not for a supernational state, but for an alliance of separate sovereignties for the preservation of the peace of the world. The Covenant recommended grew out of the fourteenth point in the President's peace program of January 8, 1918. That point was an essential part of the program which embraced the evacuation by the enemy powers of occupied territory, the restoration of Alsace-Lorraine to France, a readjustment of the frontiers of Italy, the opening of the Dardanelles to the commerce of all nations, and the erection of a new and independent Polish State. These territorial readjustments naturally required security for their preservation. The fourteenth point provided for this in the following language:

"A general association of nations must be formed under specific covenants for the purpose of affording mutual guarantees of political independence and territorial integrity to great and small states alike."

In his Mt. Vernon speech of July 4, 1918, the President's thought found a somewhat broader expression in the inclusion of the following among the statement of peace aims:

"The establishment of an organization of peace, which shall make it certain that the combined power of free nations will check every invasion of right and serve to make peace and justice the more secure by affording a definite tribunal of opinion to which all must submit and by which every international readjustment that cannot be amicably agreed upon by the peoples directly concerned shall be sanctioned."

The Peace Conference, on January 25, 1919, adopted resolutions declaring it to be essential to the maintenance of the world settlement which the associated nations were met to establish,

"that a League of Nations be created to promote international obligations and to provide safeguards against war,"—

a league which should be an integral part of the general treaty of peace and should be open to every civilized nation which could be relied upon to promote its objects.

Speaking in support of those resolutions, Mr. Wilson said that the United States should feel that its part in the war would be played in vain if there ensued upon it abortive European settlements.

"It would feel that it could not take part in guaranteeing those European settlements unless that guarantee involved the continuous superintendence of the peace of the world by the associated nations of the world."

The dominant thought in both the resolutions and the address was, that the territorial settlements about to be made must be protected by an association of the powers. A few days later (February 3d) in the French Chamber of Deputies, the President thus referred to the proposed League:

"The nations of the world are about to consummate a brotherhood which will make it unnecessary in the future to maintain those crushing armaments which make the people suffer almost as much in peace as they did in war."

Quite logically, therefore, the preamble to the Covenant reported to the Conference on February 14th, recited the purposes of the Constitution of the League to be

"to promote international coöperation and to secure international peace and security. . . ."

These objects, it was recited, were to be accomplished by open dealings among the nations, by the establishment of international law as the actual rule of conduct among governments, and by the maintenance of justice and a scrupulous respect for all treaty obligations in international dealings.

But a place was found in the body of the agreement for certain provisions regarding labor, and provisions concerning commerce. These provisions are not directly requisite to the attainment of the objects recited in the preamble, but they have a material bearing upon the purposes of a world league as advocated by the various conferences of representatives of labor.

Mr. Wilson, in reporting the draft covenant to the Conference, said:

"It is not in contemplation that this should be merely a league to secure the peace of the world. It is a league which can be used for coöperation in any international matter. That is the significance of the provision introduced concerning labor. There are many ameliorations of labor conditions which can be effected by conference and discussion."

The provision thus referred to is Article XX of the Covenant, which reads as follows:

"The high contracting parties will endeavor to secure and maintain fair and humane conditions of labor for men, women and children, both in their own countries and in all countries to which their industrial and commercial relations extend; and to that end agree to establish as part of the organization of the League a permanent Bureau of Labor." *

Lord Robert Cecil, after stating that the problem before the Conference was to devise some really effective means of preserving the peace of the world consistent with the least possible interference with national sovereignty, said:

"I do not regard the clause which deals with labor as any such interference, for it is quite certain that no real progress in ameliorating the condition of labor can be hoped for except by international agreement. Therefore, although the conditions of labor in a country are a matter of internal concern, yet, under the conditions under which we now live that is not so in truth, and bad conditions of labor in one country operate with fatal effect in depressing conditions of labor in another."

Mr. Barnes' interpretation of the article ran beyond the limitations of its language to an expression of his hope of what might be accomplished under it.

"I gladly note the insertion of a clause providing for the formation of international charters of labor," he said. "Hitherto, nations have endeavored to protect themselves against low-paid labor by the imposition of tariff barriers. I hope we shall, in the future, under the authority of the League of Nations, seek and find a better way of abolishing low-paid labor altogether. We hope to raise life and labor from the mere struggle for bread on to higher levels of justice and humanity." †

In its general form and scope, Article XX of the Peace Covenant as originally reported was more in accord with the

---

* In the amended Covenant adopted April 28th this Article is revised and amplified to read as follows:

ARTICLE XXIII.

Subject to and in accordance with the provisions of international conventions existing or hereafter to be agreed upon, the members of the League (a) will endeavor to secure and maintain fair and humane conditions of labor for men, women and children, both in their own countries and in all countries to which their commercial and industrial relations extend, and for that purpose will establish and maintain the necessary international organizations; (b) undertake to secure just treatment of the native inhabitants of territories under their control; (c) will entrust the League with the general supervision over the execution of agreements with regard to the traffic in women and children, and the traffic in opium and other dangerous drugs; (d) will entrust the League with the general supervision of the trade in arms and ammunition with the countries in which the control of this traffic is necessary in the common interest; (e) will make provision to secure and maintain freedom of communication and of transit and equitable treatment for the commerce of all members of the League. In this connection the special necessities of the regions devastated during the war of 1914-1918 shall be in mind; (f) will endeavor to take steps in matters of international concern for the prevention and control of disease.

† Article XXIII of the revised Covenant seeks to give practical effect to the sentiments expressed by Mr. Barnes, and, adopted after the report of the Commission on Labor Conditions, pledges the powers to furnish the machinery for putting into practical application the recommendations made in that report.

organization of the International Association for Labor Legislation than any of the other forms of league or association suggested for the consideration of the conferees. That association was formed in 1900, to serve as a means of communication between those who in different industrial countries considered protective labor legislation necessary, and to organize an international labor bureau whose mission should be to publish in French, German and English a periodical collection of labor legislation in all countries or to lend its aid to a similar publication.

But while the labor provision in the Constitution of the League of Nations was limited to the simple outlines above quoted, another far more complicated and more far-reaching plan of international machinery has been in the making by a different, but associated, official agency.*

On January 25, 1919, the Peace Conference at Paris, among other subsidiary committees and commissions, created a Commission on International Labor Legislation, consisting of two representatives of each of the five great powers and five representatives of the other powers, charged with the duty

"to inquire into the conditions of employment from an international aspect and to consider the international means necessary to secure common action on matters affecting conditions of employment, and to recommend the form of a permanent agency to continue such inquiry and consideration in co-operation with and under the direction of the League of Nations."

The representatives of the United States on that Commission were Mr. Hurley, Chairman of the United States Shipping Board, and Mr. Samuel Gompers, President of the American Federation of Labor (with two substitutes, viz.: Mr. H. M. Robinson and Dr. J. T. Shotwell). Mr. Gompers was later elected Chairman of the Commission. The report recently submitted by the Commision and unanimously adopted by the Peace Conference, recommends the adoption of a proposed treaty between all the powers members of the League of Na-

* The adoption of the report of the Commission on International Labor Legislation made necessary a change in the Labor Article of the Covenant which was expanded into Article XXIII, quoted in note (†) above. That report provided for the establishment of a Labor Bureau, and other machinery to carry out the mutual agreements of the revised Article, so it was unnecessary to include a provision for it in the Covenant.

tions, creating a permanent organization for the promotion of the international regulation of labor conditions. It proposes to make participation in this organization a condition of membership in the League. It proposes conferences to be held at least annually, consisting of delegates nominated by each of the powers; but in order to insure the character of representation, it is provided that each government shall send four delegates, two of whom shall be directly appointed by the government and the other two chosen in agreement with the industrial organizations representative of their employers and workpeople, respectively. Each delegate may be accompanied by advisers, not exceeding two in number for each item on the *agenda* of the meeting, and when questions especially affecting women are to be considered by the conference, one at least of the advisers should be a woman. Each of the delegates is to vote individually, the theory being that if the conferences are really to be representative of all concerned with industry and to command their confidence, the employers and work-people must be allowed to express their views with complete frankness and freedom, and that the employers' and work-people's delegates should be entitled to speak and vote independently of their governments. The organization is to function principally through an International Labor Office, under the control of a governing body of twenty-four members, to be constituted as follows:

Twelve representatives of the governments, six members elected by the delegates to the conferences representing the employers, and six members elected by the delegates representing the work-people. Of the twelve members representing the governments, eight shall be nominated by the powers which are of chief industrial importance, and four by the powers selected for that purpose by the government delegates to the conference, excluding the delegates of the eight states above mentioned; the question as to which are the powers of chief industrial importance to be decided by the Executive Council of the League of Nations. The members of the governing board are to hold office for three years.

The functions of the International Labor Office include the collection and distribution of information on all subjects relating to the adjustment of international conditions of indus-

trial life and labor, and particularly the examination of subjects which it is proposed to bring before the conference with
a view to the conclusion of international conventions, and the
conduct of such special investigations as may be ordered by
the conference. It is to prepare the *agenda* or program for all
meetings of the conference; and to edit and publish a periodical paper in the French and English languages and in such
other languages as the governing body may think desirable,
dealing with problems of industrial employment of international interest. The expenses of maintaining this international
labor organization are to come from the general funds of the
League of Nations. There are elaborate provisions as to what
shall or shall not be included in the *agenda* to be discussed at
the periodical conferences. When the conference has decided
upon the adoption of proposals with regard to an item in the
agenda, it is to rest with that conference to determine whether
or not those proposals shall take the form: (*a*) of a recommendation to be submitted to the high contracting parties for
consideration with a view to their being given effect by national legislation, or otherwise, or (*b*) of a draft international
convention for ratification by the high contracting parties.
In either case, a majority of two-thirds of the votes cast by
the delegates present is required on the final vote for the
adoption of a recommendation or draft convention, as the case
may be, by the conference. Each of the contracting parties
agrees within the period of one year after the conference to
bring the recommendation or draft before the authority or
authorities within whose competence the matter lies, for the
enactment of legislation, or other action. It is also provided
that in the case of a federal state, the power of which to enter
into conventions on labor matters is subject to limitations, it
shall be in the discretion of the government of such state to
treat a draft convention to which such limitations apply as a
recommendation only. Machinery is provided whereby a state
which fails to carry out its obligations, or to enforce a convention which has been ratified, may be subjected to economic
measures, to compel it to do so. Thus, if a complaint be made
to the International Labor Office by an industrial organization
of employers or work-people, that any of the contracting
powers has failed to secure in any respect the effective observ-

ance within its jurisdiction of any convention to which it is a party, the governing body may communicate this representation to the state against which it is made, inviting such statement on the subject as that state may think fit. If none is received within a reasonable time, or if, when received, it is not deemed satisfactory by the governing body, the latter shall have the right to publish the representation and the statement, if any. Any of the powers party to the treaty also is to have the right to file a complaint with the International Labor Office, if it is not satisfied that any other party is securing the effective observance of a ratified convention. The governing body in its discretion may either communicate such complaint to the state against which it is made, or apply for the appointment of a commission of inquiry to consider the complaint and report thereon. In the latter event, the commission of inquiry is to be constituted as follows:

Each of the high contracting parties agrees to nominate, within six months of the date on which the convention comes into effect, three persons of industrial experience, one of whom shall be the representative of employers, one of work-people, and one a person of independent standing. These nominees together shall form a panel from which the members of any commission of inquiry shall be drawn. The qualifications of the persons so nominated are to be subject to scrutiny by the governing body, which, by two-thirds of the votes cast by the members present, may refuse to accept the nomination of any person whose qualifications, in its opinion, do not comply with the requirements of the article. On application of the governing body, the Secretary General of the League shall nominate three persons, one from each section of the panel, to constitute the commission of inquiry, designating one of them as president of the commission. The high contracting parties agree to place at the disposal of the commission all information in their possession bearing upon the subject-matter of the complaint. The commission shall make a report embodying its findings of fact and recommendations and shall indicate the measures, if any, of an economic character against a defaulting state which it considers to be appropriate and which the other states would be justified in adopting, which report shall be communicated by the Secretary General of the League of

Nations to each of the states concerned, and published. Every state so affected, within one month after the receipt of such · report, shall inform the Secretary General whether or not it accepts the recommendations of the commission, and if not, whether it proposes to refer the complaint to the permanent court of international justice of the League of Nations. If any state shall fail, within the specified time, to take action as above mentioned, any other of the states parties to the compact shall be entitled to refer the matter to the permanent court, and the decision of that court shall be final. The permanent court may affirm, vary, or reverse any of the findings or recommendations of the commission of inquiry, and shall indicate in its decision the measures, if any, of an economic character against a defaulting state which it considers to be appropriate and which other states would be justified in adopting, and in the event of any state failing to carry out, within the time specified, the recommendations, if any, contained in the report of the commission of inquiry, or the decision of the permanent court, as the case may be, any other state may take, as against that state, the economic measures indicated in the report or decision. It is further provided that in no case shall any nation be asked or required, as a result of the adoption of any recommendation or draft convention by the conference, to diminish the protection afforded by its existing legislation to the workers concerned.

The proposed convention is made extraordinarily difficult of amendment. Amendments must first be adopted by the conference by two-thirds of the votes cast by the delegates present, and then ratified by the states whose representatives compose the Executive Council of the League of Nations, and also by three-fourths of the states whose representatives compose the Body of Delegates of the League.

In view of the novelty of the entire scheme, it would seem that it were wiser to make the plan more flexible by facilitating rather than preventing amendment. Any question of dispute relating to the interpretation of the convention, or any subsequent convention concluded by the parties pursuant to the provisions of this convention, is to be referred for decision to the permanent court of international justice. Pending the creation of such a court, disputes which, in accordance with the convention, should be submitted to it for decision, are to be referred to a tribunal of three persons appointed by the Executive Council of the League of Nations.

The first meeting of the conference is appointed to be held at Washington, D. C., in October, 1919. The Commission itself has prepared and published the *agenda* for that meeting. The subjects thus determined upon for discussion are the following:

1. Application of the principle of an eight-hour day or forty-eight-hour week.
2. Question of preventing or providing against unemployment.
3. Women's employment.
   a. Before and after childbirth, including question of maternity benefit. b. During the night. c. In unhealthy processes.
4. Employment of children.
   a. Minimum age of employment. b. During the night. c. In unhealthy processes.
5. Extension and application of the international conventions adopted at Berne in 1906 on the prohibition of night work for women employed in industry and the employment or use of white phosphorus in the manufacture of matches.

Besides reporting the proposed treaty or convention, the Commission adopted a resolution expressing the hope that as soon as possible an agreement should be arrived at between the high contracting parties with a view to endowing

"the international labor conference, under the auspices of the League of Nations, with power to take, under conditions to be determined, resolutions possessing the force of international law."

The Commission further reported that its members are unanimous in thinking that their work would not be completed if it were simply confined to setting up permanent machinery for international labor legislation. While it was not within their province, or within their terms of reference, to deal with specific questions relating to industrial conditions and to work them out with the detail necessary for the framing of proposals which could be accepted in binding form, nevertheless, they were so impressed with the urgent need for recognizing certain fundamental principles as necessary to social progress, that they decided to submit a series of declarations for insertion in the peace treaty. These recommendations they have made merely in general form, some recommended by a majority, some unanimously, which are to be submitted to the high contracting parties for their consideration. They do not ask the high contracting parties to give immediate effect to these principles, but only to endorse them generally. It will be the duty of The International Labor Conference to examine them thoroughly and to put them in the form of recommendations or draft conventions elaborated with the detail necessary for their practical application. The recommendations are as follows:

"1. In right and in fact the labor of a human being should not be treated as merchandise or an article of commerce.

"2. Employers and workers should be allowed the right of association for all lawful purposes.

"3. No child should be permitted to be employed in industry or commerce before the age of fourteen years. In order that every child may be ensured reasonable opportunities for mental and physical education, between the years of fourteen and eighteen, young persons of either sex may only be employed on work which is not harmful to their physical development and on condition that the continuation of their technical or general education is ensured.

"4. Every worker has a right to a wage adequate to maintain a reasonable standard of life having regard to the civilization of his time and country.

"5. Equal pay should be given to women and to men for work of equal value in quantity and quality.

"6. A weekly rest, including Sunday, or its equivalent for all workers.

"7. Limitation of the hours of work in industry on the basis of eight hours a day or forty-eight hours a week, subject to an exception for countries in which climatic conditions, the imperfect development of industrial development or industrial organization or other special circumstances render the industrial efficiency of the workers substantially different.

"The International Labor Conference will recommend a basis approximately equivalent to the above for adoption in such countries.

"8. In all matters concerning their status as workers and

social insurance, foreign workmen lawfully admitted to any country and their families, should be ensured the same treatment as the nationals of that country.

"9. All States should institute a system of inspection in which women should take part, in order to ensure the enforcement of the laws and regulations for the protection of the workers."

Very useful progress may be made by the acceptance of this program for discussion at the Washington meeting. Debate by delegates from all these countries of such subjects as those suggested by the Commission must be of great value in forming public opinion and inducing intelligent and wise legislative action. As Mr. Mackenzie King, the Canadian Minister of Labor, recently pointed out, there are four parties to industry: Labor, capital, management and the community. The problem of the right adjustment of the interests of neither one of these can be determined without regard to the others. It has seemed at times that the interests of the community at large more sorely than any other need representation and protection from the consequences of industrial disputes. If the machinery devised by the Paris Conference shall accomplish the end of creating a medium for the discussion and clarifying of thought upon these vital subjects, which shall command the confidence of all parties affected, it will have rendered a conspicuous service to mankind.

It has not yet been announced from Paris whether it is proposed to submit the convention recommended by the Commission on International Labor Legislation as a separate treaty, or as a part of the Covenant establishing the League of Nations, or as a part of the general peace treaty. It should be considered on its own merits, separately from both the general peace treaty and the Covenant establishing the League of Nations, because, while it is intertwined with the provisions for the League of Nations, it is susceptible of separate treatment, and some of its provisions ought to receive most careful consideration on the part of Congress before it is adopted.

But on the whole, I think no one can read the proposed convention without being struck with the care, the restraint and the balance with which it has been prepared. The whole scheme is a notable advance in the consideration of questions affecting working-men, women and children in all lands, and promises, if carefully considered and wisely administered, a very marked and very notable improvement in the civilization of the world, so far as it affects those people upon whom fall the greatest brunt of the world's burdens.

I have felt, personally, that if this war came to an end and we returned to our pre-war occupations without having accomplished some tangible, definite step forward, some step which promises to secure the peace of the world as long as it is possible to preserve it, every living man and woman in this generation would be derelict to his sacred duty.

I also feel that unless something be done towards extending the benefits of our civilization—the better protection of life, liberty and property, to those who are most defenseless—again we would fail to perform the duty which is laid upon this generation. We must consecrate the victory that has been won to the advancement of the interests of mankind, and we must do it by sacrificing something of our own preconceived notions and of our own selfish concerns, to the general welfare of mankind.

PRESIDENT JOHNSON: General Wickersham's scholarly and intensely interesting address has put us all under deep obligations to him. There are, however, several speakers that we desire to hear, and I shall not permit myself to make any observations upon what others say.

I think most of you know that the National Institute of Social Sciences, in addition to its aim of having meetings and gatherings such as this and the publication annually of a volume called the Journal, has also the purpose—and to many of us it seems perhaps the most worthy purpose—of deciding each year what men and women have made the most notable contribution to the welfare of humanity and of their country, and to recognize those so selected by the award of an appropriate medal. In the past, men like President Taft and President Wilson, to whom I referred at the opening of our program of addresses, have been recognized; also men like General Gorgas, General Goethals, Mr. Henry P. Davison, Mr. Oscar S. Straus, and in the field of scholarship men like Dr. Henry Fairfield Osborn. Sixty-two individuals have been recognized by appropriate gold and presentation medals during the past six years.

This year it seemed clear to the Medal Committee of the Institute that there were two fields in which achievement deserved first consideration. They were the fields of labor leadership and of medical science. There could be no question as to the man who should receive the medal for achievement on behalf of labor. The first gold medal was awarded to Mr. Samuel Gompers.

THE MEDAL TO SAMUEL GOMPERS

PRESENTATION SPEECH BY GEORGE GORDON BATTLE, LL.D.

Mr. Chairman, Ladies and Gentlemen; Mr. Gompers:

This Institute esteems it a high privilege to be able to present this medal to you, Mr. Gompers, as one of the citizens who have rendered valuable service to our country in these past five critical years. During this time there is no name that stands higher on that noble list—I say it advisedly—than yours! At the beginning of this epoch upon which so much depended, at the very beginning of the cataclysm that has rocked and is still rocking the world, it was evident that the success of the cause of humanity and of justice depended chiefly upon the attitude of labor, upon the attitude of the wage workers of the world. To us in this, the greatest of all industrial countries, it was especially vital that our wage workers, the great element of labor upon which all the welfare of the country depends, should take from the very beginning the correct position upon this question.

You stood, sir, in the forefront of that movement, you had already earned and enjoyed the respect and the confidence of the wage workers of America, and, indeed, of the wage workers of the world. You had already earned the confidence of the country, you had already earned the confidence of forward-looking and honest men and women throughout the world. And so, sir, you stood in a position to influence public opinion and to guide and direct that great force of labor, organized and unorganized, which you represented. From the first, there was never a doubt as to your position. You had the keenness of perception to apprehend and the intelligence to firmly comprehend the crucial fact that the cause of the Allies was the cause of humanity, the cause of justice; and you threw on the side of that cause the weight of your great influence with the cohorts of labor led by you.

And this determination you followed with unswerving zeal, intelligence and energy, you labored in season and out of season, you labored morning, noon and night, you labored overseas and on this side of the sea, for the cause of our country, for the cause of the Allies, for the cause of humanity! Your efforts have been crowned with a glorious success. You have won an imperishable glory, and you have earned the undying gratitude of your fellow citizens.

And so, sir, the Institute counts it an honor to present to you this medal for those services. But let me say in closing that there is another aspect to which I wish to call your attention and the attention of those who are here to-night. Gratitude has been said to be an appreciation of favors to come, and, indeed, it is largely true that our sense of gratitude for the past is rendered keener if we can look forward to a continuation of the same benefits in the future. And in that sense, sir, this country and the world still looks to you for a continuance of your aid, your assistance, your counsel and your advice, because we still stand on the eve of perilous times. We have not yet passed from out of the era of danger; indeed, I may say that we are just entering upon a period when questions no less important, no less vital than those of the war are to be solved. Peace has its victories no less renowned nor less important than war; it may also have its defeats, even more disastrous. We must look forward, and do look forward, to an immediate future, in which these problems must be met and must be solved. We must look to your assistance, to your advice, as well as to the advice of other leaders, to guard us against the dangers of reaction, unthinking reaction on the one hand, and of violence and disorder on the other. We must look to your safe and sane intelligence, to your patriotism, to your honesty of purpose, to your zeal and to your splendid and indomitable courage, to guide us in the future, as you have guided us in the past, by the compass of justice and of truth; so that the gratitude which we owe you for the past may be redoubled for your services in the future.

And now, sir, with thanks, with deep and sincere, gratitude for what you have done for your country and the world in the past, and in the confident anticipation that we can look forward to your assistance in the future, I beg to present to you, on behalf of the Institute, this medal.

PRESIDENT JOHNSON: Mr. Gompers, before handing you the medal which has been conferred, I wish to read a few words which Mr. John Mitchell would have added to Mr. Battle's appreciation, had Mr. Mitchell been able to be here to-night. Mr. Mitchell says:

"Few men in America have rendered greater service in the cause of all our people, few men have contributed more to the success of the war and to the enthusiasm of our people in the prosecution of the war than has Mr. Gompers. His whole life has been consecrated to the constructive advancement of humanity. His name will live in the hearts of the American people; his achievements will be recorded in history."

Mr. Gompers, I have the honor to confer upon you the gold medal of the National Institute of Social Sciences.

THE REPLY BY MR. GOMPERS

Mr. President, Ladies and Gentlemen: I doubt if any one can experience the conflicting emotions which come over one in such a trying hour as this, except the one who is the recipient of so great an honor. If it hadn't been for the fact that General Wickersham had anticipated me in my speech, I might have been better prepared to say something. Just before sitting down to dinner this evening he related to me—and I think within the hearing of the President—that quite recently he was invited to a dinner where he was given a theme upon which he was to address the assembled guests. He had made some little preparation for that address and upon that theme, and then at the dinner he was politely informed that for want of time they had cut out that theme and assigned to him another.

May I say this? That I was deeply impressed with the address of General Wickersham this evening. He has done for you and for me, and for our country, and for the world, a great service. The succinct review of the work of that International Conference held in Paris will be of great historic value for the future. It will be a ready reference, even to those who were intimately connected with the work, and surely it will help the students of history in understanding this great achievement in the interest of the working people of the whole world, and in the interest of common humanity.

I find myself in the same position that General Wickersham found himself in at that dinner, only he has done it very much better than I could even have hoped to have done it.

First, may I say, Mr. President and members of this Institute, a few words of the deep gratitude I feel for this honor which you have conferred upon me? This medal, expressive of your appreciation of that which I have *tried to do,* is something that touches my very soul. You will observe that I have emphasized the words "tried to do," for, after all, it isn't given to everybody to have the opportunities of doing, of achieving, and the man or the woman who tries to do the right is as deserving of honor and recognition as the one who has had the better opportunity and who has achieved.

May I interpret this honor as not alone conferred upon me, but upon the men in the Labor Movement of America, who have stood one hundred per cent in coöperation with me, and in loyal service to our country and its cause?

I have been honored in the past; marks of recognition have been given me, but I venture to say that none has touched me quite so deeply as the presentation of this medal and all that it implies. For there are quite a number of the officers and directors and Medal Committee, men and women with whom I have scarcely any acquaintance, and to have this recognition coming so voluntarily touches me so closely and so deeply that I cannot find words to adequately express my gratitude.

And so I accept it, with all that I would like to say, and which I find myself incapable of saying, but I trust that you may take the will for the deed and understand that which is in my heart and in my mind to say.

May I take your time to say this? That in the splendid presentation of the work of the International Commission for Labor Legislation, two items, perhaps, ought to be added: One, that no international convention or treaty can be adopted by the international labor conferences at their annual sessions unless it is approved by at least two-thirds of the delegates to the conference; and the other, that for the protection of America and for the protection of the countries in which the higher standards prevail, standards of life and work, a protocol was adopted by the International Commission and approved by the Plenary Peace Council sitting at Paris, that no country may be asked, or requested, to enforce any standard adopted by an International Conference, when the standards existing within the country are higher than those which are provided in the convention.

Now, a little personal reference, if I may indulge myself. At the opening meeting of the International Conference I was elected its president, as the Dean of the Labor Movement of the World, and as one who has given more years of continued service than any other living man. It was a great honor, and one which I deeply appreciated. But very soon I found myself in a hopeless minority of one; and that procedure continued for more than nine weeks. It wasn't all easy going. It was contest and conflict from the opening session until within a day of the final session.

Senator Burton is on the platform, and he has presided in that great, honorable position of President of the Senate, either pro tem., or at various times. He, as well as every other man or woman who has presided at any legislative gathering, will understand the rather peculiar position of the presiding officer being in an absolute minority of one.

However, it was on the last day of the session; that is, legislative day, when unanimity was accomplished by means of the protocol to which I have just made brief reference. It was impossible for my associate and myself to stand as America's representatives in that International Commission, when it might be possible that an International Labor Conference, as provided in the convention, might impose conditions upon the American workers inferior to those which have been achieved by and for the American workers. Nor could we tolerate, or permit to be enacted in that convention any provision that aimed a blow at the Constitution of the United States of America!

There may come a new concept of our form of government

—I have reference to the exaggerated notion of state rights—
and yet the maintenance of the principle of state rights, and
particularly in reference to international legislation affecting
the powers of the several states of our Union. It was a very
great shock and a cause for general discussion and criticism,
that the Supreme Court of the United States had swept aside
as unconstitutional the Child Labor Law, enacted by the Congress of the United States; but the situation was as it was,
and we had to do the best we could with the organization of
the government of the United States, and even though there
may have been, in the judgment of my associate and myself,
the thought that there was too great an emphasis placed upon
state rights, when it came to legislation of the character with
which our commission had to deal. Yet the Constitution was
as it was, and we were not going to be parties to the violation
of the principles of the Constitution of our country.

But the work was done. It was a hard piece of work
to construct a machine, an organism which could function
aptly, effectively, and yet do no violence to any law, constitution or right of any country. The languages of the Conference were English and French, and every word uttered
in one language was interpreted into another, until my lin-
guistic ability in the French language was quite notable, particularly for the merriment of my associates.

If you have put in about nine weeks, nearly every day,
in sessions from three to seven hours, in which a language
with which you are fairly familiar and another of which you
know little are spoken, you have found a task I would not
wish upon everybody—and there was contending for every
feature and point in order that justice might prevail.

I know this will interest you, when I say that the first point
which the International Commission recommended for adoption in the Peace Treaty was that declaration contained in the
Clayton Law, that the labor of a human being is not a commodity or article of commerce; and that humane declaration
of the Congress of the United States is now recognized as an
international principle!

I know that General Wickersham will appreciate this fact:
that when the Clayton Law was enacted, Mr. Wickersham
wrote an opinion as to the effect of that law, and he said that

under its provisions no case could again be brought in the courts of the United States as was brought in the Hatter's case; and I assure you that his review of the Clayton Law, and particularly the labor provisions of that law, confirmed me that we were on the right track. It was a great source of comfort that the General sustained the principle of that law.

Now, just a word—I shall not detain you much longer. We have won the war; that is all there is to it: we have won the war! We entered the war not alone because of the murder of our innocent men and women and children, but because the spirit of America was aroused! It was not only a menace to the democracies and the civilization of the peoples of Europe, but it was a menace and a challenge to the Republic and the Spirit of Freedom of the American people!

We entered the war high-spirited, and maintained that spirit all through. Labor, before the war was declared (three weeks before), held a conference in the city of Washington, and there declared that come what may, whether in peace or in war, the American workers would stand faithfully behind our Republic to the end! And, better than all of the declarations, they stood true to their faith to the end.

We have all done our share, as time and opportunity gave it to us, and with that same spirit of high-mindedness, of courage, of the sense of justice, the duty to make it possible that we might live our own lives and work out our own salvation as a free people, and to give the people of the world the same opportunities, there has been a merging of men and women, there has been a merging of spirit, a better understanding and a better concept of the rights of all.

And now that the war is practically over—and God grant that it may not be renewed for any cause—and the cloud that is now hovering above the Peace Commissioners in Paris may soon be dispelled and entire agreement reached—the war is practically at an end; technically it is not, but it is at an end for all practical purposes, and now we are confronted with the trying hours and times of peace, the problems of peace. We must understand that the world is in the remaking; the relations between man and man must take on a new concept, we must deal fairly by each other and have the consideration among our own people, that the men who have sacrificed their all, the men who have returned from the fighting fronts, the men of labor, must have the opportunity to live, and to live rightly, as becomes the sovereign citizenship of our country.

Only within quite a few hours I learned that in one great establishment, in one of our cities, there are 60,000 men who are unemployed in one industry and under one management. To the men who come back from France and find that their employment is gone, that they have not the means of self-support and the maintenance of those dependent upon them; to try and make them understand that we have had a triumphant, glorious victory will mean nothing to them! We can understand that in a militarist country, where their government and their armies have been depleted, that discontent, a feeling of humiliation and resentment may take possession of the people. But in a country with the wealth and the genius of our people and our land, tell the man, or the group of men who are unemployed, through no fault of their own, that they have won a glorious victory for humanity, and it will be meaningless to them. We must find the way out. It devolves upon employers, it devolves upon workers, it devolves upon publicists, it devolves upon the government, the Congress and the Legislatures of our country, to see to it that the era of peace and reconstruction shall have a new meaning in the affairs of the people of our Republic! Nothing can be more harmful than a situation where men, after having returned from a victorious struggle, find that the spirit of industrial autocracy has taken the place of political autocracy. There must be better understandings, a mutual recognition of each other's rights, and a fair and honest effort to reach a conclusion beneficial to industry and commerce, and particularly to humanity.

I appeal to you, ladies and gentlemen, and through you, to whom it may concern, to understand this fact: That the American Labor Movement, as represented by the American Federation of Labor, is a movement for the protection and the promotion of the rights and interests of all the people of our country. It aims to destroy nothing worthy of its existence. It aims to make to-day a better day than yesterday; to-morrow a better day than to-day, and each recurring to-morrow a better day than the one that has gone before. It aims at a constructive policy. It aims to help, it understands its rightful position in the affairs of our nation; it asks that it be accorded rights and freedom for justice and for democracy, and for a right life.

Gentlemen, if the attitude of employers of labor shall be one of relentless antagonism to the voluntary system of organization of the workers for the constructive and normal and rational development of the interests of the working people of our country; if that antagonism finds its repetition in relentless, bitter antagonism and policies, you may possibly destroy our movement—it is just likely that that can be done. I have very grave doubt that it is possible to do that, but if it be possible to do it, if our movement can be either destroyed or weakened, you will have another element to deal with. It is not a wish, but it is a forecast—as the weather man at Washington predicts, from the reports which come to him, the likelihood of the weather in the next twenty-four or forty-eight hours, so in the industrial and the sociological world I receive reports from all over the country, and I am no more responsible for what may follow, because I forecast it, than is the weather man for a snowstorm or a blizzard.

The men of labor in America, organized in the trade unions, and the women organized, are the militant body who are contributing their time and their means for the purpose of promoting the rights and interests of all the workers, and while it may be true that primarily they may have their own membership in view, there isn't a thing that they can do, either in the way of an advance or a check of retreat, but what must have its beneficial influence upon the unorganized.

A country does not send all its men to war. It organizes an army of a number of its men, and these men must bear the brunt in order to protect the men and the women who are left at home. And so with the organized labor movement, they bear the brunt of cost, of time and heartache, for the great mass of labor. There isn't a law passed by the Congress, or by the legislatures, or by any municipality, for the working people that can affect the men and women in the organized labor movement alone—it affects all who work! There isn't anything that can be done by organized labor that does not find its reflex in the home and the life and the work of all the toilers of our land.

I am pleading for this common action among all our people. I speak to my fellow workers in plain terms, so that there can be no misinterpretation placed upon what I say. I speak to you, ladies and gentlemen, and I speak to employers of labor wherever I may be, in terms that leave no room for misunderstanding. It is a common duty that devolves upon all of us to see to it that this great time and opportunity which has come to us shall not be lost or frittered away.

It is a great privilege to have lived and to have been of some service to the cause of justice and freedom and democracy! It was a great privilege to work in order that our fighting boys on land and sea might be sustained. It was a great work to help in stabilizing the good will and the energy of the peoples of the various countries, our own included. The glamor of war and the enthusiasm which war arouses does not exist to-day, and it is difficult to arouse men and women to understand and to act in this trying time of peace.

It is the purpose that I have to prevail upon my fellow citizens, men and women, employers and workers, men in public life, men of influence, to mold the judgment and action of our people, men and women of labor, to do their all, to perform their full duty in order that the tranquillity of our nation may be maintained; that this Republic of ours shall be not only the political but the industrial leader of the world, the land which gives to the whole world a better concept of right life and right living, and the relations between man and man, and between nation and nation. In that hope, in that thought, and with the best utterance that I can give forth—if we fail, the light of hope will go out all over our land. Men and women, don't let that occur!

THE MEDAL TO MR. CHARLES M. SCHWAB

PRESENTATION SPEECH BY HONORABLE DE LANCEY NICOLL

Mr. President, I consider myself very fortunate on this delightful occasion, where there are assembled so many intellectual men and so many intellectual and beautiful women, to have been chosen by the Institute to make one of the presentation addresses.

Ever since the armistice there have been many honors and

decorations conferred upon many persons who contributed to the great victory, but I think I may venture to say that no one is more deserving of the honor which the Society confers to-night than the distinguished gentleman to whom I am asked to present a medal.

Before the war our friend, Mr. Schwab, was known throughout America, and indeed throughout the world, as one of the greatest captains of industry, one of the master builders, one of the men who had accomplished great things. At the early age of thirty-six, I think, he was the president of the Carnegie Steel Company. At the age of thirty-nine he was the president of the United States Steel Corporation, which was really the product of his own genius. Later on he rescued the moribund Bethlehem Steel Company, and made it as it is to-day, one of the greatest manufacturing concerns in the world!

When the war in Europe came on, he deemed it to be his duty to devote himself to the manufacture of munitions for the Allies. He was consulted by the representatives of England and France. They have testified in writings, which you have all seen, what he was able to do for them. I think it is no exaggeration to say that the assistance which the Bethlehem Steel Company gave to the Allies, before we came into the war, was one of the greatest contributions to the victory which ultimately came about.

When our war came on, in April, 1917, he devoted himself with patriotic fervor and redoubled energies to the manufacture of munitions for the United States. He converted the great Bethlehem Steel Company into a munitions plant, and devoted himself entirely to the manufacture of articles of war.

I have read somewhere the extraordinary results which he accomplished. The figures are so astounding that I find it difficult to carry them in my mind, but some of them I have, and I may briefly state them. I believe the Bethlehem Steel Company produced, in finished guns, from the 14-inch gun down to the 2-inch gun, something like 3,319 guns. In addition to that, the company produced 55,000,000 pounds of steel forgings, which represented uncompleted guns; and when those guns were completed the Bethlehem Steel Company had provided for the Allies and the United States something like 13,-

ooo guns, with all the accessories accompanying them. And
after our war, out of the total number of 55,000,000 pounds
of forgings, the Bethlehem Steel Company completed 35,000,-
ooo pounds of steel forgings. Indeed, the company actually
produced over 65 per cent of all the American guns which
went to the Allies and the United States during the war!

The company furnished 18,000,000 or 19,000,000 rounds
of ammunition for these guns, and 1,500,000 of projectiles.
And not only that, but it added three great plants and two or
three great testing grounds, for the different kinds of ammunition that it produced. And not only that, but it produced
58 merchant vessels, 25 destroyers, and when the war came
to an end it had 35 more destroyers, and any number of ships
in course of construction.

Now, ladies and gentlemen, that was an extraordinary
achievement in itself, and if our distinguished friend whom
we are honoring to-night had done nothing more, he certainly
had done enough to entitle him to the honor medal of this
Society. But there came a time in the history of the war
when he was called upon to do something more. He was
called upon to speed up the belated program of ship construction. You all recollect the critical situation in which we found
ourselves when Mr. Schwab was called to Washington and
was asked to give up for the time, the management of the
Bethlehem Steel Company and become the Director General
of the Emergency Fleet Corporation. No doubt it was a great
sacrifice for him to make, but he did it cheerfully and accepted
the office which the President conferred upon him, and devoted
his extraordinary energy and unrivaled executive ability to
the great and necessary business of speeding up the ship construction; and as we now see it, indeed, as all the world sees it,
that was the real thing which helped to win the war! The
problem was *ships and more ships,* and ships in the quickest
possible time. Who was the man to get the ships? What man
in the United States could be found who could produce the
ships—for ships were necessary to win the war. And the
undertaking fell to Mr. Schwab, and you know how he discharged it; you know that in an incredibly short space of time
he produced the results which were necessary to win the war.
We all recollect how he did it, how he went around to all of

the shipyards in the country, and in a series of eloquent speeches aroused the men who were working in the yards to a sense of their duty; how he was able to call more men to the shipyards, and keep them working at the very top of their ability.

There are a great many different views about what won the war, but I say that the man who built the ships, more than anybody else, won the war!

I have the greatest admiration and gratitude for the achievements of our heroes who went to France and fought the battles which brought about the final result. No one has a greater admiration for them than I have. My bosom swells with pride when I think of what they did. At Cantigny and Château-Thierry, at San Mihiel, in the Argonne Forest, through the Hindenburg line, across the Meuse and at Sedan they took the German beast by the throat and drove him to his lair! Thousands of them gave up their lives for the safety of the world and the welfare of mankind. The plains of Flanders and France are watered with their precious blood and their bodies lie in the gory fields, where they fought so valiantly and so well. But of what avail all this matchless valor, this wonderful bravery, this unsurpassed fighting, unless we had the ships to take them to France, the ships to give them the munitions of war, the ships to give them the necessary supplies. The man who contributed to the establishment of the Great Armada, who took our heroes and their munitions and supplies to France, is one of the men who made the greatest contribution to the war.

We have a great many other reasons for giving the medal to our friend Mr. Schwab. He has many other qualities besides his wonderful executive ability, his great breadth of vision, his unparalleled energy and his powers of concentration, and all the other elements of greatness. Those of us who know him well know him as a man who loves nature, a man who loves art, a man who loves his country, and, greater than all, a man who loves his fellowmen.

It is for all these qualities, in addition to his great achievements, that we honor him and honor ourselves to-night by conferring this medal upon him. I thought it was going to be my privilege to give him the medal, and I was prepared to kiss him on both cheeks, but I see that is coming to the President.

THE REPLY OF MR. SCHWAB

Mr. President, Ladies and Gentlemen: The hour is late; I shall occupy little of your time. I accept this splendid medal of your appreciation with all the eloquent words, repeated, with which my friend, Mr. Gompers, so splendidly responded a few moments ago. I want to say that I accept it in the same spirit with which the great Marshal Foch, when I first met him in Paris, replied to me. As every true-hearted citizen would have done, I complimented and thanked him for the splendid contribution he had made to the war. His reply was that the great staff conducting the war was like an orchestra, that it was necessary for each instrument to play its part in complete harmony with the entire orchestra; and that the baton that fell to his hand was but chance and good fortune, and that he had only done his duty to the extent that every other member of that great orchestra had done his duty.

And so, Mr. President, in accepting this honor at your hands, I do so with the feeling that I am accepting the honor for myself and the staff which assisted and coöperated with me as harmoniously as the orchestra of the great Marshal, in the accomplishment of the task that was before us, and not in the personal sense, so flatteringly stated by the gentleman who made the address of presentation to me.

I have been a fortunate man in life—fortunate in many things—health, family, wealth, all that—but the one piece of good, great fortune that came to me at the beginning of this war was to have owned and controlled the one great munition works, free of the war, that I could turn over to my country for its protection.

And, above all, to feel what was of still greater pride, the sensation that comes to every true American citizen, that no sum of money, however great, could ever divert his patriotic thought for one moment from opportunity offered to do good for his country.

This works and the staff which operated it (the Ship Works) have done their share, but we did it under the spur of approval of the people and the citizens of the United States.

Such action as yours, Mr. President and gentlemen of the Society, has been my own ideal of how the great and successful things in life may always be accomplished; never under the spur of carping criticism, but always under the stimulus of encouragement and approval; and whatever may come to one in life, to the man that is worth while there is nothing which will live in his soul and memory so long, so lastingly and with such effect as the approval of his fellowmen.

I would like to make acknowledgment of something in the second article of Mr. Gompers' reply, which to me is the most important of all, and which I heard with much interest: "Employers and workers should be allowed the right of association for lawful purposes."

I have known my friend, Mr. Gompers, for a great many years; we have differed materially in our opinions at times, but I am obliged to say that I think that second paragraph of more importance than all the rest of the document together. The time has arrived when employers and employees must be one. In our great establishment we adopted a year ago the plan of having our workmen elect their own representatives to confer and sit at boards with our management, to discuss all phases of pay and employment of labor, and, although I had opposed it in principle for many years, I am now obliged to say publicly that under no condition would I go back to the old system of labor employment.

Mr. President, there is much that I might say on this subject, but there is one thing I would urge upon this great country of ours, in corroboration of all Mr. Gompers has said, and that is, while we can spend billions for war, in this great social change that is about to come over our country this government should be prepared, if necessary, to spend billions for all sorts of internal improvements and extensions to the industries, railroads and public utilities of our country, if for no other good purpose than that of keeping our work people during this period fully employed.

I thank you, Mr. President; I thank the Society; I thank you, Mr. Nicoll, for your prejudiced eulogy, the eulogy of a friend who speaks what is in his heart—perhaps not always the truth. I thank you all for your kindly reception, and, above all, for the honor which you have conferred upon me.

And so, in that spirit of gratefulness, with the humility that comes to one who feels he has not done as well as he might have done, but who under all the circumstances did his best, I accept the medal from your Society with the deepest possible appreciation.

THE MEDAL TO HARRY A. GARFIELD, LL.D.

PRESENTATION SPEECH BY PROFESSOR SAMUEL McCUNE LINDSAY

Mr. President, Ladies and Gentlemen: The distinguished and genial President of Williams College will appreciate, I am sure, our difficulties amid the warmth and plenty of this festive occasion, in bringing back a very vivid recollection of the meatless days, the wheatless days, the fuelless days, the lightless nights, and the gasless Sundays of a year or more ago.

It was a great and difficult task to which Dr. Garfield was called by the government during the war emergency, and I think that in this country we have two examples, the only two examples in the world, of men who were called to perform the duties of Food Administrator and Fuel Administrator, and survived many months of administration. We have still the two men in office who began that work and performed it to the satisfaction of their fellow citizens until the end of the war.

Dr. Garfield's great success as Fuel Administrator, of course, is well known to us all. It may not be, perhaps, so vividly in our minds that before he was Fuel Administrator he was equally distinguished as a practical business man, as a coal operator, as a lawyer and as a Professor of Law and of Political Science. He brought a great many qualities and much valuable experience from the Food Administration with him when he organized the Fuel Administration.

There are three things that distinguished Dr. Garfield's service which have already, I think, received widespread recognition and will be permanently recorded in the history of the war. First, the public interest was supreme in the plans of the Fuel Administration. Tireless energy and an eye single to the public interest with never the slightest suspicion that political influence affected any of his acts, were characteristic of Dr. Garfield's daily routine. He faced every problem—and they were extremely difficult problems that he had to face—with calmness, with clearness of vision and with absolute impartiality. Second, a social spirit dominated the task which was so clearly stated by him in the very first official document he issued, namely, to secure the maximum coal production, with reasonable profit to the producer and the lowest possible cost to the consumer. I am inclined to think from what I have heard of the record of the Fuel Administration of other countries that we had by far the best record of any country in the world, in the accomplishment of those purposes. We got the maximum production of fuel in this country during the war, with reasonable profit to the producer and at a lower cost to the consumer, I believe, than in any other country in the world. Third, the co-operation of the public with the Fuel Administration was its best achievement. Dr. Garfield's administration was characterized not only by the calm social spirit in which the somewhat arbitrary and necessarily dictatorial orders of the Fuel Administrator were executed, but by a high degree of voluntary co-operation on the part of those affected by those orders. Throughout it all Dr. Garfield always appealed to the sense of obligation and opportunity to serve a common cause on the part of all groups in the community. His regulations in the case of the gasless Sundays, as they were called, furnish the best illustration of what I mean. His orders were often not commands at all; they were appeals to the social spirit of America, they were appeals to the patriotism of America, and in some of those appeals he set a very high standard of government achievement in the difficult science and art of public administration.

Especially during the period of the war we have had to undertake great and new tasks of government, and it looks, from what has been said here this evening as well as from many other indications, that we shall have to look forward in the future to undertaking many more new tasks of government. One thing is sure, we do not want the spirit of the bureaucrat in America—we do want a great deal more of the spirit of the administrator of the type of Dr. Garfield, the administrator who doesn't rely solely upon the authority that he possesses—great as that authority may be—but realizes that something far more effective than the authority of law is the appeal to the conscience and the sense of right in the people over whom he exercises authority. It is in this third respect that Dr. Garfield seems to me to have rendered the greatest and most lasting service to the nation as Fuel Administrator.

I take great pleasure, Dr. Garfield, on behalf of the National Institute of Social Sciences, in telling you that the medal of the Institute has been awarded to you as a mark of esteem and the high regard of your fellow citizens for you personally and appreciation of the great value of your public service.

THE REPLY OF DR. GARFIELD

Dr. Johnson, Ladies and Gentlemen: We have been engaged in the delectable task of making one another's speeches to-night. You will observe that each speaker has made the same point by way of introduction, and I certainly wish to follow the same course.

It had occurred to me, as I entered the room, that we who were to receive medals would be expected to make the best bow we knew how to make, and that that would be all that would be required of us; and when I was told by our President that a few words of appropriate thanks would be expected, I framed in my mind what I thought to be a happy expression of appreciation, only to find it taken out of my mouth first by Mr. Gompers and then by my friend, Mr. Schwab.

What I had in mind to say, however, I am going to say like the boy who has learned his speech and must get it off, for lack of anything else; namely, that I accept the medal not for myself, but for those whom I represent.

And, in very truth it is so; not only do I represent the Fuel Administration, for without the many thousands who coöperated with me in the task I was called upon to perform, it would have been impossible to have achieved even the measure of success which Dr. Lindsay has indicated was achieved, but also the great body of men outside the Fuel Administration, with whom we were called upon to deal, and without whose coöperation achievement would likewise have been impossible.

From the very outset it was my task to bring together, to attempt to reconcile the operators and the mine workers. I felt a good deal as the judge on the bench feels who seeks to bring together husband and wife. He takes them into his private room and says to them, "My friends, you must find a way to get on together." And the wonderful thing about it to me was that capital and labor engaged in the fuel industry got together; they sank their differences. The question of union or non-union, which was uppermost in the minds of the men and of the operators, was adjourned as soon as the men and the operators found that the government insisted that we had one great task to perform and that was to produce the coal, all the coal that could be taken out of the ground and carried to the factories.

There was one, almost only one, failure in coöperation. I have never told the name of the individual until to-night, but I am going to tell it now. On one occasion a gentleman came to my office—I am telling this because he is here to-night—and said to me, "Mr. Garfield, I ordered a few tons of coal the other day, and when it was put down on the sidewalk and carried into my cellar, I discovered more rock than I did coal." I said, "You are exactly the man I am looking for. We have established our regulation against dirty coal; we have set up the penalty, but we haven't been able to prosecute anybody for violating the regulation because nobody has been willing to come forward and stand as the prosecuting witness." "Oh, no," he said, "no, no, I will not do that, because I realize that I must have more coal after this is gone." I said, "But, Mr. Gompers, how can you expect me under those circumstances to secure clean coal?"

Mr. Gompers was so good a coöperator in all other respects that I must at once exculpate him from the charge I have laid at his door.

But I wish to say just this in conclusion, that coöperation is no longer a theory to my mind; we have practiced it and lived it for two years. It was coöperation not only between capital and labor brought together by the Fuel Administration, but it was coöperation between capital and labor combined on the one side and government on the other—government representing the great consumers of this country. And the experiences of these two years have convinced me that nothing will solve the problems of peace which have been commented upon here to-night until the three necessary parties in interest—the public represented by government and capital and labor— learn to sit down together and discuss freely and openly every question that is involved in any industry. That is the way of accomplishment, I believe. The experience not only of the Fuel Administration, but of many another administration during this period of stress and strain has taught us the lesson, and I believe we will profit by it, that in this new era procedure will in some form or other be adopted in the great attempt to solve the problems that are before us.

Mr. President, as representative of the Fuel Administration, I accept with appreciation and with great pleasure the medal which you have presented to me to-night.

PRESIDENT JOHNSON: Medals as announced on the program have been awarded in addition to those conferred tonight to Dr. William Henry Welch, to Mr. Robert Scott Lovett, to Mr. Harry A. Wheeler, to the Right Rev. Charles H. Brent, to Mr. Raymond B. Fosdick, to Dr. Carl Koller and to Mr. Frederick Layton. These medals must necessarily be conferred *in absentia.*

THE MEDAL TO RIGHT REV. CHARLES H. BRENT CONFERRED IN ABSENTIA

PRESENTATION STATEMENT BY RIGHT REV. JAMES H. DARLINGTON

President Johnson and associates of the National Institute of Social Sciences:

I consider it an honor and a privilege to present to-night in your name as well as in my own the Institute Presentation Medal to my friend and brother, Bishop Charles Henry Brent, for his many and distinguished services both in the United States and abroad.

I regret that as he is now on the sea, returning to this country, he cannot be with us to-night.

Charles Henry Brent was born in Newcastle, Ontario, Canada, on the 9th day of April, 1862. He is the son of the Reverend Canon Henry and Sophia Frances Cumings Brent. After being graduated from Trinity College, Toronto, with classical honors, in 1884, he was ordained by Bishop Sweatman in 1887, and became assistant in St. Paul's, Buffalo. Subsequently he held several positions in Boston until he was elected Bishop of the Philippine Islands in 1901. He has also been elected twice as Bishop of Washington, once as Bishop of New Jersey and finally Bishop of Western New York, which position he has recently accepted.

Bishop Brent is most distinguished as an author and his devotional books are widely read and much quoted. In addition to his works as Missionary Bishop at the time when the United States was not only changing the government, but the educational and social life of the Philippines as well, he acted as Chief Commissioner for the United States, as President of the International Opium Commission in 1908-9. At the session of The Hague Conference in 1911-12 he was honored by being elected as its president.

General Pershing, who had formerly been in command in the Philippines and knew the ability of Bishop Brent, and desiring his war help, asked him to leave the Philippines and assist him by acting on his staff as head of all the Chaplains. Bishop Brent accepted the position as a patriotic duty, and has been at the fighting front with General Pershing continuously until the present time.

It is therefore in grateful and fitting acknowledgment of Bishop Brent's many sided life and on account of his multiplied and successful services to the Church, to Literature and to Society, and to the State, that this medal is awarded by the National Institute of Social Sciences to-night.

Honor virtutis præmium. Palmam qui meruit ferat.

THE MEDAL TO MR. RAYMOND B. FOSDICK CONFERRED IN ABSENTIA

PRESENTATION STATEMENT BY MR. LEO ARNSTEIN

Of the several factors which played an important part in bringing the war to a successful conclusion none was more important than the maintenance of morale in our army. Morale is to the spiritual being what physical vigor and condition is to the body, and it was no mean task to maintain this morale in an army composed of four million men who had been suddenly torn from their normal environments, separated from their customary associations and placed in surroundings which were strange and often unsympathetic. Half of these four million men were in foreign lands, where the language was strange and communication with those at home more than casual.

In the very first month of the war, in April, 1917, the importance of this aspect of the work was recognized and there was created by the War Department a "Commission on Training Camp Activities," and with admirable judgment the man chosen to head this activity was Raymond B. Fosdick, who had won the respect of this community by his splendid work while associated with our late beloved Mayor, John Purroy Mitchel.

.The new commission undertook two main functions: First, to furnish to the army, composed largely of young men, many of them mere boys, a substitute for the recreational and relaxational opportunities to which they had been accustomed, and second, to prevent and suppress certain vicious conditions traditionally associated with army and training camps.

Through coördinating the efforts of existing organizations within the camps, and by organizing the social communities adjacent to the camps, the commission succeeded in reëstablishing some of the old social ties, and, in a sense, rationalized the bewildering environments of the war camp.

The splendid accomplishment of this commission is too well known to require any detailed description of its specific activities, and we are gathered here to-night to pay tribute, among others, to Raymond B. Fosdick, the guiding spirit of this work, who, modestly keeping out of the limelight, directed its every move and is responsible for its success. Surely no one could better have served his fellow men than by keeping this great body of soldiers happy and contented, and by guarding their health so that disease not only did not flourish, as was its wont in military camps, but actually was materially reduced. His work required imagination of a high degree, coupled with true human sympathy and a rare executive talent; possessed of all of this, he gave of himself unsparingly for the sake of his country, and by awarding this medal to him the National Institute of Social Sciences is honoring itself as well as Raymond B. Fosdick.

THE MEDAL TO CARL KOLLER, M. D., CONFERRED IN ABSENTIA

PRESENTATION STATEMENT BY WENDELL C. PHILLIPS, M. D.

The privilege of presenting the medal of the National Institute of Social Sciences to you, Dr. Koller, is keenly appreciated. A man who contributes a remedy or appliance which ameliorates human suffering or prolongs human life becomes not only a benefactor to his generation, but is a benefactor to the future generations for all time. Jenner, Lister, Pasteur and discoverers of general anesthesia stand out as the world's greatest benefactors along this line. The medical history of the world war wherein smallpox, typhoid fever and sepsis were almost unknown speaks louder than any words of mine for the strides which preventive medicine has made. Strange as it may seem, these great achievements have largely appeared within the last one hundred years. For the purpose of contradistinction, may I for a moment place in comparison a type of individuals, prominent representatives of which are the notoriety seeking neurotic opponents of animal experimentation who well-nigh wrecked the work of the American Red Cross in France in its efforts along the lines of preventive medicine. Your discovery of the anesthetic properties of cocaine has been one of the marked contributions to surgery and especially the surgery of the eye, nose and throat. I well remember in '83 when your first article appeared and with what pleasure I made use of it in minor operations on the nose. This discovery has entirely revolutionized surgery of the nose and throat, for it permits operations of considerable magnitude without the necessity of general anesthesia. In the business world your discovery would have brought not only the fame which is yours, but also a great fortune; but with true altruism and loyalty to the sacred oath you have made this contribution to mankind without financial gain.

THE MEDAL TO MR. FREDERICK LAYTON, CONFERRED IN ABSENTIA

STATEMENT SUBMITTED BY HONORABLE JAMES G. JENKINS, MILWAUKEE, WIS.

In 1888 Mr. Layton founded the Layton Art Gallery, located at Milwaukee, expending for the lot and building the sum of $125,000. He also gave to the trustees of the corporation controlling it the sum of $100,000, as an endowment fund for the maintenance of the gallery, and has expended in paintings and works of art which are contained in the gallery a sum approximating $200,000. He has given to the upbuilding of this gallery constant attention and care, purchasing many of the pictures in Europe. The gallery is one of the monuments of which Milwaukee is proud. It is designed to cultivate a taste for art, and for four days in the week, including Sunday, is open to the public free of charge. It contains many choice paintings and has a fine reputation, both at home and abroad.

Mr. Layton has always evinced great interest in the Milwaukee (Passavant) Hospital, founded by the Reverend William A. Passavant, D. D., of Pittsburgh, in 1863. He has been not only a large contributor to its maintenance by annual subscription, but at his private expense, in 1904, made a park out of the Milwaukee Hospital grounds and erected an ornamental fence, involving an expenditure of over $20,000. He has also endowed three free beds in the hospital for deserving poor patients, at an expense of $15,000. In 1907-1908 he constructed upon the hospital grounds at his own expense a home for incurables, at an expense of over $61,000, and for the first years subsequent to its opening contributed annually $4,000 towards the current expenses. In 1913 he transferred to the authorities of the Milwaukee Hospital as an endowment fund for the maintenance of the Home for Incurables securities to the amount of $100,000. This home will accommodate thirty-two patients besides the attendants and help. Those patients unable to bear in whole or in part the cost of their maintenance are supported there without cost to them. Since 1908 there have been one hundred and fifty-five patients supported in the home.

He also erected in his native village a home for the support of the aged and endowed it with a sum sufficient for its upkeep and the support of the inmates.

These are, briefly stated, the public charities which have distinguished Mr. Layton, and which have made him known and beloved by the public of Wisconsin, but, in addition, his life has been marked by constant private charities of which the world knows nothing.

His life has been unassuming, retiring, seeking no notoriety, contented to perform good works for the benefit of humanity, without thought of recognition; his home is like himself, modest and unpretentious, such as would be maintained by a comparatively poor man, or one of quite moderate resources. At the age of ninety-one he still retains his mental faculties, and employs himself in going about doing good. He is universally beloved because he is one who loves his fellowmen.

THE MEDAL TO HONORABLE ROBERT SCOTT LOVETT, CONFERRED IN ABSENTIA

PRESENTATION STATEMENT BY MR. A. J. COUNTY

I deeply regret that Judge Lovett could not be present this evening to receive some tangible evidence of the public appreciation of his railroad and governmental service. It is a pleasant duty and an honor for me to be selected to present to him the medal awarded by the National Institute of Social Sciences in recognition of his long and distinguished public service. His name is inseparably connected with the great Union Pacific System, as legal adviser and later as chief executive. Under his direction the program for its physical and financial rehabilitation was continued, until the system reached a high physical standard, securely founded on well established credit. During the great European war he rendered constructive service to our country, especially as Priorities Commissioner of the War Industries Board, and later as Director of the Division of Capital Expenditures under the United States Railroad Administration. With the war ended he resumed the presidency of the Union Pacific System, and as a railroad executive and a railroad statesman the public and his associates will rely upon his sound judgment and leadership to aid in solving the problems that still confront our transportation systems. His career is an inspiration, and is one of the best exemplifications of the achievements possible in a country whose laws and institutions depend upon the loyalty of its citizens and which allow of private initiative and ownership by those citizens of those great enterprises which have added so much to its prosperity and none more so than our railroads. I congratulate the Institute upon its wisdom in selecting Robert Scott Lovett to be the recipient of this honor which he so justly deserves for a lifetime spent in public service, and which the Institute now asks him to kindly accept.

THE MEDAL TO WILLIAM HENRY WELCH, M. D., CONFERRED IN
ABSENTIA

PRESENTATION STATEMENT BY HONORABLE THEODORE MARBURG

Centralization is not always a gain. In certain spheres,
unless controlled, it may be deadening. But there is one activity which lends itself preëminently to centralization—the gathering and subsequent dissemination of knowledge. And here
the process of centralization is wholly beneficial. A central
bureau, by keeping in touch with parallel endeavors of individuals or groups who may be ignorant each of the other's
work, spells economy of effort. It likewise heightens the value
of all progress by making it generally and immediately available not only for the public, but also for the investigator who
may continually readjust his effort to the progress already
made. Gathering the waters of knowledge in a great central
reservoir to be distributed through innumerable channels and
tapped at will for countless needs—to this beneficent process
none object.

It was to such work of organizing knowledge in the fields
of medicine and sanitation for the purposes of the war that
Dr. William H. Welch was summoned when America responded to the call of outraged justice. And seldom has a task been
better performed.

Throughout the period of the war Dr. Welch's services to
the government has been recognized as of exceptional value.
His knowledge of scientific medicine, sanitation, public health
and medical education, derived both from wide reading and
experience, was of material aid to the medical profession both
in the army and outside. When the National Academy of
Sciences was asked by President Wilson in 1916 to name a
committee to inquire into and define the scientific needs of the
country in peace and war, Dr. Welch, who was the president
of the Academy, forthwith began the organization of the National Research Council. In company with Professor George
Hale, he visited France and England in the summer of 1916
and acquired a knowledge of the latest practices in medicine
and in sanitation in time of war. The organization of the
National Research Council was then effected and before the
United States entered the war this council had laid out the

work to be done and mobilized the workers, assigning to each task the men best qualified for it. The National Research Council became officially the body to which all scientific matters were referred, and it is to Dr. Welch and Professor Hale that its effective organization is due. Dr. Welch's wide acquaintance with the best men in the medical profession and his accurate knowledge likewise gave especial value to his services as a member of the executive board of the Medical Section of the Council of National Defense. It was the urgent duties in connection with this latter service that drew Dr. Welch's attention away from the side of research to be devoted to organizing methods for caring for the health of the army. In this connection he became a member of the executive staff of the Surgeon General. He was constantly consulted in all matters pertaining to the equipment and personnel of laboratories in the camps. With General Gorgas he visited most of the larger camps and made a detailed study of the efficiency and needs of each laboratory. His opinion was sought not only in regard to laboratory matters, but in the broader subjects of the control of communicable diseases. And there was no one connected with the government whose opinion on such matters was more valued. Aside from the influenza epidemic, which defeated all efforts to analyze and control it, the death rate in our camps and cantonments was without parallel in the history of the mobilization of armies, and this result was due largely to Dr. Welch's advice. Even with the great havoc wrought by the influenza, the death rate from disease in our army was lower by far than that recorded for any army in previous wars.

Passing tribute must be paid, in this connection, to Dr. Victor C. Vaughan, who was associated with Dr. Welch during the entire period of the war and whose services were of very great value to the country.

Dr. Welch was also a member of the Medical Advisory Board of the Red Cross. By reason of his acquaintance with scientific men in Europe and because of the knowledge acquired during his trip abroad, Dr. Welch was able to render to this board a service which no one else could have rendered. He likewise served on various subcommittees, such as the Pneumonia Board. His advice was constantly sought, freely given and always valuable.

Dr. Welch has long been known as the father of scientific medicine in this country. No man has done more than he to raise the standards of medical education and to place the best medical schools of this country on their present high level.

Not the least of Dr. Welch's claims to our gratitude is his splendid example of patriotic service. More than that of any other man it stimulated the medical profession to such service. By common consent he is worthy of every honor that can be bestowed upon him and the National Institute of Social Sciences honors itself in honoring him with this medal.

THE MEDAL TO HARRY A. WHEELER, LL. D., CONFERRED IN ABSENTIA

PRESENTATION STATEMENT BY EMORY R. JOHNSON, SC. D.

It was seven years ago that Harry A. Wheeler realized the need for the establishment of a national organization that would really represent the business sentiment of the country. Previous efforts to build up a national society for this purpose had failed, but Mr. Wheeler in bringing about the establishment and development of the Chamber of Commerce of the United States has created an organization which has been completely successful. During the first two years of the life of the Chamber of Commerce Mr. Wheeler was its president. He retired at the end of the second year and started a precedent which was followed subsequently by the Chamber, a president being elected every two years. When, in 1918, the time came for the selection of a president to guide the work of the Chamber during the period of the war, Mr. Wheeler was again drafted to the presidency and during the past year has given the larger part of his time to the work of the Chamber. Since the armistice was signed, the Chamber of Commerce, under the leadership of Mr. Wheeler, has been specially active in developing plans for the revival of business and for the enactment of legislation made necessary by the period of reconstruction through which business is passing.

In addition to his other duties, Mr. Wheeler has acted as Food Administrator for the State of Illinois and during the war he gave a portion of each day to that work. Without thought of the business sacrifice made necessary by his devotion to public services and without considering the heavy strain which his many duties placed upon him, Mr. Wheeler devoted himself unreservedly to the needs of the country. Few men have rendered more valuable wartime services than he has performed.

It is in recognition of these services and of the high standard of devotion to public duties which Mr. Wheeler has maintained that the National Institute of Social Sciences has awarded him its medal.

ANNUAL MEETING

The Sixth Annual Meeting of the National Institute of Social Sciences was held at the office of the Institute, 225 Fifth Avenue, New York, January 17, 1919, at 4:30 o'clock, President Emory R. Johnson presiding.

President Johnson read the Minutes of the Annual Meeting held January 18, 1918.

Miss Alice Lakey, chairman of the New Jersey State Liberty Medal Committee, read the report of the Liberty Service Medal Committee for Miss French, secretary of the Liberty Medal Committee.

In the absence of Henry P. Davison, treasurer, Dr. Johnson read the treasurer's report, showing a balance of $3,808.75.

Miss Lillie Hamilton French was nominated assistant treasurer for 1919.

The President reported the ballot returns received from the members regarding the officers for 1919, signed by the Nominating Committee.

The President was authorized to appoint an Executive Committee, Medal Committee, Finance Committee and Liberty Service Medal Committee.

The President was authorized to employ and fix the compensation or salary of the clerical force of the Institute.

SPRING MEETING

The Spring Meeting of the National Institute of Social Sciences was held at the Hotel Astor, April 25, at 3 o'clock. The subject under discussion was, "What Shall Be Done With the Railroads?" Professor Emory R. Johnson presided.

Speakers: Honorable Theodore E. Burton, formerly United States Senator from Ohio; Honorable William Church Osborn, Mr. George A. Post, chairman of the Railroad Committee, Chamber of Commerce of the United States; Mr. Paul M. Warburg and Mr. A. J. County, vice-president of the Pennsylvania Railroad Company.

REPORT OF THE LIBERTY SERVICE MEDAL COMMITTEE

A report of the Liberty Service Medal Committee was published in April, 1918, and sent to the members of the National Institute. In this report the citations and replies for the year were given.

Eighteen State Committees were formed.

CHAIRMEN OF STATE COMMITTEES

California	Hon. Curtis H. Lindley
Colorado	Tyson S. Dines
Connecticut	Arthur R. Kimball
District of Columbia . .	Hon. Harry A. Garfield
Illinois	Franklin H. Martin, M. D.
Kentucky	Mrs. Geo. C. Avery
Louisiana	A. L. Metz, M. D.
Maryland	Hon. Theodore Marburg
Minnesota	Mrs. Chas. P. Noyes
Missouri	Percival Chubb
New Jersey . . .	Miss Alice Lakey
Ohio	Marshall Sheppey
Pennsylvania . . .	Hon. Joseph Buffington
Rhode Island . . .	Mrs. C. Lorillard Spencer
Texas	Hon. Geo. E. Barstow
Virginia	Edwin A. Alderman, LL. D.
Washington . . .	Prof. F. M. Padelford
Wisconsin	Hon. James G. Jenkins

In March, 1918, Ephraim Douglass Adams, Ph.D., conducted for the National Security League the campaign of the New England District against premature peace with headquarters at Cambridge. Becoming interested in the need of patriotic education, he succeeded in bringing together the Lowell Normal School, the public schools of the city of Lawrence, and the National Security League, organizing them into one body, the aim of which is to discover in what ways American public schools may best help to make and keep its children genuine patriots and good citizens. The Lawrence Plan Leaflets issued by the National Security League are a development of this activity.

At Stanford University, in July, he organized, with the approval of the Security League, a similar experiment under the direction of the Los Angeles State Normal School and known as "The Los Angeles School for Patriotic Education."

These experiments he believes to be the "first attempts made to determine by what may be called laboratory methods the means of patriotic education in our common schools." Dr. Adams wrote a series of papers for the Third Liberty Loan and distributed 110,000 along the Pacific Coast.

President Edwin A. Alderman, University of Virginia, made public addresses in various cities and communities during 1918 and wrote many papers intended to "stimulate patriotism, to strengthen the national will to win a just war, and to teach young men the deeper meaning of their country." "Seminaries of learning," says President Alderman, "have been the scenes of great difficulty during this period. It was a vital thing to keep alive the spirit and agencies of sound learning, and yet not to deny to the nation the services of its best youth. . . . Perhaps the finest proof of the strivings of American teachers is contained in the proud record of the American college and university in this great crisis."

Mrs. Fannie Fern Andrews sailed for France December, 1918, at the request of the United States Commissioner of Education, authorized by the Secretary of the Interior, to represent the United States Bureau of Education at the Peace Conference. Mrs. Andrews is secretary of the executive committee of the National Conference on Education, which is aiming to secure the educational codes and laws promulgated in all the states of the world since 1900, with special reference to those since 1914. The object of this investigation is to discover to what extent states use their educational systems to further the national ideal.

Mrs. Andrews is secretary of the American School Peace League, which since the war has concentrated on supporting President Wilson and his policies.

In October, 1918, Leo Arnstein was commissioned as Lieutenant-Colonel in the army and assigned successively to the Bureau of Commissioned Personnel and Division of Operations of the General Staff. On December 20, 1918, Colonel Arnstein was honorably discharged.

Before receiving his commission he had, for nine months, served as chairman of the Executive Committee of the New York Chapter of the American Red Cross, in active charge of the chapter work.

Dr. Raymond F. Bacon, Director Mellon Institute of Industrial Research of Pittsburgh, Pa., was commissioned Lieutenant-Colonel in the Chemical Service Section of the National Army on December 1, 1917. He left for France on January 9, 1918, to assume charge of the Research Laboratory of the American Expeditionary Forces at Puteaux, near Paris. Upon the organization of the Chemical Warfare Service, A. E. F., Dr. Bacon was advanced to the grade of Colonel and was appointed Chief of the Technical Division of the Chemical Warfare Service. In that positional capacity he had supervisory charge of the experimental field near Chaumont, as well as of the Research Laboratory at Puteaux. A full account of Dr. Bacon's activities is presented in the January number of the Journal of Industrial and Engineering Chemistry. Dr. Bacon returned to this country on November 17, 1918, and was honorably discharged from the Chemical Warfare Service on December 16, 1918, at which time he resumed the directorship of the Mellon Institute.

Harlan H. Ballard, Librarian and Curator Berkshire Athenæum and Museum, Pittsfield, Mass., under the title of "Adventures of a Librarian," has revealed himself as "detective, psychologist, raconteur, scholar, lover of mankind, all in one."

Dr. W. H. Ballou regards as his greatest accomplishment in 1918 the capture on rod and reel of two ten-pound weakfish and one six and three-quarters pound bluefish in Barnegat Bay, N. J. Incidentally, he conducted an "eat more fish" propaganda for the National Food Administration and has begun a new propaganda under the head of "Everybody go fishing." "If you catch fish you eat 'em," he states, "and save other foods to ship to starving peoples abroad." Also, he wants people to either collect and eat more wild mushrooms for the same purpose, or else propagate and eat more of the cellar mushroom. The despised "toadstool," he demonstrates, is an all-around food, containing the elements within its cap of meats, fish and vegetables. Those who find the mushroom or fish hard to digest can readily correct the difficulty by taking a tablet of pepsin after eating. "A little pepsin," he declares, "either in form of powder, essense or tablet, is a perfect defense against indigestion and offsets possible poisons and ptomaines in foods. Pepsin also destroys toxic bacteria and toxic flagellated worms in food, since it has no part in the digestive apparatus of any known parasite."

Miss Jessie H. Bancroft, founder and first president of "The American Posture League," founded and served as first president of the "American Cooked Food Service"—that boon to tired housekeepers and to households without servants.

This organization, which delivered from 50 to 100 hot meals to homes, was organized as a war measure. It released women for war work, coöperated with the Food and Fuel Administrations in all conservation measures, and placed at the service of the public the skill of trained dietitians, buyers and cooks.

The meals are cooked at central stations planned to feed each a maximum of 500 persons (about 150 families) per day. The cooked food is packed in a series of bowl-shaped aluminum insets that stack, one on another, so that each forms the cover of the one below. These insets are then clamped together and inserted in a cylindrical shell that is insulated. In these containers the food will keep steaming hot, without change in condition or flavor, for over two hours.

These containers are delivered to the homes by motor service and called for the following day. With each is returned the next menu checked to indicate the choice for the next day's dinner. Luncheons are also served. In opening the container the food is found in the order of courses. Cold dishes and breads are carried in a separate container. As a health measure the balanced menus have been very effective, though the dishes do not differ from those of refined tables. Special dietary of various kinds can also be had.

The first station of the American Cooked Food Service was opened February, 1918, on West Seventy-ninth Street, New York City; a second one in Princeton, N. J., toward the close of that year, and plans are under way for others. This service in the original stations is designed to reach the great middle-class homes of the salaried or professional type—the independent homes that can neither accept charity nor pay for luxuries, and that suffer keenly but silently in times of financial stress. When the main features of this type of service have been standardized it is hoped the special problem of an industrial service may be worked out that will go a step farther than the usual community kitchen and deliver to the home of the working man or the shop girl, or its immediate vicinity, suitable meals, hot, well cooked and reasonable in price.

Financially the service has been organized as a self sustaining welfare movement, ranking in that way with the City and Suburban Homes Company, the Provident Loan Society, the Morris Plan, and the National Employment Exchange. It is incorporated under the business laws of the State of New York, but the preferred stock is limited to 6 per cent dividends, so that the prices may be kept within reasonable limits for moderate incomes. The amazing demand for this service from all parts of the country indicates that labor and other conditions make it a greatly needed part of the social reconstruction following the war, indicated, indeed, for a long time before that catastrophe. This phase of the movement appealed equally with the war service to the group of persons who financed the Cooked Food Service, or who, on the consulting or other honorary boards, have given a large volunteer service to start the movement. The need of dietetic guidance for the masses of the people, during times of high food prices especially, has presented an urgent phase of public health that has enlisted the physicians associated with the movement. And all realize that the enormous increase of the "mealing out" habit in this country has made a serious inroad on home life, and shows that a new era in household economy must come to the rescue of family life.

Mrs. Clarice M. Baright has been engaged in working out a bill to be presented to the Legislature having for its object the creation of a great State farm for mental derelicts who to-day are sent to prison, but who instead of punishment should receive hospital attention and be given a chance to work out their own salvation.

Mrs. Baright was the first woman to be admitted to the State Bar Association; to defend a man before a court-martial, and to sit as a member of a lunacy commission.

The Honorable George E. Barstow has been devoting the major part of his time to addresses and writings in connection with the Liberty Loans and those of the Red Cross and the Y. M. C. A. Ward County, of which Barstow is the county seat, went "over the top" in every quota assigned her, and so far over in one loan that to this county the Federal Government assigned the naming of a battleship.

Mr. Barstow's "Carry On—Whither" has been published in pamphlet form and distributed throughout the country.

Lieutenant-Colonel Vilray P. Blair remained in the office of the Surgeon-General until March 30, 1918, and then went to France as Senior Consultant for the Maxillo-Facial Surgical Service for the American Expeditionary Force and was stationed at Neufchâteau. On completion of the organization of this service he returned to America, December, 1918, and took up the work for the cases returning to the United States and was appointed, in addition to other duties, the Consultant in Maxillo-Facial Surgery for this country.

For two years past Cornelius N. Bliss, Jr., has given practically all of his time to the work of the American Red Cross.

Marston Taylor Bogert, LL. D., from April, 1917, to January, 1919, served on thirteen different boards: (1) as member Executive Board of National Research Council; organizer and first chairman of its Division of Chemistry and Chemical Technology, with thirty-two subcommittees; also member of various other of its committees; (2) member, Raw Materials Division War Industries Board, and of its predecessor, General Munitions Board; (3) member U. S. Board on Gas Warfare from its organization to its disbanding; (4) Consulting Chemist, U. S. Bureau of Mines; (5) member Scientific Staff, U. S. Bureau of Standards; (6) member Advisory Committee, U. S. War Trade Board; (7) member Advisory Board, Materials Production Division, Signal Corps, War Department; (8) in consulting capacity U. S. Federal Trade Commission; Military Intelligence Division of General Staff, War Department; Bureau of Investigation, Department of Justice; Postal Censorship, U. S. Post Office Department, and less frequently with other branches of the Government. Commissioned Lieutenant-Colonel and appointed Chief, Chemical Service Section, National Army, and Assistant Director, Gas Service, March 9, 1918; (9) upon consolidation of the Chemical Service Section with other units into the Chemical Warfare Service, under Major-General Wm. L. Sibert as Director, promoted to full Colonel July 13, 1918. Served as Chief of its Relations Section, and of its Intelligence Section; member of its Board of Review, its Claims Board, and of its Headquarters Staff. (10) Chairman, Army Commodity Committee on Chlorine and Chlorine Products, and Chairman of Army Chemical Commodity Committee Chiefs; Purchase, Storage and Traffic Division, General Staff, U. S. A. (11) Liaison Officer for Chemical Warfare Service with Committee on Education and Special Training, General Staff, U. S. A. (12) Member Standardization Section, Purchase Branch, General Staff, U. S. A.

In 1916, Bishop Brent went to England as special emissary, representing his Church. This gave him an opportunity to visit all the fronts, where he was granted every courtesy and did much to interpret the true feeling of America to the warring nations. On the entrance of America into the war he preached before the King at St. Paul's Cathedral in London, outlining the true position of America and her ideals in respect to the world war. Returning to America, he spent some time in reasserting his impressions before Americans, and then left for the Philippine Islands, arriving in August, 1917. After two months devoted to his work among the Moros, he was called to the American Expeditionary Forces in France as a special agent of the Y. M. C. A.

On his arrival in France, General Pershing, a close friend, requested him to prepare a scheme for organizing the various welfare agencies operating in France with special attention to army chaplains, who until then had occupied regimental positions without corps or organization. The Bishop's scheme proving satisfactory, the Commanding General asked him to work it out, and appointed him Senior Chaplain of the American Forces at General Headquarters. The complete unity of purpose in the Chaplain's Corps and the absence of denominational distinction were due to Bishop Brent's leadership.

His work took him to all parts of France, with constant visits to England. In July, 1918, he carried a message from the American Expeditionary Forces to the Grand Fleet in Scapa Flow. He was one of the first three American officers to enter Germany after the signing of the armistice, passing ahead of the advance troops to arrange for hospitalization in the territory to be occupied. After arranging the Chaplains' organization in the Army of Occupation, he returned here in February, 1919, for two weeks, bearing special messages from the Commander-in-Chief to the Secretary of War. After a short visit to Buffalo, the seat of his future activities as Bishop of Western New York, he returned to France in February to close his work.

The Bishop's plans for the American Expeditionary Forces include, first, the "Chaplains' Fellowship," an organization comprised of all the chaplains in the service; and, second, "Comrades in Service," comprised of those who have served in the American army during the world war, whether in foreign service or at home. As soon as this task is completed he will take up his work in Western New York. By virtue of his dual citizenship, as he is an American citizen of Canadian birth, his presence in Buffalo will give him an opportunity to bind strongly together the English-speaking peoples in this continent.

Christian Brinton, M. A., Litt. D., prepared from original sources an illustrated lecture on Contemporary Russian Painting, and during 1918 delivered it before the Washington Society of Fine Arts, at the National Museum, Washington, D. C., and the Haverford Union, Haverford College, Pa. He prepared the Official Illustrated Catalogue of the works of the Russian decorative painter, Boris Anisfeld, first exhibited in America at the Brooklyn Museum, October, 1918. He also prepared for the Ministry of Information, London, and the Worcester Art Museum, the Official Illustrated Catalogue of War Paintings and Drawings by British Artists, first exhibited in America at the Corcoran Art Gallery, Washington, D. C., January, 1919.

Mrs. William Adams Brown has been active as first vice-president of the National War Work Council of the Y. W. C. A., which since the beginning of the war has raised and expended more than sixteen million dollars for the benefit of women replacing men in industry, for the women relatives of men in service and for girls and women whose lives have been affected by changed living conditions in time of war, in the United States and overseas. The work done for the women in the service of the United States Government abroad and for the munition workers of France has won the commendation of General Pershing and of the French Government.

Mrs. Brown has also served as the national president of

the Woman's Land Army of America, a war emergency organization created in 1918, in response to the demand of the government for increased food production. Groups or "units" of women were formed to aid the farmer, supplying his need for seasonal labor at a moderate price. Land Army units were in operation in more than twenty States in the summer of 1918, with an enrollment of 15,000 "farmerettes." More girls applied, both college and industrial, than it was possible to place. While much prejudice had to be overcome, the farmers at the close of the season were found to be so favorable to this new type of labor that the United States Department of Labor proposed an affiliation between the Woman's Land Army and the United States Employment Service which still exists. It was also found that the "units" tended to become community centers in the rural districts where they were established.

F. Kingsbury Bull served from June to December, 1918, as secretary of Region No. 2, Resources and Conversion Section, War Industries Board, with headquarters at Bridgeport, Conn.

Luella Clay Carson, LL. D., since September, 1917, has been Dean of Women in Drury College, Springfield, Mo., founded in 1873 by Congregationalists and occupying a remote territory (no other college of its rank being within two hundred miles). Drury College claims to reach a population more purely American than any other in the country—earnest, single-minded, "and ready for the best that modern ideals can give them."

In the big drives for the Red Cross Fund and the Liberty Loans, Enrico Caruso set aside a sheaf of tempting offers and devoted his time to singing for patriotic purposes. The result of his actual sales for the Third Liberty Loan totalled $3,060,-000; for the Fourth Liberty Loan, $4,300,000. He sang for the Italian Reservists, the Italian War Relief in Washington, D. C.; at the Metropolitan Opera House, for three benefit performances—the Italian Red Cross, the American Red Cross, U. S. Navy Benefit. At Sheepshead Bay he sang for the Police Reserves. In recognition of this work, Commissioner Enright presented Caruso with an illuminated parchment in the name of the city, and Mr. Wanamaker appointed him Captain in the Police Reserve. He sang also for the Lafayette Day at the Waldorf-Astoria; for the people of New York—Mayor Hylan's popular concerts—in the open air in Central Park; before President and Mrs. Wilson for the Italian Blind in the Metropolitan Opera House; for the United War Work campaign in Madison Square Garden, and the U. S. Navy Benefit at the New York Hippodrome. In recognition of his work for the sailors, Admiral Usher presented Caruso with a medal, accompanied by a letter of thanks from Secretary Daniels.

Because of the many and continued generosities of Signor Caruso, the City of New York, on his twenty-fifth jubilee in the Metropolitan Opera House, presented him with a flag of the city.

Mrs. Catherine R. Chenoweth in 1918 served as member in public city work on War Camp Community Service. In February, 1919, she went as delegate to the convention of the League to Enforce Peace, which is now conducting an educational campaign on the subject.

During 1918 Russell H. Chittenden, LL. D., Yale University, represented the U. S. Government on the Inter-Allied Scientific Food Commission, which met in Paris, London and Rome during the spring and early summer of 1918.

Mr. Percival Chubb, president of the Drama League of America, is making every effort to perpetuate the recreational features of the training camps by establishing peoples' theatres in every community. The camp theatres, as he points out, have opened the way to a people's drama and an era of Peoples Theatres. He says in his appeal:

Camp achievements have revealed new potentialities in popular education and recreation; they have set new levels, opened new doors and liberated new resources. The camps have put the schools to the blush. Just as they have hopefully started to convert a songless into a singing America—which the schools had failed to do—so they may develop a new dramatically minded America out of the evening diversions of our soldiery. Rude beginnings in song have evoked here and there a higher kind of lyrical folkcraft. Academicians may squirm at "Good Morning, Mr. Zip," but just as a wincing musician confessed to me that he had become tolerant of this effervescent jingle because it leads on to "Joan of Arc," "Land of Mine," the "Marseillaise"—and beyond; so a stiff-jointed advocate of the "legitimate" may see in a vogue of soldiers' minstrel shows the promise and potency of a new national drama.

This is part of a great issue—that of the changes in our civilization which war-time effort may effectuate. . . . The situation in the large is this: *Hundreds of thousands of our boys have been living in camp a kind of life that is cleaner, comelier and richer than the life they knew before.* . . . Are these lads to return to their old life, lacking in the resources and opportunities they have enjoyed in camp? . . . Or are we to catch these new nascent interests and connections, provide for them and carry them forward? . . . Here, for example, is a division that leaves camp, after skillful handling by a dramatic specialist, ready to *supply itself* for a year ahead with a never-ending variety of entertainment—vaudeville, comic operas, plays: is that to lead nowhere after they get back? . . .

The Drama League of America . . . must bring every influence to bear to get the Heroes' Funds which are beginning to be raised for war "monuments" applied to this end.

Isaac M. Cline, M. D., during 1918 continued the issue of forecasts and warnings for the agricultural, live stock and commercial interests of the southwest, embracing Louisiana, Arkansas, Oklahoma and Texas. It was Dr. Cline who, in 1895, introduced into the United States Weather Bureau the issue of forecasts, stating the expected degrees of temperature for the next succeeding twenty-four to thirty-six hours in connection with warnings of coming freezes, for use of sugar cane and truck growers in protecting their crops. Similar warnings are now being issued by the bureau for use in protecting nearly all interests.

In emphasizing the value of these warnings the *New Orleans Times-Picayune* in an editorial says:

"Our ability to presage a freeze has minimized the possibility of injury to crops and has cut down the losses of the farmers millions of dollars. There was a time when a sudden and unexpected freeze in the sugar district of Louisiana meant a half crop or less. . . . It is not possible to ward off freezes altogether, but by windrowing the cane, which can be done if sufficient notice of the approach of Boreas is given, and protecting of orange groves by smudges and other means of protecting the fruit from the cold, the saving will be a hundred times the cost of the Weather Bureau. The farmers have learned this lesson and are profiting by it."

Harold J. Cook, F. A. A. S., writes: "We maintain and operate a free private museum and laboratory devoted to vertebrate paleontology here, and also include certain types of minerals and archæological specimens. This is visited by numerous people from all parts of the country, and lectures are given to nearly all parties who desire it on the geological history and life record of the earth, and with special reference to the phases represented by the tertiary deposits of the west. Facilities for examining the Agate Springs fossil quarries, where the skeletons of prehistoric creatures lie imbedded in the rock, are provided." Mr. Cook has discovered new and undescribed forms of vertebrate life during the past year, as during many years past. These are studied and results are published from time to time. He also is interested in general phases of geology and oil development work, vocation, ranching and stock farming.

Donald J. Cowling, president of Carleton College and of the Association of American Colleges, served in 1918 as president of the American Council on Education, Washington, D. C. When the armistice was signed, preliminary courses for the training of nurses were being organized by the Council at the request of the Surgeon-General. The Council entertained the British Educational Mission, headed by the Vice-Chancellor of Cambridge University, and had charge of the French

Educational Mission. One hundred and twenty French girls and twenty-five invalided student soldiers were brought to this country on scholarships.

Among his many other activities, President Cowling served as a member of the executive committee, Pilgrim Memorial Fund, a foundation of five million dollars to provide retiring allowances for Congregational ministers.

Henry F. Cutler, principal of Mount Hermon School since 1890, reports that 1,350 of their students have been in military service, and 45 names are marked with the gold star. "The war has interrupted our work in some ways," he says, "but we are glad our boys could do their part to help in bringing in peace."

Bishop James Henry Darlington of Pennsylvania served in 1918 on the following committees: To dispose of the Verdun medals; to receive the Alsace and Lorraine delegates, and to welcome the Archbishop of Greece to New York City.

He acted as chairman for the Serbian Relief Fund and prepared the Sons of the Revolution Memorial cabled to Lloyd George.

France gave him the Legion of Honor; Greece and Serbia have awarded him decorations.

Charles B. Davenport, Ph. D., Department of Experimental Evolution, Cold Spring Harbor, L. I., was for the latter two-thirds of 1918 in the Surgeon-General's Office, Washington, D. C., engaged in statistical studies on the results of the selective draft, with especial reference to defects found in the American population by race and the variation of dimensions of recruits drawn from different sections of the United States inhabited by representatives of different European races.

Henry P. Davison, LL. D., was requested by President Wilson to represent the United States at an international conference of the Red Cross Societies of the Allied nations, to be held after the signing of the treaty of peace. The conference has as its purpose the coördinating and coöperating of civilian relief work.

General Charles G. Dawes, Chief of the American Purchasing Service, was made Commander of the Legion of Honor.

For two years Miss Elsie De Wolfe served with the Third and Tenth French Armies, as a member of the Ambrine Mission on the Western front. For this she was given the "Médaille des Épidemiés" and the "Croix de Guerre" with the bronze star, awarded only to women who have been under fire. The presentation was made by General Humbert of the Third Army.

Besides helping to equip a hospital in Versailles, known as the American Women's Hospital, Miss De Wolfe raised a flotilla of eighteen ambulances, presenting them to the Service de Santé. Some of these ambulances were destroyed by bombardment. So active was the service they performed that two of the chauffeurs received the "Fourragère."

Miss Nina Larrey Duryea, president of the Duryea War Relief, was the first American civilian to cross the battlefield at Ardennes and Argonne, thirteen days after the German retreat in October, 1918. The French Government had given her three motor vans filled with food and clothing for distribution among the blasted villages. Hers was the first organization to carry help to Arras. Again in November, 1918, she crossed the Somme battlefield with Mrs. Seth Barton French, carrying supplies to Lille, where a depot of distribution was established, and where, with the aid of the famous Mayor of Lille, they distributed a carload of garments entrusted to them by the French Government. Milk was also shipped to all the tuberculosis stations of France.

The Duryea War Relief, while in sympathy with the Red Cross, has remained independent for two reasons; first, because the French Government has honored it by replacing the suspended War Relief Clearing House, transporting its cases free, directly and quickly from New York to their Paris depot;

and, second, because its work goes straight from its own hands to those of the poor waiting in France.

The activities of the late Samuel T. Dutton, LL. D., during the past year, in spite of failing health, have been directed to the interests of the World's Court League and its magazine, the Constantinople College for Women, of which he was treasurer, and the work of the American Committee for Relief in the Near East, of which he was chairman of the executive committee.

The World's Court League continued to publish a magazine, to keep its readers informed concerning a League of Nations, and sent it to leaders of international thought in all Allied countries and South America, as well as to statesmen in Washington. As it was finally deemed best to merge several organizations interested in establishing a permanent peace, the name of the "League of Nations Union" was adopted. The first organizations to combine were the World's Court League and the New York Peace Society.

As treasurer and American director of the Constantinople College, Dr. Dutton did much work in keeping the college in funds during a trying period, when the prices of necessities were from five to twenty times greater than in normal times. A new staff of professors and instructors was necessary to replace those disabled by hard work. Classes have been begun in medical training and nursing, the training of teachers and teaching of such practical arts as agriculture and fruit raising.

As an officer of the American Committee for Relief in the Near East, several results were attained meaning much for the suffering peoples involved. The committee, in coöperation with the Red Cross, in the spring of 1918 sent a commission to Palestine under the general direction of John H. Finley. Substantial contributions for the relief of sufferers by this commission were made. Later it sent a distinguished group of medical men and missionaries to Persia, the Caucasus and Mesopotamia, to organize industries and various forms of relief.

Under its auspices, early in January, 1919, a commission of six gentlemen went to Great Britain and France to prepare for extensive relief operations in what has been known as the

Turkish Empire. Three naval ships laden with all kinds of medical and food supplies, vehicles, tractors, etc., to the value of $3,000,000 were dispatched to Constantinople and a carefully selected group of workers numbering 300, including doctors, nurses, sanitary engineers, mechanics and general workers, conveyed by American and British transports.

George W. Elkins is one of the main supporters of the Philadelphia Orchestra, which has won for itself such eulogies from both the critic and the public.

Professor Charles A. Ellwood, University of Missouri, contributes the opening chapter, "The War and Social Evolution," to a new book on reconstruction, entitled "America and the New Era," and edited by Mr. Elisha M. Friedman of the War Finance Corporation. Among Professor Ellwood's contributions to various publications are "The Reconstruction of Education Upon a Social Basis" (The Educational Review for February, 1919), and "Making the World Safe For Democracy" (The Scientific Monthly for December, 1918).

Since we entered the war, Professor Henry W. Farnam, Yale University, has served as chairman of the New Haven Branch of the National Security League; as member of the Publicity Committee of the State Council of Defense, and of the War Bureau of New Haven. During the summer of 1918 he accepted the chairmanship of the Community Labor Board, connected with the United States Employment Service, and also of the executive committee for the Relief of the Near East.

James L. Fieser, during 1918, served as Director, Department of Civilian Relief of the Lake Division of the Red Cross, which also includes Ohio. To Mr. Fieser belonged the responsibility of caring for families of enlisted men, returning soldiers, and victims of disaster. He was chairman of the Committee on Influenza directing the distribution of nurses; president of the Ohio State Conference of Social Work, and member of the Ohio State Council of Defense.

Eugene L. Fisk, M.D., Medical Director of the Life Extension Institute, reports that during 1918 the Institute made over 110,000 periodic health examinations, these examinations being included in services rendered to life insurance policyholders, to individual members of the Institute and to employees of industrial and commercial organizations. In addition to these, many thousands of individuals were examined for the Red Cross, Y. M. C. A., Knights of Columbus, Salvation Army, War Camp Community Service and similar organizations prior to qualifying for overseas service. Interest in the principle of periodic health examinations has been manifested in France, England, Australia, South Africa and even in Japan and China. The book, "How to Live," by Irving Fisher, former president of the National Institute of Social Sciences, has been translated into Japanese, Chinese, Spanish and French. The royalties from this book were used for printing one million pamphlets prepared by Dr. Fisk on the results of the draft examinations and in devising and publishing methods by which those rejected in the draft should receive proper instruction and guidance as to the nature of their troubles and to possible remedial measures. Many life insurance companies and corporations responded to the Institute's appeal, and nearly two hundred important concerns have taken its service.

A community program has been arranged in Grand Mere, Canada, whereby an entire community is to receive the benefits of the health program outlined and supervised by the Life Extension Institute dealing with the fundamental preventive measures, periodic examinations, health inspection, community welfare work, recreation facilities, hospital facilities, etc.

The Institute's book, "Health for the Soldier and Sailor," has been approved by the Secretary of the Navy and placed in all the naval libraries. That 38 per cent of our young men were declined for military service has startled the nation and the work of the Institute has been directed quite as much toward arousing the public mind on these matters as to the reclamation of men for the army.

Mrs. Paul Fitzsimmons (Mrs. French Vanderbilt), since the opening of the Y. W. C. A. Naval Training Station at Newport, has been serving as chairman, a position bringing her into touch with the women enlisted as yeomen and the families of sailors in training at the station. The presence of this important station in Newport has of necessity created various and vital problems, which are not to be solved by the signing of peace. The work therefore will still go on.

Mrs. Fitzsimmons also served as vice-chairman of the Newport Chapter of the Red Cross and head of the Department of Military and Naval Relief.

Professor Henry Jones Ford, Princeton University, has since our entrance into the war published in the Atlantic Monthly "Rights and Wrongs of Pacifism," "The War and the Constitution," "The Growth of Dictatorship," all strongly upholding national authority and the subordination of the rights of the individual to those of the community. "Washington and His Colleagues," covering the first two administrations under the Constitution has been published. "The Cleveland Era," 1880-1896, and a new biography of Alexander Hamilton are nearing completion as we go to press.

Lee K. Frankel, Ph.D., was elected in 1918 Commissioner of the State Board of Charities of New York State and President of the American Public Health Association.

Mrs. Robert A. Franks has, during the past four years, devoted herself to formulating for the "busy woman a simple workable plan for the administering of her household upon the same principles which her husband has found successful in business." Her first book, "Efficiency in the Household," began a nation-wide movement, and since its publication every domestic science school teaches business administration in the household. Mrs. Franks organized in Orange, N. J., a class of fifty-three women who were taught by a local science teacher, Mrs. Franks herself prefacing each lesson with a fifteen minute talk on some question of domestic economy, afterward published in book form. Diplomas were given to the graduating classes at the end of two winters' work. Her "Daily Menus for War Service" were made out for three classes of income—liberal, medium and economical—each and all giving a balanced ration, with calories for every dish and substitutes for meats, butter, sugar and wheat flour which war conditions made needful.

C. Stuart Gager, Director of the Brooklyn Botanic Garden, reports that Volume I. of the Brooklyn Botanic Garden *Memoirs* was published in 1918. This volume of 521 pages contained 33 papers which were presented at the dedication of the Botanic Garden buildings in April, 1917. The endowment of the Botanic Garden was increased during 1918 by $12,500 in two funds—one of $10,000, to be known for the Benjamin Stuart Gager Memorial Fund, and the one of $2,500 for the Martha Woodward Stutzer Memorial Fund. The Botanic Garden has been active in conducting and supervising war gardens throughout the Borough of Brooklyn, and giving lectures at the Garden and other centers on subjects pertaining to gardening.

During the first part of 1918 Virginia C. Gildersleeve, LL.D., Dean of Barnard College, served as chairman of the Columbia University Committee on Women's War Work; as chairman of the Advisory Committee on the Y. M. C. A. Conferences for Women Overseas Workers (a training school conducted at Barnard College for the women who were going over to work in the "Y" huts abroad), and as a member of the Committee on War Service Training for Women College Students of the American Council on Education. Dean Gildersleeve is now the chairman of the Committee on International Relations of the Association of Collegiate Alumnæ, which is undertaking to aid in bringing about closer educational relations between the United States and our Allies.

Armistead C. Gordon, LL.D., published in 1918 a "Life of Jefferson Davis" as one in a series of "Figures of American History." (Scribners.)

In June, 1919, Dr. Gordon retired from the office of Rector of the University of Virginia, after a longer service than that of any other incumbent of the position since the founding of the University by Thomas Jefferson, its first Rector.

John W. Green, in writing present-day differences of opinion, says: "Let us not be unfair to those who differ from us upon government policies. The Union Veterans, and we Confederate Veterans, are both now solidly for the Union and the Constitution, and those who have carefully studied the struggle between us realize that the large majority of both North and South in those dark days were anxious that the Constitution and the Union should be preserved."

Captain Selskar M. Gunn has been in France since July, 1917, working with the International Health Board, the Red Cross and French government in introducing American methods adapted to the psychology of the country in the interests of anti-tuberculosis work and the lessening of infant mortality. On January 2, 1919, he was decorated by the French Government with the Cross of the Legion d'honneur.

Dr. Samuel H. Halley served as chairman of the Committee on Agriculture, Kentucky Council of Defense. As Kentucky is an agricultural state, the work of Dr. Halley's Committee assumed unusual importance. "When scarcity of labor and the demand of farm hands for unprecedented remuneration in the wheat harvest threatened the good feeling between the farmers and the harvest hands this committee, in conjunction with the County Councils of Defense, fixed the price to be paid wherever dissatisfaction arose and in this way serious trouble was obviated and the crops were saved."

Mrs. William Pierson Hamilton opened a camp at her country place, Table Rock Farms, Sterlington, New York, near Tuxedo, for the New York State Land Army workers. As vice-president of the Woman's Land Army of America she was appointed its delegate and sailed for England and France to study conditions of women as an aid to agricultural work.

Hastings H. Hart, LL.D., of the Russell Sage Foundation, at the request of Governor Charles Henderson of Alabama, made in 1918 a study of the Social Institutions and Agencies of Alabama, as related to War Activities. Dr. Hart had previously made similar studies of West Virginia, South Carolina and Florida. His method has been to visit the charitable and correctional institutions and to talk to people informed on such subjects, including convicts and paupers, in this way making a thorough and exhaustive study of the subject. His conclusions after his visit to Alabama are embodied in a report published by the Russell Sage Foundation, and appear as letters to the Governor and to the people. In his letter to the people he says: "When you open any page of a volume of national statistics, the first name you see is Alabama. . . .

"But when you come to the record of her social development, you find Alabama second or third in the profit derived from the labor of her convicts, but far down the list in her efforts for their reformation; high in illiteracy, but low in public school education; high in the quality of care for the insane, but absolutely without care for the feeble-minded who are even more in need of it; high in her receipts of donations from northern states for the support of educational institutions for the negroes, but low in appropriations for the state university; high in protection of the health of hogs and cattle, but low in protection of the health of the people."

In this report his endeavor has been to secure a complete change of the financial administration of the State.

George A. Hastings was for some months during 1918 the executive of the war work department of the National Committee for Mental Hygiene coöperating with the Surgeon General's office in providing facilities for the mental examination of soldiers and for the treatment of nervous and mental disorders developing in the U. S. military forces here and abroad. As executive secretary of the New York Committee on Feeblemindedness and the Mental Hygiene Committee of the State Charities Aid Association, he has helped direct public and legislative attention to the further needs of the insane and feebleminded in New York State, and helped to promote the statewide campaign for prevention of mental disorders.

The Honorable David Jayne Hill was elected president of the National Association for Constitutional Government, the purpose of which is as follows:

"It shall be the object of the Association to propagate a wider and more accurate knowledge of the Constitution of the United States, and of the distinctive features of constitutional government as conceived by the founders of the Republic; to inculcate an intelligent and genuine respect for the organic law of the land; to bring the minds of the people to a realization of the vital necessity of preserving it unimpaired, and particularly in respect to its broad limitations upon the legislative power and its guarantees of the fundamental rights of life, liberty, and property; to oppose attempted changes in it which tend to destroy or impair the efficacy of those guarantees, or which are not founded upon the mature consideration and deliberate choice of the people as a whole; and to this end, to publish and circulate appropriate literature, to hold public and corporate meetings, to institute lectures and other public addresses, to establish local centers or branches, and generally to promote the foregoing objects by such means as shall from time to time be agreed upon by the Association or by its governing bodies."

The Honorable Edward W. Hines, in October, 1917, was appointed chairman of the Kentucky Council of Defense and, according to his report of January 1, 1919, made the following committee assignments: on Agriculture, Finance, Health and Education, Industry, Labor, Military Affairs, Public Safety and Publicity. One of the first activities of the Council was to coördinate its efforts with those of the Woman's Committee, which had for some time been in active existence. Regular meetings of the Council were held twice a month; the Executive Committee met twice each week or oftener as emergencies arose. The late William D. Cochran, chairman of the Committee on Health and Education, died under the strain, his latest work having been "the organization of the 'Back to School' drive for the purpose of returning to the schools those who, during the war, attracted by the high wages of war work or for other reasons, had left such institutions."

Mrs. Ripley Hitchcock, in 1918, organized the Art War Relief, serving as its chairman. Under its initiative over five hundred landscape targets were painted by eminent artists for machine gun instruction in our training camps. Mrs. Hitchcock, under the Surgeon General, also assisted in organizing the War Service Classes, from which one hundred students were graduated as hospital aids in craft work for the reconstruction of disabled soldiers and sailors.

She was asked to organize the National Committee of One Hundred on Memorial Buildings, having as its object the creation of living tributes to those who served in the Great War. The erection of useful community buildings was advocated, and in two months the coöperation of some 400 towns was secured. As a member of the Woman's Roosevelt Memorial Association, Mrs. Hitchcock has been active in organizing plans for the purchase and restoration of Theodore Roosevelt's birthplace at 28 East 20th Street, New York. At her suggestion it was agreed to purchase the adjoining dwelling, making it a center for civic, historic and patriotic Americanization, thus making the memorial a vital factor in national development.

The Honorable Charles B. Hubbell, on August 1, 1918, was appointed by Governor Whitman as Public Service Commissioner, 1st District, State of New York, to succeed the Honorable Oscar S. Straus.

During the summer of 1918 George W. Hunter, Ph.D., served as Educational Director in the Washington District, an area covering at one time twenty-one camps and about 100,000 men.

"The work, before the signing of the armistice," says Dr. Hunter, "was directed mainly to making our men better fighters, much emphasis being placed on French and on the teaching of English. Since the signing of the armistice, morale work has superseded the class work and a definite program of vocational guidance, vocational education, better citizenship and general morale lectures. While the work is given to fewer men the problem becomes an increasingly difficult one now because of the rapid movement of troops."

Ellsworth Huntington, Ph.D., Yale University, prepared in 1918 a volume entitled, "World Power and Evolution." The book is primarily a study of the effect of varying conditions of health upon fluctuations in business, in history, and in evolution.   A detailed examination of about 9,000,000 deaths in the United States, France and Italy from 1899 to 1915, a still more detailed study of 400,000 deaths in New York City from 1877 to 1884, and a more general study of 50,000,000 other deaths all over the world show that health is affected by daily, weekly and seasonal variations in the weather far more than by any other cause.   "Incredible as it may seem," Dr. Huntington says, "the ebb and flow of business seems to follow the march of health to a most extraordinary degree.   A comparison of bank clearings, prices, immigration and other conditions with fluctuations in health from year to year suggests that as a factor in sociology health has an importance which has only begun to be realized."

In addition to writing "World Power and Evolution," Dr. Huntington served in the Army as captain in the Military Intelligence Division, where he is still stationed.

William Mann Irvine, Ph.D., LL.D., celebrated, April, 1918, the 25th anniversary of his installation as Head Master of the Mercersburg Academy, Mercersburg, Pennsylvania. During that time the school, known to all the great educators of the world, has grown from an entry of forty boys and four instructors, to one of four hundred boys and forty-four instructors, representing every state in the Union and eighteen foreign countries.   Among the philanthropic activities cultivated among these boys, is the support of a Medical Missionary in China; educational work among the negroes of the South, and the education of six Chinese boys at an American college in China.   During the Great War 760 Mercersburg boys were in active military service, one being the first American to win the Italian War Cross, while another, who landed with General Pershing, won the Croix de Guerre.

At the suggestion of LeRoy Jeffers, who is Manager of the Book Order Office of the New York Public Library and Librarian of the American Alpine Club, an association was formed in 1916, of which he is the secretary.   Under the title of the Bureau of Associated Mountaineering Clubs of North America, it now comprises 24 organizations with an individual membership of about 24,000. The distinctively mountaineering and outdoor clubs are the American Alpine, Adirondack Camp and Trail, Appalachian Mountain, British Columbia Mountaineering, Colorado Mountain, Field and Forest, Fresh Air, Green Mountain, Hawaiian Trail and Mountain, Klahhane, Mazamas, Mountaineers, Prairie, Rocky Mountain Climbers, Sagebrush and Pine, and Sierra. Associated with these, and having many aims in common, are the American Game Protective Association, American Museum of Natural History, Boone and Crockett Club, Geographic Society of Chicago, Geographical Society of Philadelphia, National Association of Audubon Societies, National Park Service, and the New York Zoölogical Society.

Apart from mountaineering activities and the exploration of mountain regions, the Association is coöperating with the National Park Service in creating, protecting, and developing our national parks and monuments. The common aim is the protection of tree and flower, of bird and animal, in their natural environment.

The secretary issues an annual bulletin of information giving the officers and activities of these members. He is also lecturing on National Wonders of the United States and Canada, and is publishing a series of articles of exploration and travel in little known regions of North America.

Mr. Jeffers has gathered a large collection of mountaineering literature and photographs in the New York Public Library, to which the American Alpine Club has added its collection; and he has compiled a bibliography of the literature.

Miss Content Johnson, vice-president of the Pen and Brush Club, organized in 1918 an Art Club, the purpose of which is educational and aimed at stimulating an understanding of art in the vicinity of Washington Square, New York City. Miss Johnson is chairman of the Art Committee, Miss Cecilia Beaux its honorary chairman. The first exhibition was arranged by Mrs. Philip Lydig, Dr. Christian Brinton and Miss Johnson. Exhibitions are to be held semi-annually. 'Miss Johnson exhibited thirty of her paintings at the Majestic Art Salon.

Emory R. Johnson, Ph.D., Sc.D., president of the National Institute, served as Assistant Director of the Bureau of Transportation of the War Trade Board until the first of June, 1918, when he began an investigation of ocean rates and terminal charges for the United States Shipping Board. That investigation lasted through 1918 and until June first, 1919. At the time this investigation was authorized, the Shipping Board was especially interested in ascertaining what rates would meet the costs of services during war-time conditions. With the signing of the armistice and with the approach of normal peace-time conditions, the Shipping Board's interest in rates has become primarily that of regulating the services and charges of ocean carriers and terminal companies. The report by Dr. Johnson upon ocean rates and terminal charges discusses the problems of regulation, and recommends a rate policy for consideration by the Shipping Board. The subject of port terminal services and charges is dealt with at length in a special report prepared by Dr. C. O. Ruggles, of the University of Ohio, under the supervision of Dr. Johnson. These reports have been published by the Shipping Board for public distribution.

In addition to these government services, Dr. Johnson has continued his work at the University of Pennsylvania, and has taken an active interest in the work of the Railroad Committee of the Chamber of Commerce of the United States. This committee has organized a series of conferences on the railroad question for the purpose of assisting in the formulation of a program of legislation to be enacted for the future government regulation of the railroads.

The literary activities of Miss Elizabeth Jordan in 1918 consisted of the serial and book publication of a new novel, "The Wings of Youth," together with the writing of numerous short stories. Her newspaper syndicate work included three articles weekly, published simultaneously in leading newspapers throughout the country. She was able to include much war propaganda and work for liberty bonds and thrift stamps. As a gratuitous work for the suffrage cause she collected and edited the suffrage novel, "The Sturdy Oak," published serially by Collier's Weekly and in book form by Henry Holt. All the proceeds of this book went to the suffrage cause.

At St. Dunstan's, Regent's Park, London, the residence of Mr. and Mrs. Otto H. Kahn, given by them to the English government for the care of blinded soldiers, one of the first things taught is dancing, "since dancing gives a sense of balance and a feeling of security in getting about." The blind learn to play checkers, dominoes and chess, and to read the Braille type. Writing on the typewriter is taught as a matter of course. "Our stenographers," Sir Arthur Pearson says, "leave with a speed of one hundred words a minute and can probably do one hundred and twenty-five. There are forty-two of our men working in offices in London, and are getting normal wages, or higher wages than they did before in their old positions. Our telephone operators do the work just as well as seeing persons. In a competitive examination of masseurs in which 342 contestants from all parts of England took part, one of our men took second place."

Robert L. Kelly, LL.D., served from July to December, 1918, as Executive Secretary of the American Council on Education of the National Publicity Campaign in behalf of the Students' Army Training Corps and of American education in general.

Under the joint auspices of the Association of American Colleges and the American Council on Education 114 French girls and over 30 disabled French soldiers were placed in American colleges and universities, on scholarships, carrying the cost of board and room, tuition and fees. This plan of international scholarships is now being extended to include representatives from other allied governments.

The American Council on Education had charge of the tours across the continent of the British Educational Mission and of the French Mission of Scholars sent by their respective governments to study educational conditions in the United States and to strengthen international sympathies.

William Kirk, Ph.D., professor of Economics and Sociology in the University of Rochester, has been associated with the

American Red Cross as Director of Education in the Bureau of Civilian Relief for the Western New York District.

John C. Kirtland, L.H.D., is chairman of a committee which, at the Phillips Exeter Academy, has planned a summer session of the school, designed to help solve the problem of wastage in American education, by putting the equipment of the school in use for a considerable part of the time in which it now stands idle, thereby "giving in larger measure the service for which it is intended." Dr. Kirtland is chairman of the summer session faculty.

Miss Mary Lois Kissell, A.M., formerly Associate Professor of Home Economics at the University of California, says that the great waste to the poor in the matter of poor fabrics manufactured into clothes, which go to pieces almost before they are worn, led to the production of her "Yarn and Cloth Making," an economic study prepared as a college and normal school text-book, as a preliminary to fabric study and as a reference for teachers. "It is an intensive study of a narrow but fundamental field with a focus upon the economic gain achieved as spindle and loom became more efficient in producing improved yarn and cloth. The plan was tested out at one of our universities, and the results of the experiment far exceeded expectation. For, as the student followed the expanding science step by step and traced the definite gain in each progressive type, she gained two important things: a clear knowledge of good yarn and cloth, together with a rich appreciation of economic values."

Strickland L. Kneass, C.E., has been assisting in the design and construction of appliances for large naval rifles used on the American front and has been awarded two additional patents for safety devices for railroad motive power operating devices.

Miss Alice Lakey was chairman of the Women's Committee of Cranford for the Third and Fourth Liberty Loans, and was credited with sales amounting, respectively, to $75,850 and $218,000. In 1918 she was appointed a member of the

Advisory Council of the Women's College of New Jersey and was also elected president of the Cranford Village Improvement Association. As a charter member of the New York Milk Committee, Miss Lakey was elected chairman of Women's Day at the National Milk and Dairy Farm Exposition held in New York May, 1918, and again in 1919. Miss Lakey is chairman of the Liberty Service Medal Committee for the State of New Jersey.

In October, 1918, Professor Frederic S. Lee of Columbia University was sent to England and France by the United States Public Health Service to investigate certain matters pertaining to war industries. These included the poisoning of munition makers by T.N.T. and other high explosives, and the methods that had been found useful to protect the workers; industrial fatigue and the status of its investigation in Europe; and the industrial work of women. Professor Lee was given unusual opportunities by scientific men and government officials to study these subjects, and since his return he has submitted a report upon them to the government. He has recently published a book, "The Human Machine and Industrial Efficiency."

Miss Luisita Leland, chairman of the New York Committee and vice-president of the National Executive of the Fatherless Children of France, a society which aims to rebuild France through the home, reports that during 1918, 150,000 orphans have been helped. The plan of the society has been to add to the small pensions given by the French Government to orphans of soldiers killed in the Great War, and so to enable the remaining parent or guardian to keep those children at home instead of sending them as waifs to an institution.

Miss Leland has the highest official authority for denying the widely spread report in this country as to the present wealth of France and the comfort and affluence of her people. "There are now," she says, "over 2,000,000 orphans of France, over 1,000,000 of whom are in great need." The society, therefore, of which she is chairman, has made a nationwide effort to interest the school children of the United States in their little allies, and has met with the greatest success.

Groups of children were formed, of a class or division, and by subscribing only a few cents a week or a month, each group was able to adopt a child and together they wrote to it, worked for it and sent it little gifts, such as children love to exchange. This has been found to have an excellent effect in stimulating interest in our school children in their lessons and outlook, and it is drawing them very close to the French children whose childish letters they receive."

Miss Leland has made many public addresses on the subject. Two hundred committees have been formed. Many of the orphans adopted by our own soldiers in France are being cared for through the Fatherless Children of France.

Mr. Adolph Lewisohn was president of the National Committee on Prisons and Prison Labor which devoted practically all its energies in 1917 and 1918 to war activities. This organization was the first to suggest the application of the "work or fight" principle. It placed at the disposal of the Federal Government its entire staff and was frequently consulted by the government on matters relating to interned enemy aliens, prisoners of war and military prisoners.

Mr. Lewisohn was a member of the War Industries Board, and of the Waste-Reclamation Section which inaugurated a system for the saving and salvage of waste materials by the use of prison and other labor. He was chairman of the Thrift Committee of the Industrial Department of the Y. M. C. A. and of the Home Gardens Committee of the International Child Welfare League. He made numerous addresses and appeals in behalf of the various liberty loans.

Miss Sophie Irene Loeb has been reëlected to the presidency of the New York City Board of Child Welfare, which in 1918 cared for 15,000 children and 5,000 widows at a cost of $1,750,000. This has been done "at a cost of 3 per cent, that is administration expenses of but three cents on the dollar, the lowest of any city or state in the United States."

Miss Loeb was also elected president of the National Union of Public Officers of Child Welfare Boards, which held a meeting in the City Hall of New York City in February, 1919, where it was agreed to promote the principle of home life for the child wherever possible, and further agreed to promote the widows' pension law in all sections of the country.

In 1918, Miss Loeb, having proved that the poorest people had to pay the highest price for coal, made a tour of the Pennsylvania coal mines. After a series of articles on the subject she laid the subject before the Coal Committee in Washington, where hearings were conducted. In January, 1919, she accompanied the Senate Committee to Pottsville, where her own previous findings were substantiated, the monopoly disclosed being so apparent as to demand government interference in fixing prices of coal.

George E. MacLean, LL.D., reports as his activities during the year beginning May, 1918: "By invitation I lectured in the University of Cambridge in the course of Local Lectures Summer Meeting, 1918, devoted to the United States of America, my topic being 'American State Universities, Colleges and School Systems'; in the autumn in Bedford College, University of London, in a course of public lectures entitled: 'Aspects of the History of Life and Thought in the United States of America.' I gave several lectures under the auspices of the Victoria League at British Hospitals in London. I became secretary of the British Branch of the American University Union in Europe and recently the Acting Director, and served under the Army Educational Commission, A. E. F., Y. M. C. A., as Director for Universities and Colleges in Great Britain and Ireland. I am on the Executive Committee of the British American Fellowship of which the Rt. Hon. the Earl Beauchamp, K.G., is president and Arthur Carlton, Esq., J.P., Mayor of Worcester, is chairman.

"I am also member of the Executive Committee of the English Speaking Union of which Rt. Hon. A. J. Balfour is president in Great Britain and Ex-Pres. Taft in the United States. I am a member of the editorial board of the 'Landmark,' the magazine of the English Speaking Union."

Mrs. Howard C. Mansfield in 1918 organized with the approval of the Surgeon General, U. S. Army, a series of War Service Classes for Training Reconstruction Aides for Military Hospitals. One hundred and two Reconstruction Aides were graduated, all of whom have appointments overseas or in the military hospitals in this country. The classes closed on January 30, 1918.

———

Dr. Franklin H. Martin, Chairman of the Committee on Medicine of the Advisory Commission and Chairman of the General Medical Board of the Council of National Defense, Colonel in the Medical Corps of the U. S. Army, was one of the leaders in the great work of coördinating the civilian medical resources of the country with the official governmental programs of the Army, Navy, Public Health Service and Red Cross. On the General Medical Board have served seventy-five of the leading physicians and surgeons of the country, formally appointed by the Secretary of War, and through the patriotic work of the more than 2,000 state and county committees appointed by the Chairman of the General Medical Board, practically the entire medical profession of the country was enrolled for war service in the Army, Navy, Public Health Service, Provost Marshal General's Department and Volunteer Medical Service Corps. Committees of the Board—other than the state and county committees in the field, have enlisted the services of 234 individual medical men in activities which the following committee titles will connote: Civilian coöperation in combating venereal diseases, dentistry, editorial (publication of medical manuals), hospitals, hygiene and sanitation, industrial medicine and surgery, legislation, medical advisory boards, medical schools, nursing, states activities, surgery, women physicians, child welfare and Volunteer Medical Service Corps. The last named body, a great civilian medical reserve of which Dr. Edward P. Davis was chairman, the organization of which President Wilson emphatically endorsed, gave notable evidence of its value during the recent influenza epidemic, its members answering successive calls from Surgeon General Blue of the Public Health Service as to elicit from him the tribute that he found it "most gratifying to certify to the prompt response." Information concerning the qualifications of about 70,000 doctors, additional to approximately 40,000 commissioned in governmental service, has been transferred to code cards and will be placed in the Library of the Surgeon

General of the Army where it will be maintained as a permanent record of the medical profession.

Dr. Martin visited England, France and Italy in November and December, 1918, on a special mission for the Council of National Defense.

Since the outbreak of hostilities in 1914, Miss Anna C. Maxwell, R.N.M.A., has crossed the ocean twice in order to visit the scene of action, personally inspecting over one hundred army hospitals. In speaking of the patriotic service rendered by the nurses of this country, Miss Maxwell refers to the fact of their having been given neither rank nor status, and that "in consequence they worked under a serious handicap, being rated below the non-commissioned officer, and securing only such authority as their own personalities commanded. Their opportunity, however, for giving anæsthetics and lending valuable and efficient aid in carrying out the treatment of wounds such as the world has never seen; their satisfaction in the knowledge that they could bring to the soldier in his extremity that atmosphere of home which only a devoted woman can create, are their inestimable reward."

During the past year Dr. N. E. McIndoo, Insect Physiologist, Department of Agriculture, Washington, D. C., has published the following papers: (1) the olfactory organs of a coleopterous larva and (2) the olfactory organs of Diptera; and now has the following in press: (3) nicotine sulphate as an ovicide and larvicide; (4) Derris (an East Indies fish poison) as in insecticide; (5) the olfactory sense of lepidopterous larvæ; and (6) the olfactory organs of Orthoptera.

Douglas C. McMurtrie, in 1918, served as director, Red Cross Institute for Crippled and Disabled Men; and as president, Federation of Associations for Cripples. He was editor of the American Journal of Care for Cripples, a member of the Active Vocational Board, office of the Surgeon General, U. S. A., and also of the National Commission on Standardization of Artificial Limbs. His "The Disabled Soldier" was published by the Macmillan Company.

Hon. Cyrus C. Miller, during 1918, served as chairman for the Borough of The Bronx of the Second Liberty Loan Campaign; chairman of the Condemnation Commission having in charge the acquisition of land for the Bronx Parkway from the Botanical Gardens to the City Line; Fuel Administrator for Bronx County; Director of Transportation and Distribution of the New York Federal Food Board; Director of Transportation and Distribution on the New York State Food Commission; member of the Commission to Investigate the Surface Railroad Situation in the City of New York on the West Side; Director, Bronx Union Branch Y. M. C. A.; Director, Bronx Board of Trade; President, Boy Scouts of America, Bronx Branch.

John F. Moore has for many years been at the head of the Railroad Department of the Y. M. C. A., establishing welfare work for a million railroad men in this country. He has also initiated similar work in China, Japan, Philippines, etc.

Dave H. Morris served as Government Appeal Agent in New York City for the State of New York Selective Service. The Selective Service Organization of the United States indicated the names of 24,000,000 men from whom the United States Army was selected. Mr. Morris states that "during the whole time there was not one serious objection to the draft," and he feels "it to be an achievement which stamps the people as worthy of the ideals of our democracy." Concerning the organization of Board 138, Mr. Morris makes the following statement:

"This organization is still in existence and it seems almost a crime that it must some day disband. It is very closely in touch with the people everywhere and is one of the few times when the Federal government has an agency to which the people in their own districts can go. This contact with the Federal power has advantages and possibilities and it is hoped that the organization can in some way survive so that these relations may continue.

"An interesting point in regard to Board No. 138 is that the district it covered contained a population of more than one third *enemy* aliens. Few realize what this means in the problems presented, not only in the raising of an army to fight the nations to which this third owe their allegiance, but also, in assimilating them to our national life and ideals. Every one who has done any war work in any capacity must feel, above all other considerations, that Americanization of our entire population is our immediate and first duty to all who live in our great country."

As chairman of the War Service Commission of the Medical Women's National Association, and as chairman of the Executive Committee of the American Women's Hospital, Dr. Rosalie S. Morton established work which resulted in the raising of $300,000 and the foundation of four hospitals in France and two in Serbia, staffed by women who are caring for men, women and children in devastated districts. Through the above and other organizations, Dr. Morton was able to aid and relieve the dependents of soldiers, sailors and marines in the North Carolina mountains, the Middle West, and other parts of the United States, besides sending supplies to Serbia, to American and French army hospitals, and to the refugees, prisoners of war, the sick and the wounded in Switzerland, Halifax, Palestine, France and Serbia.

Dr. Morton began her war work in 1914. In 1915, at the request of the New York secretary of the Grenfell Association, she spent the summer in Labrador to relieve the deficit of doctors working in the mission hospitals. The summer and autumn of 1916 she gave to a study of war hospitals in England and France and to service in Macedonia. On going to and from Salonica, she served on French hospital boats. In 1917 she organized and helped get in readiness the Woman's Army General Hospital, authorized by General William C. Gorgas to receive wounded American soldiers.

Mrs. Frederick Nathan has accepted the chairmanship of the Woman's Roosevelt Memorial Association, and is serving as one of its executive committee. She is also a director of the Women's Pan-American Board Table, vice-president of the Association to Promote Better Housing Conditions and has been elected one of the executive board of the Girls' Community Club House at 109 East 30th Street, New York. Mrs.

Nathan still retains her office in the National State and City Consumers' Leagues, as vice-president in the National and State Leagues, and as honorary president in the City League.

Mrs. Charles P. Noyes, president of the Y. W. C. A., St. Paul, Minnesota, during 1918, served on the State Suffrage Board, the N. W. Field Committee of the Y. W. C. A., the City Americanization Committee, the Police Woman's Committee, and the Social Service Committee of the federated churches.

On August 1, 1917, when Lieutenant-Commander Thomas M. Osborne assumed command of the Portsmouth Naval Prison, there were 486 men confined in the prison. There were 30 or more armed guards on duty at all times. No man was allowed to think for himself, being governed entirely by the set rules as enforced by the armed guards. Few men were permitted to return to the service. At the expiration of a sentence a man usually got a dishonorable discharge and was returned to civilian life, unprepared to meet the obstacles created by his misfortune.

Since August 1, 1917, owing to the increased enlistment in the Navy, 5,133 men have been convicted by general court-martial and confined in the prison, making the total number of men under Mr. Osborne's command during the period he has been in command of the prison 5,628. Of this number 1,905 have been restored to duty and thus far but 271 have been reconfined by reason of breaking their probation. There have been certain offenses which by reason of the regulations would not permit of the offender returning to duty. Of these men there have been 1,684 dishonorably discharged and many of this number have immediately enlisted in the army and in a few cases become officers, while others have entered important civilian employment.

The prison, under Mr. Osborne, is run almost entirely by prisoners, with but three guards stationed at the entrances and eight sentries guarding the prison reservation. The system of the Mutual Welfare League, as instituted at Auburn and Sing Sing prisons, is in full sway at the Naval Prison and working satisfactorily. Trade schools have been established and a school of letters maintained, where instruction is given by the most intelligent prisoners to the less fortunate. From an educational point of view remarkable results have been obtained. The prison has supplied over a thousand men each day for work in the Navy Yard.

Each individual is allowed to think for himself, talk with his fellow prisoners or with any officer at the prison, and the general atmosphere of the prison is that of striving for better living, a higher sense of honor and justice to mankind. The loss of liberty with the disgrace involved in a prison sentence is sufficient punishment for errors committed, and the present system is building up character instead of returning the men to society broken in spirit and ready to commit crime at the first opportunity.

Charles L. Pack, LL.D., is president of the National War Garden Commission.

The 5,000,000 war gardens established by him raised in 1918 over $535,000,000 worth of food. Trinity College of Hartford, Conn., conferred on him the honorary degree of LL.D., June, 1919, in recognition of these services.

As president of the American Forestry Association, he commenced in 1918 to advocate the planting of memorial trees in honor of the soldier dead.

He was made chairman of the French Agricultural Committee of the American Society for Devastated France and is a member of the Executive Board. He accepted in 1919 an invitation from the French Government to attend a conference in France relating to French reforestation, and as president of the American Forestry Association, he has assumed the work of aiding France, Belgium and England in their plans for reforestation. The losses to their forests during the war have been enormous, and help must come from America as most of their mother, or seed-trees, were destroyed.

The Honorable John M. Parker, Federal Food Administrator for Louisiana, reports that the work in his state was marked by "the highest degree of coöperation and patriotism on the part of practically everyone in every walk of life," so that "in the final check on sugar, there was a report of less than two per cent in the amount allotted and amounts issued according to cards." That which made the work of the Louisiana Food Administration of vital importance during the war was the fact that "Louisiana is not only one of the greatest sugar and rice producing states, but that the City of New Orleans stands second in the United States in export."

Dr. Raymond Pearl was engaged throughout the year 1918 as Chief of the Statistical Division of the United States Food Administration. At the request of Mr. Hoover, he spent the months of October and November in Europe in connection with the work of the Interallied Scientific Commission on Nutrition. In July, 1918, Doctor Pearl began the organization of the Department of Biometry and Vital Statistics, of which he is in charge in the School of Hygiene and Public Health of Johns Hopkins University. After March 1, 1919, his entire time will be devoted to this work at the Johns Hopkins University.

During 1918 Professor William Lyon Phelps served as a United States Four-Minute Man, speaking in Connecticut, New York and Michigan. He also served as a delegate to Win the War Convention in Philadelphia, and Limit Man in War Savings Stamps.

Two books of his were published during this time: "The Advance of English Poetry in the Twentieth Century Theatre" and "The Twentieth Century Theatre."

During the past year the members of the international society known as the Associated Observers of Mars, of which Professor W. H. Pickering is the secretary, have continued their investigations of this interesting planet. Thirty-six drawings of its surface by nine of their leading observers have been published in Popular Astronomy for January, 1919. These give the most complete and recent views of its more striking features. Other reports published in 1918 deal with the latest theory of the canals and other matters of interest. Twenty-one of these reports have now appeared, the last one dealing with the seasonal and other changes that are continually occurring upon its surface, and also with the curious doubling effect that has been noted by several observers.

Mrs. Cornelia B. Sage Quinton, Director of the Buffalo Fine Arts Academy, arranged sixteen special exhibitions during 1918. Among these were exhibitions of war posters; selected paintings by American artists; paintings of the late Henry Golden Dearth; paintings by soldiers of France and arranged by Monsieur Ludovic Leblanc; "Carry On" by Edwin Howland Blashfield, and in December the work of the Students of the Art School in the class of Occupational Therapy.

Fifteen life members were added to the list of the Academy and the city of Buffalo appropriated $30,000 for its use for the fiscal year, 1918-1919.

Joseph Edward Raycroft, A.B., M.D., Professor of Hygiene and Physical Education, Director of the Department of Physical Education, Princeton University, served in 1918 as member of the War Department Commission on Training Camp Activities, and chairman of the Committee on Athletics. As chairman he formulated and put into operation a program of physical and bayonet training for use in our army. A demonstration of its value in training recruits and of its group games and mass athletics has influenced the plans now being considered for physical and athletic games in our schools and colleges.

William E. Ritter, Ph.D., Director, Scripps Institution for Biological Research of the University of California, La Jolla, gives as the basal ideas of his "War Science and Civilization": (1) War is a primitive and usually ineffective attempt to solve problems which only statesmanship, jurisprudence, science and ethics are competent to solve; (2) The highest aim of science in its application to practical affairs is to relieve all mankind from the fear of physical want and disease; (3) Civilization is organic evolution on the plane of man's spiritual nature.

Dr. Ritter has made several contributions to the bulletins published monthly by the Society to Eliminate Economic Causes of War of Wellesley Hills, Massachusetts.

Mrs. Lucy H. Robertson, President Emeritus of Greensboro College, was for a year chairman of the Child Welfare Department of the North Carolina Division of the Council of National Defense.

Hon. Simon W. Rosendale, former Attorney-General of the State of New York, in a letter addressed to Congressman B. Sanford, September, 1918, says regarding the Jewish movement known as "Zionism": "This project has not had and does not have the general sympathy or approval of that large religious organization of citizens known as Reform Jews of America, nor of a representative body in Great Britain known as the League of British Jews—headed by such prominent Englishmen as Claude Montefiore and others.

"It should be stated at the outset that the great body of Reform Jews in this country maintain that they are Jews by religion only and Americans by nationality."

Speaking for the Reform Jewish Congregation of America, of which the late Rabbi Isaac M. Wise was the leading spirit— a union numerically in the majority until the great influx of Jews from Russia, Galicia, Roumania—Mr. Rosendale claims that there is no such thing as a Jewish flag, and that the Jews of America recognize only the Stars and Stripes.

Leo S. Rowe, LL.D., has since April 17, 1917, been serving as Assistant Secretary of the Treasury.

H. H. Rusby, Dean of the College of Pharmacy, Columbia University, among his other activities in 1918 instructed a Unit of the Students' Army Training Corps in the School of Pharmacy at Columbia University.

Mr. and Mrs. William Salomon continued during 1918 the support of their hospital, St. Katherine's Lodge, Regent's

Park, London, which was designed especially for reconstructive or orthopedic work for wounded American officers.

S. J. Shwartz, in October, 1917, was appointed State Merchant Representative of the United States Food Administration, Louisiana, working in conjunction with John M. Parker, and having charge of all publicity matter for the state. He was also appointed a member of the War Economy Committee of the National Retail Dry Goods Association, which provided ways and means for releasing men for war service and putting women in their places and originated the slogan "Carry it home and keep it," thereby encouraging customers to carry their bundles so as to save horsepower and gasoline. In November, 1917, he was appointed Director, Bureau of Supplies, American Red Cross, handling all finished supplies to Louisiana, Mississippi and Alabama. He installed a fumigating plant for fumigating all knitted garments and a cutting wheel for cutting gauze for bandages.

During the past year, and after leaving the hospital for French wounded where they had worked for two years, Madame Basil de Sélincourt (Anne Douglas Sedgwick) and her husband have been with the A. R. C. in France, working in the Department of Civil Relief. They have been especially interested in the refugee problem at Evian and in the campaign carried on by Dr. Lucas at Lyons. With her husband, Madame de Sélincourt has also made a study of conditions of life in a French commune for Lieut.-Col. Homer Folks. The report is to be embodied in book form.

Mrs. Ernest Thompson Seton sailed for France early in January, 1919, to operate the Women's Motor United, of Le Bien-Etre du Blessé, which she organized for the French Government in 1916.

Wilbur H. Siebert, A.M., Department of European History, Ohio State University, was, during 1918, acting dean of the Graduate School of the Ohio State University; member of the executive committee of the Historical Commission of Ohio created by Governor Cox to collect and preserve the war records of the state; contributor of articles on the independence of Armenia and joint translator of a brief history of modern Armenia; teacher of some of the men who enlisted in the Students' Army Training Corps; member of the War Records Committee of the Ohio State University.

Frank H. Simonds has been made a Knight of the Legion of Honor, in recognition of his incomparable articles on the Great War with his estimates of French generalship.

Colonel Lorillard Spencer, 369th Infantry, A. E. F., received two French citations and the Distinguished Service Cross of our Army. The French citation reads: "For showing the greatest bravery in leading his battalion the 26th of September, 1918. Seriously wounded at the head of his men."

'Mrs. James Speyer in 1918 perfected plans for looking after the First Provisional Regiment, Aqueduct Guard, which when war was declared was hurriedly summoned to protect New York City's water supply. Several of the camps were located near Scarborough, Mrs. Speyer's summer home, and in driving among them she discovered that many of the men were almost entirely destitute of even the proper comforts. Those in her immediate neighborhood she provided for some time with necessities for cold weather and provisions on holidays. As, however, the guard was composed of more than 2,000 men stationed all along the Aqueduct and often in lonely places, she appealed to one hundred prominent citizens from the five counties in which the men were located, organized committees and raised funds to supply the needs of the men. Mrs. Speyer served as chairman of the Comforts Committee.

Mrs. Speyer is still treasurer of the St. Mary's Free Hospital for Children, Board of Associate Members, and vice-president of the Girls' Branch of the Public School Athletic League, organized by her thirteen years ago. She is also treasurer of the Women's Auxiliary of the United Hospital Fund and in 1918 raised over $35,000 for this worthy charity.

Under her presidency of the New York Women's League for Animals, thousands of animals belonging to the poor were treated without charge at the League's Free Animal Hospital;

drivers were helped with advice and instruction, and useful garments distributed to the men and their families; sixty car-loads of ashes were scattered on the streets in slippery weather and chained shoes given to drivers. A number of watering stations for horses were opened in the summer and light-weight bridles and fly-nets distributed. One watering station was kept open all night for the market men coming in from the country.

After serving for thirty-five years as treasurer of the Irene Club for Working Girls, Mrs. James Speyer, on the death of the president, was elected in 1918 to that office.

Colonel Henry Lewis Stimson, A.M., Secretary of War in the Cabinet of President Taft, was in May, 1917, appointed Major Judge Advocate, promoted in August, 1917, to Lt.-Colonel of Artillery and assigned to the 305th Field Artillery at Camp Upton. In December, 1917, he sailed for general staff instruction and duty abroad, and served with the 51st Highland Division of the British Expeditionary Forces before Cambrai in January and February, 1918. During the succeeding months he was at the General Staff College of A. E. F. at Longres; in line with the 26th Division, A. E. F.; in line again with his own regiment, the 305th Field Artillery, in Lorraine, his Battalion firing the first shot of the National Army Artillery against the Germans. In August he was promoted to full colonelcy and assigned to the 31st Field Artillery then training at Camp Meade. The signing of the armistice brought to a close the activities of his regiment, mustered out of service, December, 1918.

Guy B. St. John, Field Agent, United States Housing Corporation of the United States Department of Labor, has been active in solving housing problems in towns and cities where large numbers of industrial war workers were employed on war contracts.

President Henry Suzzallo, University of Washington, Seattle, Washington, served during 1918 as chairman, First Red Cross War Campaign, Seattle, 1917; chairman, Washington

State Council of National Defense, 1917 and 1918; one of ten National Umpires for the National War Labor Board, 1918; adviser to War Labor Policies Board, as chairman of a group to prevent employment difficulties in the munitions industry, 1918. By a proclamation of Governor Lister he was made Joint Adviser to the Governor, along with the Attorney General, during the recent Revolutionary General Strike on Puget Sound, 1919. As President of the University of Washington he was in charge of coöperations with the U. S. Naval Training Station—ten schools—and with the U. S. Shipping Board—three schools—1917 and 1918.

Joseph M. Thomas, Ph.D., was elected president of the National Council of Teachers of English for 1919.

Professor Edward L. Thorndike, Teachers College, Columbia University, has served as member of the Psychology Committee of the National Research Council from its inception, and also as member of the Committee on Classification of Personnel in the Army, from its inception, in the Office of the Adjutant General, and later in the general staff. He was a member of the Advisory Board of the Division of Psychology, Office of the Surgeon General, and of the board appointed by the Director of Military Aeronautics to consider problems of selection and training of officers and enlisted men in the air service under peace conditions.

Professor William Trelease served as President of the Botanical Society of America during 1918.

Mrs. George Montgomery Tuttle, chairman, Executive Committee, American Friends of Musicians in France, reports that by the end of March, 1919, $45,000 had been sent to France where terrible conditions prevail among the musicians, especially in districts evacuated by the Germans. Fifty per cent of those returning to their old homes have died because it was too late to save them.

Branches of this society have been formed in twelve cities of this country.

At the request of the Surgeon General of the Army and on the recommendation of the Surgeon General of the Navy, Professor Milton Updegraff, U. S. N., was, in July, 1918, placed on duty at Prescott, Arizona, to supervise meterological observations at Whipple Barracks. For climatic reasons General Hospital No. 20 of the Army was located at Whipple Barracks, and the meteorological observations are of great importance.

Situated on the southern edge of the elevated mountain region of northern Arizona, Prescott has an elevation of 5,300 feet, with a semi-arid climate, but with sufficient rainfall to maintain an abundant growth of native trees, and is ideal for the recuperation of invalid soldiers of the war.

Miss Mary Van Kleeck, director of the Woman in Industry Service of the U. S. Department of Labor, was appointed when the service was first organized in July, 1918. She came to this position from the Ordnance Department where she had been chief of the Woman's Division of the Industrial Service Section. While with the Ordnance Department from January, 1918, to July, 1918, Miss Van Kleeck supervised the conditions of employment of women in the government arsenals and plants operating under government contract. She thus had the opportunity of safeguarding the women who were being so rapidly recruited into the government service by regulating the conditions under which they were employed, at the same time insuring the maximum output of munitions which were so urgently needed by the Army.

As Director of the Woman in Industry Service she has been in close touch with all government agencies and has assisted in the solution of their problems regarding the employment of women. Her position as the only woman member of the War Labor Policies Board gave her wide influence in the forming of policies for the employment of women. The standards for the employment of women in industry which were formulated by the Woman in Industry Service and adopted by the War Labor Policies Board are being widely used as guides by employers and by organizations working for the betterment of conditions for working women.

In addition to establishing standards for general conditions, the employment of women under unusual circumstances has been considered by this service.   Special studies have been made of women working in the chemical industries of one city, of the women in the metal trades in one state, of women candy makers in another city, and of the employment of negro women in industry.   Assistance has been given in several states with a view towards recommending or furthering improved legislation.   The service also has an advisory relation with the War and Navy Departments regarding the conditions affecting the employment of women in government arsenals and navy yards.

T. Wayland Vaughan, Ph.D., after the entry of the United States into the World War, was called upon as an officer of the United States Geological Survey to furnish Army and Navy officials information on water supplies, road building material, the nature of foundations for different kinds of structure, and other information of military value.   He was diverted from his geologic and oceanographic researches for the greater part of two years.

Mrs. Henry Villard has during 1918 continued her activities as president of the New York Diet Kitchen Association; the Babies Welfare Association, and as vice-president of the Armitage House Settlement and the Froebel Kindergarten Association.   She has continued her work for Woman's Suffrage as one of its foremost leaders, and, having inherited from her father, William Lloyd Garrison, her sympathies for the colored race, she has championed the negro's cause on every occasion.

Mrs. Antoinette Van H. Wakeman during 1918 devoted herself to securing suitable employment for women, who, accustomed to comfortable living, had been left destitute by the misfortunes of war.   The title of Mrs. Wakeman's new novel is, "Where the World was New."

The Henry Street Settlement (sometimes called the Nurses Settlement), founded by Miss Lillian D. Wald in 1893, made with its present staff of 158 nurses during 1918, 302,543 visits and gave nursing care to 43,946 patients in their homes in Manhattan, Bronx, Richmond, etc. When the epidemic of influenza and pneumonia struck New York City in October, 1918, Miss Wald, as chairman of the Nurses Emergency Council, coördinated within twenty-four hours the work of every agency in the city, municipal and private, which could give nursing care or relief in the home. When the epidemic was controlled, Miss Wald drew up a plan for after-care stations where influenza patients could receive physical examinations and follow-up care. The plan was accepted by the Department of Health which coöperated in the conduct of these stations for a period of six weeks.

During the war Miss Wald served as chairman of the Committee on Home Nursing of the Section on Sanitation of the Committee on Welfare Work of the Committee on Labor of the Council of National Defense—represented public health on the Conference Board of the Council of Women's Organization of Committee of Women on National Defense—and was a member of the Committee on Nursing of the General Medical Board of the Council of National Defense, New York State Committee of the Committee of Women in Industry of the Advisory Commission of the Council of National Defense, Food Administration Campaign, New York City, etc.

Mr. Charles Sumner Ward, at the request of Mr. Henry P. Davison, organized the first national campaign for the Red Cross. In the second campaign he served as chairman of the Advisory Committee for the national campaign and the campaign in New York City. He served also as chairman of the Food Administration and was Field Organizer for the United War Work Campaign last fall. The amount contributed in the campaign for which Mr. Ward has been largely responsible is $548,000,000.

E. W. Watkins, Executive Secretary of the Boy Conservation Bureau, reports that in 1918 ninety-seven boys were rescued and sent to Home Industrial Schools. When the United States declared war, seventy of the boys saved from the streets in other years by the Bureau enlisted in our Army and Navy.

Two were killed in action.   During the seven years of its existence 557 boys have been provided for by the Bureau. Scores of these boys are now holding honorable positions in banks, insurance and other offices in this city.

Miss Maude Wetmore is chairman of the Woman's Department of the National Civic Federation. Just prior to the war she accepted the chairmanship of the National League for Woman's Service, an organization formed for the training of women to meet emergencies in national life.

In April, 1917, she was appointed a member of the Woman's Committee of the Council of National Defense, and served until it was dissolved March, 1919.

She is third vice-president and director of the American Committee for Devastated France.

In February, 1919, Miss Wetmore was made a member of the Republican Woman's National Executive Committee acting with the Republican National Committee.

Benjamin Ide Wheeler, LL.D., during the past year has served as chairman of the Committee on Resources and Food Supply, California State Council of Defense, and as chairman, California Branch of The League to Enforce Peace. He was the personal representative of Governor William Dennison Stephens at the Food, Fuel, Price Conference, called by the Federal Trade Commission, April 30, 1917, in Washington; and again at the Conference of the states called by the Council of National Defense, May 2 and 3, in Washington.

He was a member of a committee to examine candidates for the Reserve Officers' Training Corps; and also of the Executive Committee, California State Council of Defense. He was appointed by President Wilson as one of the Board of Visitors to the U. S. Naval Academy at Annapolis.

Joseph A. White, M.D., having been past the age limit for overseas service, was made civilian chief of the Aviation Unit, in Richmond, Virginia, serving from January 1 to April 1, 1918. He was then elected chairman of the Virginia Council of Defense to enroll the doctors of Virginia for army and navy service. He also served as a member of the Selective Service Board.

Harris P. Wilder, Ph.D., together with Mr. Bert Wentworth, a private detective and finger-print expert, published in August, 1918, a book on "Personal Identification." "The science of individual identification through the various bodily peculiarities has now," he claims, "quite outgrown the prison walls, and is ready to fill the place which the growing needs have made for it." The book lays before the reader all known methods of personal identification, including, of course, the system of measurements inaugurated by M. Bertillon, and the now famous system of fingerprints devised by Sir Francis Galton, and put into actual use by Sir E. R. Henry. It also introduces two new methods, those based upon the friction-skin configuration of the palm of the hand and the sole of the foot, which, although their possibilities have been previously exploited in technical journals, appear here for the first time in practical form for general use.

At the December meeting of the American Society of Zoölogists Dr. Wilder was elected vice-president.

In addition to his official work at the Maine Agricultural Experiment Station, Charles D. Woods, Director, was chairman of the Local Public Safety Committee, having charge of the fuel wood supply for the state, under the Fuel Administration. He also served as a member of the State Public Safety Committee on Food Production.

Mrs. Mary Schenck Woolman, formerly professor of Domestic Art in Teachers College, Columbia University, and first Director of the Manhattan Trade School for Girls, New York City, gave up her regular work early in 1918 to accept service on the War Emergency Bill of the United States Department of Agriculture. Her duty has been to increase thrift in the household, training consumers in a more intelligent purchase of textiles and clothing. As her former training had been on textiles, Mrs. Woolman could put her knowledge to use in war service. Her headquarters are at Amherst, Mass., where she has just completed a book on "Thrift in the Household" for the use of social workers, leaders in clubs and home-makers.

Miss Mary V. Young, Ph.D., Department of Romance Languages, Mount Holyoke College, served with the committee of the College Entrance Board in preparing entrance examinations in French.

INDEX